Aspects of Subjectivity

Medieval & Renaissance Literary Studies

General Editor:
Albert C. Labriola

Advisory Editor:
Foster Provost

Editorial Board:
Judith H. Anderson
Diana Treviño Benet
Donald Cheney
Ann Baynes Coiro
Mary T. Crane
Patrick Cullen
A. C. Hamilton
Margaret P. Hannay
A. Kent Hieatt
William B. Hunter
Michael Lieb
Thomas P. Roche Jr.
Mary Beth Rose
Humphrey Tonkin
Susanne Woods

aspects of subjectivity

society and individuality
from the middle ages
to shakespeare and milton

anthony low

duquesne university press
pittsburgh, pennsylvania

Copyright © 2003 Duquesne University Press
All Rights Reserved

Published in the United States of America by

Duquesne University Press
600 Forbes Avenue
Pittsburgh, Pennsylvania 15282

No part of this book may be used or reproduced, in any manner whatsoever, without the written permission of the Publisher, except in the case of brief quotations embodied in critical articles or reviews.

Library of Congress Cataloging-in-Publication Data
Low, Anthony, 1935–
  Aspects of subjectivity: society and individuality from the Middle Ages to Shakespeare and Milton / by Anthony Low.
     p. cm. — (Medieval & Renaissance literary studies)
  Includes bibliographical references and index.
    ISBN 0–8207–0337–0 (acid-free paper)
1. English literature — Early modern, 1500–1700 — History and criticism. 2. Self in literature. 3. Literature and society — England — History — 17th century. 4. Alienation (Social psychology) in literature. 5. Individuality in literature. 6. Subjectivity in literature. I. Title. II. Series: Medieval and Renaissance literary studies.
PR438.S45 L69 2003
820.9′353—dc21
                                       2002151237

∞ Printed on acid-free paper.

Publication of this book has been aided by a grant from the Abraham and Rebecca Stein Faculty Publication Fund of New York University, Department of English.

In memory of Douglas Bush, Herschel Baker,
Francis P. Magoun, Henry Osborn Taylor and
William H. Armstrong:
Splendid and generous teachers

Contents

	Preface	ix
One	Exile in the Tenth Century: Alienation and Subjectivity in *The Wanderer*	1
Two	Privacy and Community: Medieval Confession and *Sir Gawain and the Green Knight*	22
Three	Sin and Penance at the Reformation: Redcrosse, the Church, and Everyman	60
Four	*Hamlet* and the Ghost of Purgatory: Intimations of Killing the Father	98
Five	"Umpire Conscience": Freedom and Obedience in *Paradise Lost*	129
Six	The Fall into Subjectivity: Milton's "Paradise Within" and "Abyss of Fears and Horrors"	153
Seven	Theoretical Considerations and Conclusion	183
	Appendix: Further Considerations on Penance	203
	Notes	211
	Index	239

Preface

This book, seven or eight years in the making, has developed from ideas I first began to think about many years ago, although, as often happens, I have learned more as the work has progressed and unfolded. I am greatly indebted to the Pew Charitable Trusts and to New York University, whose combined generosity enabled me to profit from a Pew Evangelical Fellowship and a year's sabbatical leave in 1995. A year of relief from ordinary teaching and administrative duties got me off to a good start with the research and writing. Among those responsible for this welcome opportunity whose names are known to me, I am grateful to Louis L. Martz, Leland Ryken, and Tony Judt.

My theme is the gradual development of subjectivity and the growing sense of the importance of the inner self and of the individual from the early middle ages to the seventeenth century. My contention is that there was nothing altogether new in the stunning early-modernist sense of a vast, inner world of the self that is exemplified most famously in Hamlet, although there was a change in attitude regarding the significance and the desirability of this inner world. In the early modern period, this ancient, natural, but normally peripheral, aspect of lived experience became more central. Just as ordinary people caught up in the turmoil of the Puritan Revolution exclaimed that the world turned upside down, so we might say that, in a similar way and at much the same time, subjectivity turned inside out. Still, the experience of subjectivity can be traced far back into the past. Probably consciousness of an inner self has always been an aspect of human experience. For example, as early as Plato or Augustine there were those who thought that the ultimate goals in life — truth, beauty, goodness, justice, the eternal Ideas, or an utterly transcendent God — were to be sought for within the soul, by means of its preternatural faculty of memory. Yet, although they thought that the traces of these supreme goals were to be found within, they believed that the goals themselves — rather than the self — were the primary and eternal reality. Gradually the balance shifted, however, until in the early modern period a seismic break occurred. This cultural transformation can be witnessed in religion in the new Protestant (as well as Counter-Reformation) emphasis on the all-important relationship between God and the individual soul, in politics in an increasing emphasis on the individual, and in literature (and therefore presumably in individual psychology) as a growing sense that true authenticity comes from within, coupled with a kind of vertiginous fall into the interior self, exemplified by Shakespeare's Hamlet and Milton's Satan. Subjectivity was not new. What was new was the sense, the feeling, the suspicion — sometimes the fear and sometimes the glad conviction — that the world within was more real than the world outside.

As we shall see in two chapters touching on confession and repentance from the time of the early Church into the Reformation, the broad movement in religion away from emphasis on community — on the institutions of the Church and the parish or congregation — toward emphasis on the individual soul and the inward spiritual life can be identified several centuries prior to the Reformation. Therefore (since the compass of the discussion only allows us to suggest rather than conclusively demonstrate) it seems likely that Protestantism was not so much the cause as one of the results or accompaniments of a long-wave cultural transformation in attitudes toward subjectivity and individuality. Indeed, the Catholic Church after the Council of Trent was also more intensely focused on the interior spiritual life than it was during the middle ages. Since my emphasis is on English literature, Protestantism plays a larger part than it might have done had I focused on such various Continental figures as St. Ignatius, St. Teresa, Montaigne, or Pascal. By the late seventeenth century, when Milton published *Paradise Lost*, the inner life — already well known to Virgil and Ovid and no doubt to others before them — could now variously be seen as a Protestant "paradise within" the individual soul, as a new Counter-Reformation emphasis on interior spirituality, as a modernist call to individual freedom and a declaration of personal autonomy, and as a shocking fall from confident possession of objective reality into the bottomless abyss of subjective relativism.

Although this book covers a good deal of territory, from the tenth to the seventeenth centuries, and although it glances even further backward and forward than that, I conceived of it from the start as a unified whole, as chapters in a book, not as separate essays. Borrowing a term from the French Annales school, I intend to keep in mind the "long wave," the extended, interlinked process of development (which has presumably not yet reached its limits) of exile, alienation, individualism, and subjectivity. I never intended to cover everything that happened or was written in those eight centuries, which would scarcely be possible, but have chosen to focus on selected literary works of great interest in themselves, works that also illustrate significant turns in the history of individuality and subjectivity and their relations to community and society. In conjunction with these literary works I look at several pertinent historical beliefs, practices, attitudes, and cultural indicators, such as the experience of exile and loneliness, the gradual development of sacramental confession from emphasis on social and communal reconciliation to personal absolution from sin, the abolition of Purgatory and of the ancient Christian sense of solidarity with ancestors and the dead, the role of conscience in the development of the self, and the rise in Shakespeare and Milton of a typically modern sense of autonomous individuality and subjectivity.

I have chosen to omit many cultural practices and beliefs that might have been included. To take the most obvious example, when the Catholic sacramental notion of Real Presence, with its implications that the Church is mysteriously but really the Body of Christ and the communion of saints, was replaced at the Reformation by notions of memorial recollection, chiefly inward and personal, that too had a decisive effect, in life and in literature, on the changing balance of notions about society, community, and individuality. Likewise, had I chosen to speak more about philosophy and less about literature, I could have begun with William of Ockham and entitled the book *The Triumph of Nominalism*. Were my focus more Continental, I might have included chapters on Petrarch, Dante, and Montaigne. But if, as I hope, my findings have substance, the results would have been much the same had I selected other literary works, other historical moments, other cultural practices, or a different balance of intellectual disciplines from those on which I have chosen to focus. I am cheered by Anthony Kemp's apt simile in his preface to *The Estrangement of the Past* (p. viii) explaining why he deliberately decided to focus on a few selected works and events over a very long period of time. "Like lightning, which varies the direction of its travel with each new pulse, seeking the direction of least resistance, this study might have achieved its result through many alternative pathways." After many years of reading I find that I value more those books that articulate a few thoughtfully chosen things well than those that strive for methodical, but sometimes plodding and predictable, completeness. My aims require me to suggest rather than demonstrate, to move cavalierly between the tenth century and the seventeenth, to neglect vast stretches of time and change that lie in between, and to shift between large theories of the long term and particular instances of the short term. In a wise caution, Sir Francis Bacon deplored rapid movement between the top and bottom of a logical chain of evidence. Bacon failed, however, to anticipate that the scientific method of hypothesis and confirmation (or sometimes refutation) would prove more fruitful than pure, methodical induction. Moreover, he knew that the advancement of learning requires the cooperative labors of many people over a long period of time. If I have omitted anything important, perhaps others will fill in the gaps in the cooperative scholarly enterprise.

As the work has progressed I have taken advantage of several occasions to present parts of it in lectures and articles. Doing so has allowed me to receive many useful comments and suggestions from audiences, from anonymous journal referees, and from editors. An early version of chapter 1 appeared in *Satura*, a Festschrift in honor of Robert R. Raymo, edited by Ruth Sternglantz and Nancy Reale, published by Paul Watkins Press. I thank the publisher for permission to reprint. I thank James Dougherty, Thomas Werge, and James Turner for inviting me to inaugurate the annual Lecture on Religion and Literature at Notre Dame, which was subsequently published in *Religion and Literature* (30 [Summer 1998]: 1–20) and now expanded as chapter 2. I thank the editors of *The Ben Jonson Journal* (5 [1998]: 1–35) *English Literary Renaissance* (29 [1999]: 443–67), and *Studies in Philology* (96 [1999]: 348–65) for permission to reprint materials adapted from chapters 3, 4, and 5, respectively. An earlier version of chapter 5 was presented as a lecture at St. Bonaventure University at the kind invitation of John Mulryan, with generous hospitality from its Miltonist President, Robert Wickenheiser. At the gracious invitation of Arthur Kinney and his associates, a version of chapter 6 was presented as the Dan S. Collins Lecture in Renaissance Studies at the University of Massachusetts, Amherst. I presented a somewhat different version at Baylor University, at the kind invitation of Maurice Hunt and Ralph Wood, where responses from the audience and my hosts suggested several refinements.

I have enjoyed conversations with Deborah Shuger about early aspects of this book. My colleague Haruko Momma gave me good advice on points of Anglo-Saxon scholarship and the current state of opinion in the field. Robert Bruce Mullin, whom I met at the 1995 summer gathering of Pew Evangelical Fellows on the shore of Lake Michigan, has answered e-mail inquiries on points of Anglican theology and worship. Fr. David N. Beauregard, O.M.V., gave helpful advice on matters theological and historical in the *Hamlet* chapter. Sally Fitzgerald, John Mulryan, William A. Sessions, Stanley Stewart, and R.V. Young also gave welcome advice and encouragement. My colleague Robert R. Raymo lent me books (some for a *very* long time and still not returned as I write this), made various suggestions for improvement, and in general has kept me from going too far astray in matters medieval. Needless to say, none of these generous friends and colleagues is responsible for errors that remain.

Before beginning the book proper, I want to devote the remainder of this preface to looking at a few passages that throw light on the early history of subjectivity, passages taken from the *Odyssey*, the *Aeneid*, and the *Confessions* of St. Augustine. All these works are much earlier chronologically than *The Wanderer*, with which the book proper opens. Yet in some ways they are more sophisticated. They may be taken to represent the periods of early, high, and late antiquity. Let us begin with a passage from Homer's *Odyssey*. Early in the tale, after Hermes at Zeus's command has told Calypso that she must release Odysseus from imprisonment on her island, she finds him gazing out to sea:

> And now her ladyship, having given heed
> to Zeus's mandate, went to find Odysseus
> in his stone seat to seaward — tear on tear
> brimming his eyes. The sweet days of his life time
> were running out in anguish over his exile,
> for long ago the nymph had ceased to please.
> Though he fought shy of her and her desire,
> he lay with her each night, for she compelled him.
> But when day came he sat on the rocky shore
> and broke his own heart groaning, with eyes wet
> scanning the bare horizon of the sea.[1]

As Erich Auerbach points out, Homer is a poet whose idea of mimesis is material, objective, and immediate. In his poetry, "a continuous rhythmic procession of phenomena passes by, and never is there a form left fragmentary or half-illuminated, never a lacuna, never a gap, never a glimpse of unplumbed depths." Yet Auerbach also recognizes that Homer's characters have and express inward feelings, that "they vent their inmost hearts in speech; what they do not say to others, they say in their own minds."[2] The primary focus of Homer's poetry is on the present moment and the material surface. Still we can hardly doubt that his characters have inner depths of feeling and a strong inner sense of themselves. True, in Homer's time that sense of self is less self-concerned, less isolated from others than is typically the case in modern times. It is more informed by rank, honor, and position in life, by social and familial ties. But readers will not be wholly mistaken if they imagine that they feel and understand something of what Homer represents Odysseus as feeling and thinking within himself in this and similar passages.

With Virgil, the solid surface of material life seems to grow more ambivalent, shadowy, and clouded, as if any object or landscape might conceal mysterious depths. In the *Aeneid* we already begin to see some of the features that have been associated with the "invention" of subjectivity in the Renaissance. Conflicts between the personal self and the social self, between desire and duty, are revealed in the minds of many of the characters. Indeed, almost always the most personal and inward passages result when Aeneas is reminded that he cannot afford to indulge his natural, personal feelings but must accept the terrible obligations of duty. His duty is not to live a life or to experience love and pleasure but to found an eternal city. Toward that end all his most intimate and natural feelings must be sacrificed. Numerous passages illustrate this necessity, but two especially may be cited. The first draws upon the passage we have just quoted from Homer. Just as Zeus sends Hermes to warn Calypso to free Odysseus in order that he may realize his destiny, so Jupiter sends Mercury to free Aeneas from loving bondage to Dido and to remind him of his obligation to fulfill his great destiny. In each case the messenger god speaks ruthlessly, as commanded by the Father of the gods, but Hermes frees Odysseus to realize his humanity by returning home to wife and family, whereas Aeneas is strictly forbidden to indulge in any such human relief. As a result of the god's harsh command to suppress his feelings and to perform his duty, Aeneas is driven into himself. Unlike the description in Homer, we are permitted to witness his painful indecision from within his mind:

> This vision stunned Aeneas, struck him dumb;
> his terror held his hair erect; his voice
> held fast within his jaws. He burns to flee
> from Carthage; he would quit these pleasant lands,
> astonished by such warnings, the command
> of gods. What can he do? What openings
> Can he employ? His wits are split, they shift
> here, there; they race to different places, turning
> to everything. But as he hesitated,
> this seemed the better plan.[3]

There is no great distance between this depiction of the internal workings of the human mind and one that we might find, say, in Shakespeare.

Even more striking is the epic simile that Virgil employs to describe Aeneas's troubled and divided state of mind when he realizes that the gods have made war between the Latins and the Trojans inevitable after he has bent every effort, with apparent success, to seal a peaceful alliance with King Latinus through marriage with his daughter Lavinia. The gods, it seems, prefer that the alliance, and with it the destined foundation of Rome, be sealed in civil war and bloodshed. Thus the violent events they precipitate savagely foreshadow the history of Virgil's own time: the Roman civil war, which brought out of struggle and doubt the brilliant Age of Augustus and the *pax Romana*. Not easily are civilizations destroyed and rebuilt.

> And so it went through all of Latium;
> and when the Trojan hero has seen this,
> he wavers on a giant tide of troubles;
> his racing mind is split; it shifts here, there,
> and rushes on to many different plans,
> Turning to everything: even as when
> The quivering light of water in bronze basins
> reflected from the sun or from the moon's
> glittering image glides across all things
> and now darts skyward, strikes the roof's high ceiling.
> (8.23–32)

W. R. Johnson points out that Virgil borrows this simile of light reflected from a rippling bowl of water from a similar image in the *Argonautica*, used to describe a young woman in love, but that in doing so he complicates and transforms it, much as he had earlier transformed the meaning of the descent of Mercury, which he borrowed from Homer's similarly placed episode.[4] Virgil's bronze basin becomes a striking image of the troubled, subjective mind under pressure to conform to fate, duty, the will of the gods, and the needs of the Roman people. Elsewhere, Virgil in a series of epic similes compares the Trojans to a hive of bees and to a company of ants, social creatures to whom individuality and subjectivity are simply unknown. Yet paradoxically he places at the very center of the Trojan hive's determined effort to rebuild their destroyed city a recognizably human individual whose personal feelings and natural, affectionate desires are constantly destined to be thwarted and suppressed. As I shall suggest in the succeeding chapters, especially chapter 1, unusual social and psychological pressures that thwart personal desires and normal cultural expectations can be important sources of increasing subjectivity and self-awareness, in literature, in the individual, and sometimes in the culture itself.

To illustrate the sophisticated delineation in antiquity of inward states of mind and psychological processes, I have focused on Homer and Virgil, partly in order to suggest that even the great poet of the material surface and the chief exponent of Roman public duty were well acquainted with the mind's inward depths. If it would not delay us too long from our main purposes, we could dwell on several other classical writers who deliberately chose to work in modes more private and personal than Homer or Virgil: among them Catullus, Propertius, and Ovid — in his *Amores* but above all in his *Metamorphoses*. Ovid's psychological mastery often involves the reader intimately in what it feels like from within to undergo a violent change. His Narcissus provided later imaginative writers and psychologists with what eventually became one of the very definitions of subjective pathology. Ovid, taught in the schools and widely imitated in the Renaissance, suggested to numerous English poets, and to their French and Italian predecessors, ways to depict intense, vivid inward experience enforced and revealed by outward events. An indirect instance of Ovid's pervasive influence on later times is Spenser's tale of Hellenore and Malbecco, told in *The Faerie*

Queene (3.10). What begins as a typical Italian fabliau ends as a terrifying Ovidian metamorphosis, with the transformation of Malbecco into Jealousy itself, an outcome that some of Spenser's astonished critics have admired but others have deplored, because it is so ruthlessly disturbing. When Spenser chooses in the end to emphasize the terror of the psychological event at the possible expense of the moral lesson, he is at his most Ovidian.

I shall conclude this necessarily brief survey of early times with St. Augustine's *Confessions*, perhaps the single most powerful and influential depiction of subjectivity in late antiquity. With Augustine the ancient prescription, "Know thyself," begins to take on new meanings, for in the tradition of Augustinian mysticism the experiential traces of God are found only within the mind and soul. In Augustine, too, we find a paradox very similar to that which we find in Virgil. The great poet of imperial *Romanitas* and self-sacrifice is also an immensely influential exponent of personal subjectivity and the inner self, the source of numerous paintings, tales, romances, and operas. It is not surprising that in later times romantic Dido oversteps her assigned place in the poem, much as Milton's arch-individualist Satan oversteps his. The temptation often proves more powerful than its resolution. Similarly Augustine, the most influential authority on predestination before Calvin, was a seminal source for thinking about free will. As discussed in chapter 5, for Augustine and Boethius free will relies on divine providence and is impossible without it.

These knotty complexities issue in Augustine's unsurpassed description of the inner workings of the mind in the conversion experience. His description, which occupies several sections of book 8, is much too long to quote. It is vivid, immediate, and experiential. Just as Augustine has earlier explained the nature of Original Sin by close observation of an infant's behavior, so he takes an experiential, even what might be called a remarkably modern experimental, approach to the problem of interior acts of the will, how they are arrived at and how executed. The experience of free will and subjectivity that he describes is all the more powerful because he shows that the mind is at once both free and bound, capable and yet incapable of choosing.

> I was deeply disturbed in spirit, angry with indignation and distress that I was not entering into my pact and covenant with you, my God, when all my bones (Ps. 34:10) were crying out that I should enter into it and were exalting it to heaven with praises. But to reach that destination one does not use ships or chariots or feet. It was not even necessary to go the distance I had come from the house to where we were sitting. The one necessary condition, which meant not only going but at once arriving there, was to have the will to go — provided only that the will was strong and unqualified, not the turning and twisting first this way, then that, of a will half-wounded, struggling with one part rising up and the other falling down.
>
> Finally in the agony of hesitation I made many physical gestures of the kind men make when they want to achieve something and lack the strength, either because they lack the actual limbs or because their limbs are fettered with chains or weak with sickness or in some way hindered. If I tore my hair, if I struck my forehead, if I intertwined my fingers and clasped my knee, I did that because to do so was my will. But I could have willed this and then not done it if my limbs had not possessed the power to obey. So I did many actions in which the will to act was not equalled by the power. Yet I was not doing what with an incomparably greater longing I yearned to do, and could have done the moment I so resolved. For as soon as I had the will, I would have had the wholehearted will. The willing itself was performative of the action. Nevertheless, it did not happen. The body obeyed the slightest inclination of the soul to move the limbs at its pleasure more easily than the soul obeyed itself, when its supreme desire could be achieved exclusively by the will alone.[5]

As Cardinal Newman has suggested in his *Confession* and *Grammar of Assent,* matters of heart and mind, of faith and will, of interior transformation and conversion, are exceedingly subtle and complicated. Unsurprisingly, the development of individuality and of subjectivity in the West often has been tied to religious beliefs and practices. But there are other motives as well, such as we have found in the *Aeneid* and will find in *The Wanderer*: the suppression of love and affection, the frustration of natural expectations, the experience of exile and abandonment, the disappointment of ambition. The tale is long and complex. Only a small part of it is told here.

Anthony Low
New York University

One

Exile in the Tenth Century

❧

Alienation and Subjectivity in *The Wanderer*

The roots of modern individualism and subjectivity may be traced back much further than is often thought. A long tradition attributes individuality to the Renaissance as opposed to the middle ages. No doubt a critical turning point was approached at some time in the Renaissance, and reached more conclusively still in the seventeenth century. In the matter of individual self-consciousness, European culture may conveniently be divided into pre-Cartesian and post-Cartesian eras, although the descriptive terminology might vary. Another long tradition attributes individuality to the Reformation and to the consequent division and disarray of Christendom in Europe, as opposed to the earlier period when for those living in the West the Church was, despite theological disputes and fringe exceptions, Catholic, universal, and comfortably taken for granted. In the debate as to whether the Renaissance represents a continuation of or a sharp break from the middle ages, the pendulum of opinion has swung back and forth. Assuredly religion grew more internalized and less corporate after the Reformation, but as Ronald Knox has shown, the Protestant turn from the institutional and corporate to the charismatic and individual had many precedents. If those earlier episodes were less decisive, nonetheless they were frequent, and they went back to the earliest days of the Church.[1]

Moreover, the Catholic Counter-Reformation of the sixteenth and seventeenth centuries, like the Protestant Reformation, took a striking turn toward inwardness in religion. That turn was not only in response to Protestantism, for both movements can be traced back to pre-Reformation sources. The major Catholic exponents of a more internalized religion, such as Saints Teresa of Avila, John of the Cross, Ignatius Loyola, Francis of Sales, and Charles Borromeo, represent continuity as well as change. They draw on traditions of spiritual renovation that go back to the fourteenth century mystics, to monastic reformers like St. Bernard, and still further back to the ancient desert fathers. True, something happened to European culture in the seventeenth century which, from our vantage point four hundred years later, looks uniquely tenacious and possibly irreversible. It was as if there were a gradual shifting of weight, and then the balance suddenly tipped. Or, to use a different trope, there was a slow undermining and then a swift collapse. Yet the roots of those sweeping changes may be traced back a long way into the past.

This long-term process of internalization was causally connected to outward social pressures and to resulting inward psychological alienation. If, as Marxist sociologists and others have often argued, the modern age is a time of extraordinary — even unique — alienation, it is not surprising that it has also been a time of extraordinarily intense individualism and subjectivity. Alienation comes in several kinds. It may be the built-in product of a systemic or "structural" defect, or it may result from a concatenation of particular, accidental circumstances. Broad causes of alienation — war, plague, tyranny, enslavement, industrialization, the unbalanced spread of the market economy — may propel wide and lasting transformations of the kind we are contemplating. Local pressures may drive individuals into subjectivity, in one degree or another, and push the more articulate among them into providing others with the linguistic and rhetorical innovations that give social transformations their means of expression.

More often than not, the determining experience that forces the individual toward subjectivity has been "exile" — that is, expulsion of the individual person from being or feeling himself to be part of the community in one way or another. This is so because, although more painful fates can be imagined, exile strikes at the core of a person's sense of identity in relation to society. It cuts him off from unexamined assumptions and, through isolation, drives him into himself. If full-blown alienation is a modern phenomenon, exile is certainly an ancient one. It has repeatedly subjected individuals to cultural and consequent psychological pressures that may, if the times are ripe, induce them to assert themselves against their cultures and ultimately lead them to a conviction of their autonomous freedom from external constraints.

The experience of subjectivity, broadly considered, cannot be new. Some of the most characteristic qualities of modern subjectivity, such as our sense that there are unplumbed regions within the mind and heart, are easily found in the works of early writers: throughout Virgil, for example, or in St. Augustine's *Confessions*.[2] Some recent critics have taken Hamlet's plangent words, "But I have that within which passes show," to represent a portentous development in the march toward Romanticism, liberal individualism, and modern subjectivity. Hamlet's words, for all their echoing reverberations from the interior depths of the imagination, are not altogether novel. What was new to culture in the early modern period was not loneliness, isolation, estrangement, or a sense of vast inner regions within the self, but rather certain moral and systematic philosophical responses to those ancient feelings of exile and loss, to being thrown back upon oneself by social pressures that are, after all, perennial.

The Beginnings of Individualism

The consensus among Renaissance scholars, who may sometimes be handicapped by too exclusive an attention to their own period, is that the birth of individualism as we now know it was largely a phenomenon of the late Renaissance. In the case of England, scholars have recently thought it anachronistic to speak about real subjectivity, or about a truly modern sense of interiority, much before the turn of the seventeenth century. As Anne Ferry points out in an authoritative survey, portents of subjectivity are evident as early as Wyatt, but not until Locke did a systematic philosophic vocabulary emerge to describe inward states of mind and to permit the development of a theory of individuality couched in terms recognizable to modern readers.[3] During the gradual transformation of cultural assumptions that led up to Locke, which allowed him to formulate his theories of possessive individualism and instrumental reason more rigorously than was earlier possible, the discoverers or inventors of modern interiority were more typically poets, lovers, and imaginative thinkers than rational philosophers. They did their work largely by means of tropes and conceits and by the gradual shifting and renovation in meaning of old words rather than the invention of new ones.

A pivotal example of this linguistic transformation is the word "individual" itself, which we know changed radically in meaning over the course of the seventeenth century. Its primary earlier meaning was that which is whole and integral and cannot be divided. "One in substance or essence," as the

Oxford English Dictionary puts it. The *OED* cites as its first example of the word used in the primary modern sense — "distinguished from others by attributes of its own; marked by a peculiar and striking character" — a passage from Sir Thomas Browne's *Pseudodoxia Epidemica* (1646). Browne, who was characteristically both a traditionalist and a scientific innovator, writes: "A man should be something that men are not; and individual in somewhat beside his proper nature."[4] Bacon, always an innovator, had earlier used the term in the related modern sense, which the *OED* defines as "of, pertaining or peculiar to, a single person or thing, or some one member of a class." In *The Advancement of Learning* (1605) Bacon writes: "As touching the Manners of learned men, it is a thing personall and individuall" (1.3.4).[5]

Of course, the meaning of words is notoriously slippery. The same writer may at different times use the word in opposing senses. The *OED* notes that in *Animadversions* (1641) Milton uses the newer meaning: "It is no individuall word, but a Collective."[6] Yet we remember that in *Paradise Lost* he reverts to the older sense, when the Father announces that all the angels are to be incorporated as one body under the rule of the Son, "United as one individual Soule" (5.610), or when Eve proclaims that — in origin and in love — she is inseparably bound to Adam, "Henceforth an individual solace dear" (4.486).

In the course of moving from one meaning to what seems at first to be its virtual opposite, a word may sometimes be used ambiguously. Milton, keenly aware of the meanings of words, usually uses "individual" in its older sense, which is related to its Latin root.[7] In the divorce tracts, however, feeling obliged to reconcile the truth of the Bible with the seemingly disparate lesson of his own experience, and thus under the difficult pressure of explaining away Jesus' plain commandment against divorce and remarriage, we find Milton using the word with shifts in meaning and with a kind of oscillation between one sense and the other. In *The Doctrine and Discipline of Divorce* (1643, 1644), he explains away the Genesis text on which Jesus drew (2:24) — and on which the marriage service traditionally drew — by asking why the Bible neglected to bring this text out of its original context to build it into Jewish law, as it did with the original institution of the Sabbath. "[N]ay rather why was not that individual institution brought out of Paradise, as was that of the Sabbath, and repeated in the body of the Law, that men might have understood it to be a command?"[8] Milton answers that the text was left where it was because it was "individual" — that is, inseparable from its context and circumstances, and therefore not to be generalized into a prescriptive law on marriage. In this use of the word, "individual" may easily, by extrapolation from the modern vantage point, be understood as meaning peculiar or unique, not to be repeated or generalized — although actually it retains primarily its older sense of inseparability.

It is noteworthy that Milton uses the word individual far more often in his divorce tracts than anywhere else. He employs it typically to prove that particular texts or admonitions, which had been traditionally understood as prohibitions of divorce, are "individual" in just such a double sense. That is, they are individual (inseparable) from their original historical circumstances; therefore they are individual (unique) in their applicability. They are not to be drawn out of context and applied universally. In Milton's hands, this development of one key word exemplifies in miniature how psychological anxieties and social pressures help generate a long-term linguistic and cultural transformation. As a particular instance, it clearly belongs to and illuminates a larger historical process. Milton's use of individual anticipates the quintessentially modern growth of, and connection between, possessive individualism and the social institution of divorce. In this lengthy historical unfolding, divorce became more and more closely intertwined with and seemed more and more beneficial to free expression of individual autonomy. As a rule, before the early modern period, divorce was viewed as a desirable convenience for rulers and men of importance who wished to put away unsatisfactory wives to perpetuate lineage and assure succession. The history of Europe from the dark ages to the Reformation saw the indissolubility of marriage gradually established as a protective social institution — protective of women especially. The Reformation marked the reversal of that process, as divorce began to be seen as a means to deliver individuals, including women, from marital oppression.[9] Milton anticipates the central modern trend (as he often does elsewhere), but he is torn by his deep need to preserve the integrity of biblical truth.

Forms of Exile

At least for a modern reader, the internal life of the speaker of the Old English elegiac lyric, *The Wanderer*, is central to the poem's meaning and impact. But before we look more closely at this inner life, we must review some points of scholarly debate. First is the question of the speaker's identity. Is the poet the same person as the wanderer, or does he describe someone else's experiences? Is there one speaker in the poem, or are there two, the wanderer and the wise man? Is it reasonable to speak of the wanderer as if he were a real person, when the figure in the poem may more probably represent an accretion of sources and experiences, if he does not simply serve as the (nonexistent) focus for restating common, impersonal wisdom and oral formulae of long standing and multiple authorship? Finally, are modern ideas of "character" or personality at all relevant when we are considering a poem that comes down to us from a culture as different from ours as the tenth century is distant from the twentieth?[10]

Recent debate started with Bernard Huppé's fairly simple question of whether the poem has one or two speakers, a question that easily combines with the old conundrum of how much any Old English poem owes to a particular poet, writer, or scribe and how much to the dispersed oral traditions on which he presumably drew when he set it down in the form we have it in manuscript. Subsequent turns in the debate suggest that the question of the speaker's individuality cannot now be separated from questions of our own subjectivity and individuality, as postmodern theory brings these qualities to a head. The end result of the long growth of individuality and subjectivity has been a breakdown of confidence in the subject's sense of his own reality. What used popularly to be called an "identity crisis" of the individual a generation ago now has broadened to become a crisis in cognition and belief that pervades the culture itself.

To all appearances, *The Wanderer* was written down in its present form toward the end of a primary heroic age, a time when the hero begins to lose his unthinking identity with the received wisdom of his culture but when it is still far too soon for him (or us) to think of that received wisdom as something wholly external to his own sense of identity. To distinguish sharply between received traditions, bits of gnomic wisdom, and verbal formulae borrowed from earlier poems and the character of the speaker who utters them is to impose modern categories anachronistically. Inwardness and outwardness, individuality and solidarity, simply could not be so easily distinguished from one another. We should keep in mind that the wanderer represents an emergence from communal unselfconsciousness into individuality. We, to the contrary, find ourselves somewhere beyond (or further into) the modern predicament of individuals in a mass culture, well described by Max Weber and David Riesman, a culture in which alienation and "other-directedness" threaten our individual autonomy. (The addition of a counterculture has only intensified this predicament, as rival cultures interweave and strive to coopt one another, at the expense of the individual autonomy each professes to support.)

Social psychologists have cogently argued that personal identity necessarily includes a large component of outward social influence.[11] Man is a social as well as a rational animal. The further a culture is from modernity — the "earlier" or more primitive it is — the more fully a person's identity derives from his society and not from a (real or imagined) autonomous center within himself.[12] Yet this is not to say that individuals can ever somehow cease to exist. If, as many prominent critics now argue, Shakespeare did not "exist" as a unique person of genius, then, *mirabile dictu*, there must have been a hole or a node in his culture that acted and wrote very much as if Shakespeare did.[13] So if we wish we may say with recent theorists that there was a place or a hole in the Old English cultural fabric where the convergence of oral formulae produced *The Wanderer*. By custom and from the example of the poem itself — just as it is convenient to call "Shakespeare" Shakespeare — so it is convenient to call that particular confluence of cultural forces the wanderer.[14] With the Old English poet, we embody cultural cross currents, historic and poetic traditions, in a person, and thus give these scattered abstractions life. It scarcely matters whether we prefer to think of the wanderer as a nexus of received beliefs, Christian and pagan (and incipient questioning of those beliefs) or as a lifelike person, who, if not the poet himself or someone he knew, represents certain characteristics at large in his culture whom poet and audience agree to recognize and admire.

There is a family resemblance among the Anglo-Saxon system of the comitatus, the feudal system with which the Normans replaced it, and the Renaissance patronage system which in turn replaced that. In each society the emphasis is on loyalty to a personal superior repaid by the giving of rings, land, security, fellowship with other vassals and followers, and other benefits, including a sense of honor and worth. Not the least of these gifts is the gift of self and of self-esteem. These institutions chiefly differ in intensity. As the bonds between leaders and followers grow more codified, regulated, and self-conscious, there is a gradual diminishment in intensity and in the assumption that they represent the natural order of things rather than a beneficial — or malevolent — cultural arrangement. Some measure of this difference may be seen in the exile suffered by the wanderer and those suffered by Sir Thomas Wyatt and Sir Philip Sidney. In the first case the result is utter desolation, which only God can solace; in the others, the results are painful discontentment and thwarted ambition, ameliorated by the opportunities that rustication affords for compensatory pleasures.[15] Even the death of a patron, with the consequent dashing of all his clients' hopes and ambitions, produces sorrows of a lesser kind, as we find exemplified in the elegies that poured forth after the death of Prince Henry in 1612. The underlying reason for the difference is the extent to which the member of a comitatus, as opposed to the client of a Renaissance patron, owes his honor, his worth, his very identity, to his relationship with his lord. To be separated from that lord and from his fellowship is to cease to exist.

In a previous book, I looked at two seventeenth century poets whom exile or exclusion from the patronage system drove to invent new ways of dealing with the isolation that results from enforced separation from society.[16] When John Donne broke with his patron, Sir Thomas Egerton, his dismissal from office thwarted his advancement for many years. This exile from public life, from the city and the court, caused him to suffer intense psychological pressures. In response, he invented a new kind of love poetry: private, antisocial, and intensely loyal and mutual between the lovers, who form a little world of two set against the larger world. Thus Donne made the best of his enforced privacy and rendered his disgrace legitimate, even inestimably valuable. Thomas Carew suffered a similar break with his patron, Sir Dudley Carleton, and with his parents and family. His fall from grace had a like disastrous effect on his career, until he seized the opportunity to transfer his allegiance to an opposing political faction led by the Duke of Buckingham. Suffering, like Donne, under intense pressures of exile and disgrace but finding himself, a generation later, in different cultural and economic circumstances, Carew justified his change of allegiance by inventing a different kind of private love poetry: not loyal and mutual like Donne's, but libertine, mobile, market-driven, and individualistic. Thus, in their own characteristic ways, as their circumstances allowed, Donne and Carew made a virtue of the necessity of exile. Pushed into themselves by exclusion from society, they fashioned new ways of living and loving. Each of them represents more than an isolated case because each was an influential poet, whose sufferings were connected with a central and prevalent crisis of his time. Clients disappointed by failures of patronage and exile from public life were regular fixtures of English Renaissance literature, as of life.[17]

Exile and Subjectivity

The plight of the Anglo-Saxon wanderer is similar in significant ways to those of Donne and Carew. Although we cannot know for certain that the wanderer is based on a real individual, we may safely posit that he represents or embodies an experience that others in his culture could recognize. Stanley Greenfield calls the topos of separation from society, on which several Old English laments and consolations were written, the "theme of exile." Robert E. Bjork adds that the prevalence of the theme of exile in Old English poetry demonstrates its broad familiarity — in the language and in the culture — and its presumed appeal to a poet's audience.[18] Poets and audiences alike must have regarded the experience of exile as an intensely painful breaking of human bonds, even as an assault on the natural order of things in this world; yet they must also have regarded those who bore exile well as heroic and admirable.

The extent to which the wanderer is embedded in his culture and takes his identity from it is a principal cause of his pain. After his exile, however, it becomes a principal cause of his, or at least of the poet's, consolation. The culture to which the poet belongs, as recent Old English scholars have recognized, is a synthesis of the heroic and the Christian.[19] One Christian lesson that the poet draws from the wanderer's enforced isolation is that an exile can put his trust nowhere in this world, but only in God. The conclusion of *The Wanderer* makes that lesson explicit:

> Wel bið þam þe him are seceð,
> frofre to fæder on heofonum, þær us eal seo fæstnung stondeð.
> (ll. 114–15)
>
> [Well is it for him who seeks favor, comfort from our Father in heaven, where all our certainty remains.][20]

When a man forced into isolation finds himself in utmost extremity, in exile from society and deprived of all the good things of the world, he is obliged to look deep into himself. There he — or the poet working and sympathizing through him — learns that only his Father in heaven can be relied on. God is the unfailing heavenly lord to whom an exile must turn, in place of the fealty he owed to the earthly lord who was taken from him. But although the poet finds this lesson in the wanderer's isolation by looking into his isolated heart, nonetheless it embodies the traditional wisdom of the poet's ancestral culture, within which the wanderer still remains although he has been exiled from his home and people and forced to the social margins.

Working from more explicit evidence in *The Seafarer*,

Dorothy Whitelock suggests that there is a connection between the protagonist's lonely voyage and the Christian tradition of pilgrimage, of "peregrinatio pro amore Dei." More recently, Clair McPherson points out resemblances between the seafarer's lonely voyage and the tradition of eremitical, ascetic spirituality that derives from the desert Fathers.[21] The wanderer's exile is forced whereas the seafarer's may be voluntary. Nonetheless, much the same may be said of the wanderer's journey through suffering and deprivation toward spiritual renewal. He undergoes a pilgrimage both inward and outward; he suffers and gains from a journey into the depths of the mind as well as through frost-cold seas. From the poem's opening, the wanderer's acceptance of a bitter combination of isolation, suffering, and deprivation results in compensatory spiritual gains:

> Oft him anhaga are gebideð,
> metudes miltse, þeah þe he modcearig
> geond lagulade longe sceolde
> hreran mid hondum hrimcealde sæ,
> wadan wræclastas. Wyrd bið ful aræd!
>
> (ll. 1–5)

> [Often the lonely one lives on to find favor,
> mildness of his lord, even though, troubled in mind,
> over the water-path, he must long stir
> with his hands the frost-cold sea,
> wander the path of exile. Fate is fixed fast.][22]

The Christian virtues that *The Wanderer* advocates, however, have not altogether driven out or repudiated the old pagan heroic virtues; rather they have formed with them a synthesis. Patience and courage in the face of suffering, loss, and defeat, are recognizably pagan virtues as well as Christian ones. To cite a group of disparate examples belonging to distinct heroic traditions, the *Iliad*, *The Tale of the Heike*, and *Beowulf* all agree in their emphatic admiration for heroism in the face of loss and defeat. Although *The Song of Roland* is combatively

Christian in emphasis, it presents us with a hero the manner of whose death evokes admiration for his proud chivalric honor. His famous embrace of defeat is Christian not so much in essence as by adoption. The hero of *The Wanderer*, forced by stressful circumstances to retreat within himself, if he is to find mildness and favor must learn that no one else but God the Father can be relied on. He must find within himself hard lessons that confirm by experience what the traditional lore, combining pagan with Christian wisdom, has already taught the poet about stoic self-reliance and the private fortitude that may be found deep within a man's heart and mind. Some of this may come from traditional Anglo-Saxon resignation to fate; some, as J. E. Cross suggests, from the literary influence of Seneca:[23]

> Ic to soþe wat
> þæt biþ in eorle indryhten þeaw,
> þæt he his ferðlocan fæste binde,
> healde his hordcofan, hycge swa he wille.
> (ll. 11–14)

> [I know for a truth
> that it is in a man a noble custom
> that he bind fast his heart's coffer,
> hold tight to his mind's treasure-chest, think what he will.]

These stoic virtues are, essentially, virtues taught by exile, cultural distress, and exclusion from the community.

In the experience of exile we may recognize the remote ancestor of alienation and of other cultural phenomena leading toward modern individualism and separation from society. Nowhere have these trends been taken further than in contemporary America, which might be called the exemplar, if not the *reductio ad absurdum*, of the modern and postmodern conditions. Significantly, a recent study of American individualist culture by Robert Bellah and his colleagues traces our strong sense of autonomous individuality and our resentment of social authority back to the early Puritan tradition of "leaving home." As Charles Taylor sums up Bellah's theory: "this has grown into the American tradition of leaving home: the young person has to go out, to leave the parental background, to make his or her own way in the world. In contemporary conditions, this can transpose even into abandoning the political or religious convictions of the parents."[24] Another good name for this modern habit — in which, as Taylor paradoxically remarks, a long cultural tradition inculcates fierce resentment of tradition — is Anthony Kemp's term, "the estrangement of the past." Kemp traces this phenomenon back to the late middle ages and Wycliff's attacks on religious traditions and institutions, and he sees it as steadily accelerating and intensifying into modern times. The exile of the wanderer is only a remote ancestor of such modern trends, for it results from what would have seemed to people at the time an "unnatural" breakdown in the culture rather than from a trend fully (if paradoxically) incorporated into the culture. This is so even though evidence suggests that Old English audiences understood that the suffering caused by exile was a recurrent problem, even a universal one.

Closely and necessarily associated with the experience of exile is separation from the community of discourse, which results in enforced silence. In discussing the interrelationship between the self and the community, one of Taylor's names for the cultural "frameworks" within which we live and from which we draw our sense of self is "webs of interlocution."[25] Expelled by fate from his cultural framework, the exile is also expelled from the web of discourse, by means of which he once defined himself:

> Oft ic sceolde ana uhtna gehwylce
> mine ceare cwiþan. Nis nu cwicra nan
> þe ic him modsefan minne durre
> sweotule asecgan.

(ll. 8–11)

> [Often before the day dawned I have lamented
> my cares alone. There is no one living
> to whom I can safely speak
> the thoughts of my heart.]

Just as the exile has been expelled from his "home," he has been expelled from the community of language and the companionable reassurance that language can give.

From our vantage point of postmodernity, we may even see in the wanderer's plight a faint anticipation — unrealized and unrealizable in this poem or by anyone in that age — of a further extremity of individualism: the Nietzschean removal of the self from any normative system of morality. Formerly, the wanderer drew on, or at least found comforting reinforcement of, a sense of right and wrong provided by the counsels of his liege lord: "his winedryhtnes / leofes larcwidum" (ll. 37–38). He could determine what to do and what not to do by consulting with those on whom he could rely, especially by consulting with the lord to whom he owed loyalty and obedience. In exile, however, he can only rely on himself and his memory to give him a basis for moral decisions. Even to raise the possibility that the wanderer's exile might in the end lead to relativism, or to a modern sense of internalized autonomy "beyond good and evil," is to speculate far beyond what was conceivable to a poet living in the tenth century or earlier. The psychosocial mechanism that connects alienation with relativism is potentially there, however, even though it will not be activated for many centuries.[26]

It would be wrong, however, to imagine that because he is not modern the wanderer has no options; that because he lives in a culture that defines his identity for him even in exile he lacks freedom of choice or a strong sense of self. As Alasdair MacIntyre argues, the Homeric hero — who inhabits a heroic culture much like the wanderer's — has choices, although they may seem to us to be restricted choices. In particular, he must decide whether to do, or whether to fail or refuse to do, whatever is right for a person of his social rank in given circumstances. "Thinking well (*eu phronein*) or soundly (*saophronein*) is a matter of reminding oneself or another of what *aretē* and *dikē* require."[27] Fate is determined, as both the wanderer and Odysseus remind themselves. Yet within the dictates of fate or the unfolding of events, one has a choice: either bravely to meet or fearfully to flee whatever happens.[28] In the Anglo-Saxon heroic culture, precisely such a degree of choice may be seen, for example, in *The Battle of Maldon*. The last of those retainers who choose to die with their lord is named Godric, the son of Æthelgar. A more notorious Godric, the "coward son of Odda," chose to flee on his lord's own horse at the first opportunity, to abandon the lord who gave him many gifts to secure his loyalty in battle. The contrast between those two sharply delimited choices — to do what is right, or to refuse to do what is right — is emphasized by the poem's closing description of the faithful Godric's death. "Godric often let spear go, slaughter-shaft fly at the Vikings. Thus he advanced, first among the folk, hewed and laid low, until he died in the fighting. He was not *that* Godric who fled from the battle."[29] A man may choose or he may reject the values of his community — or, exceptionally, he may raise them to a higher level as Achilles does in response to Priam's plea for the return of Hector's body — but he may not alter them at his convenience or deny their validity for him personally. The only right choice for the wanderer in his circumstances is not to give up: to accept his fate, to bear his exile bravely, to keep his thoughts to himself, and in the poet's view, to take comfort from his unfailing lord, his Father in heaven.

Exile and isolation bring the wanderer a further lesson and choice. By driving him into himself, they produce a vividly realized, sharply felt inner world, the remarkable intensity of which arouses the workings of the poet's imagination. The beauty of the poem itself is a direct product of the wanderer's isolation, which is so painful to him that his suffering brings him to the point of sensory deprivation and hallucination:

> ðonne sorg ond slæp somod ætgædre
> earmne anhogan oft gebindað.
> þinceð him on mode þæt he his mondryhten
> clyppe ond cysse, ond on cneo lecge
> honda ond heafod, swa he hwilum ær
> in geardagum giefstolas breac.
> Ðonne onwæcneð eft wineleas guma,
> gesihð him biforan fealwe wegas,
> baþian brimfuglas, brædan feþra,
> hreosan hrim ond snaw, hagle gemenged.
>   . . . Sorg bið geniwad,
> þonne maga gemynd mod geondhweorfeð;
> greteð gliwstafum, georne geondsceawað
> secga geseldan. Swimmað eft on weg!
> Fleotendra ferð no þær fela bringeð
> cuðra cwidegiedda.
>
>   (ll. 39–48, 50–55)

> [Then sorrow and sleep together
> bind fast the lonely man.
> It seems in his mind that he embraces and kisses
> his liege lord, and lays on his knee,
> his hands and head, as he used to do
> in the old days at the gift-throne.
> Then he awakens, the lordless man,
> sees before him the tawny waves.
> Sea birds bathe, preen their feathers;
> frost and snow mingle with hail.
>   . . . His sorrow is renewed
> as the memory of kinsmen passes through his mind.
> He greets them with glad words, eagerly looks on them,
> warrior companions. Then they swim away over the water.
> These fleeting spirits bring him
> no familiar spoken utterance.][30]

Thus in *The Wanderer* we find a well-developed instance in poetry of what critics usually define as a typically Romantic or modernist phenomenon.[31] The poet, here identifying himself with the wanderer in his poem, retreats within himself in response to cultural dislocation and psychic malaise. There within he finds another world of beauty, embodied in imagery that is at once hallucinatory and artistic in nature. There he finds in the compensatory rendering of suffering into poetic language — as well as in turning to religion and to the folk wisdom of his culture — a means of consoling himself and his sympathetic audience for the losses of exile.

The wanderer finds inside himself a world of space, time, memory, and feeling, the boundaries of which seem fully as large as Hamlet's inner world. The discovery of vast inner spaces in early writings is sometimes described as a roaming of the soul beyond the confines of the body, rather than as a journey into the interior.[32] But the difference is more in the descriptive metaphor than in the seeming nature of the experience. The poet of *The Wanderer* employs both kinds of imagery. His protagonist travels into the interior — the "hordcofan" — of his mind and heart, at the same time that his soul fares forth across the waves and the years to visit his lost home. The combination of imagery is not so very different from what we find in much later poetry. For example, Milton's Satan insists that "The mind is its own place" (1.254). He often journeys within vast inner regions of the self where he encounters unexpected depths beneath depths. Speaking of similar psychic experiences, Belial evokes the alternative image of "thoughts that wander through Eternity" (2.148). If at such moments we think of *Paradise Lost* as a strong precursor of Romanticism, we might likewise think of *The Wanderer* — or of Virgil and Augustine — as more distant precursors.

Premodern Subjectivity

To conclude, we find in *The Wanderer* many of the special marks that have been thought characteristic of — or even unique to — early modern and modern internalization and to the supposed late birth of "subjectivity": the sense of isolation and of separation from society and the world, the sense of a vast world within, the feeling of painful estrangement under external pressures, the need for self-reliance that requires no help from others, and the urge to transform psychic distress and loneliness into art. But the alienation experienced by the wanderer as interpreted by the poet is not fully developed in the modern sense. It evokes a distinct combination of Anglo-Saxon self-reliance and Christian *contemptus mundi*, with the stoic acceptance of events that cannot be changed. It is not a typically modernist repudiation of the traditional values that the wanderer held earlier while he belonged to the comitatus — still less the typically modernist conviction that the values which give life meaning can only be discovered from within, never learned from or imposed by society from without. The wanderer looks within, but finds there the ancient wisdom of his community. Although the poem may and sometimes has been read as a conversion of its speaker from pagan warrior to Christian penitent, close reading does not support such a view. The wanderer undergoes a conversion only in the sense that painful experience deepens the traditional wisdom of his culture and makes it real for him, as for the poet and his audience. The wanderer is what he is; what he learns, he learns not from late, external advice, but from suffering and memory.

What the subjectivity of the wanderer, as an individual in the tenth century, possesses is a well-developed sense of interior depths, of exile from society, and of the creative forces of the poetic imagination (although, of course, without his having at his disposal any of the formal terminology and theoretical framework that Locke or Coleridge would later popularize). What the subjectivity of the wanderer lacks is any sense of a purely autonomous self, of possessive individualism, of Lockean political liberalism, or of Nietzschean rebellion against social conventions. Those are the inventions that we may properly assign — in their various, unfolding degrees — to early modernism, to the Enlightenment, to Romanticism, to modernity, and to postmodernity. They may also be said to mark one of the essential differences between two otherwise similar psychic experiences: exile and alienation.

Probably these two modes of estrangement differ from each other more in degree than in kind. Still it is a modern illusion to think that "subjectivity" — insofar as it means having a well-developed sense of oneself as a person, who may choose between alternatives and experience depths of interiority — requires a concomitant politics of possessive individualism, civic humanism, or habits of resentment and dissent. Typically these characteristics are conjoined in various proportions in the modern individual — but not of necessity. Exile is the enabling ancestor of alienation but not its necessary cause. Exile and alienation represent two stages on a path of historical development. They are markers on the long wave of subjectivity that leads from the far past into the present moment. One might plausibly imagine alternative developments.

Two

Privacy and Community

❧

Medieval Confession and *Sir Gawain and the Green Knight*

The Place of Religion in Cultural Criticism

Toward the end of the millennium, many literary scholars turned from New-Critical formalism and poststructuralist theory to cultural criticism. True, much cultural criticism as now practiced in America preserves the heavy baggage of deconstruction and of neomarxist materialism. Stanley Fish argues, "if there is now no vigorous discussion of deconstruction in the academy, it is because its lessons have been absorbed . . . [and its implications] extended far beyond the realm of aesthetics and philosophy to the very texture of everyday life."[1] Nevertheless the current turn to culture provides new openings for kinds of criticism that are not deconstructive, and in particular affords us the opportunity to see the relationships between literature and religion with new eyes. Until the latter part of the twentieth century, criticism of religion and literature, like other kinds of literary criticism, emphasized the private and psychological at the expense of the social and political. The most interesting religious poetry was private devotional poetry. Some pioneers in the field were Helen Gardner, Louis Martz, and, later, Barbara Lewalski. Now, although cultural criticism is often based on secular materialist assumptions, there is growing recognition that we cannot talk about culture, especially in earlier periods, without talking about religion. That is hardly surprising, since "culture" derives from the Latin *cultus*, a word with roots in religion, sacrifice, ritual, and communal ontology.

A generation ago, when fruitful criticism of Christian devotional poetry was mainly related to the private and the psychological, the best criticism moved beyond reductive modern approaches, such as Freud's, which assume that religious faith is an illusory neurosis. Similarly, to understand the full cultural implications of religious poetry a critic should move beyond reductive approaches, such as Stanley Milgram's, which implicitly treat religious faith as superstition on the part of its victim and as an instrument for "social control" on the part of his masters. The concept of social control assumes that the purpose of religion is to manipulate people by internalizing the rules that support leaders in power. Instead of controlling people by brute force through the police or the magistrates, you teach their consciences to do the job subtly from within. Instead of putting down rebellion with the sword, you persuade people that rebellion is sinful and that they should love their rulers. If you succeed, their consciences do the job for you. There is, of course, something in such theories. From a variety of motives, political authorities are tempted to manipulate their subjects. Still, a secular theory of social control (new historicist hegemony) insufficiently explains why people are religious because when religion grows purely instrumental, a tool in the hands of politicians, in one way or another it usually stops working. Christianity, for example, can be used instrumentally for a while, but it remains a dangerous tool. It can subvert the intentions of the user who seeks control over others, because, like Judaism, it condemns pride, self-interest, injustice, and abuse of power.

To digress briefly, another useful way to distinguish between social control and the enabling of genuine repentance and forgiveness — necessary and practical to ease guilty consciences and heal social breaches — is that one is the outward correlative of the Freudian "superego" and the other the correlative of the Christian "conscience." The Freudian concept of the superego describes the involuntary imposition by outward authorities of inward, mental control, which begins with the introjection of parental authority in a child's mind and leads in extreme cases to loss of will, weakening of the sense of self, and unhealthy "heteropathic identification" with others. Although conscience includes a sense of obligation, which Kant calls, with reference to moral choice, the categorical imperative, it differs from the seemingly similar introjected authority wielded by the superego because it respects, indeed constitutes, an individual sense of self and of personal integrity. As John F. Crosby points out in a seminal article on the distinction between Freudian superego and Christian conscience (both concepts that have a considerable basis in practical human experience), "we are capable of understanding moral imperatives, of understanding where they come from and why they can bind us; we are capable of approving them with our own insight." A child's "act of understanding enables him to will what his parents will and to remain completely intact as a distinct person; his understanding lets him act with his own will. This remains true even when that which he understands is a moral imperative calling for a kind of moral obedience."[2] By contrast, the superego, which represents introjected authority, does not develop through the free and rational consent of the child but is imposed, by sleight or repetition, without regard to his freedom to choose.

Twentieth century criticism of literature and religion has thus addressed both the private and social. To these, we may add a third term, communal. Religion is the locus where, in most premodern cultures including early Christian Europe, the psychological meets the social and the communal, and various balances are struck. Extrapolating from Victor Turner's distinction between society and community,[3] by social I mean those aspects of the Church having to do with hierarchy, canon law, external control, and worldly relations: that which is sometimes referred to as the Petrine Church. By communal, I mean those aspects of the Church having to do with love, mystery, and friendship, signified by such concepts as the communion of saints, the body of Christ, the fellowship of believers, and, on the local level, the parish community. Community in the local parish or congregation is more readily understood today than that wider community (as opposed to institutional structure) of the Church that was familiar to earlier cultures.[4] As we have already noticed, while glancing at the literary criticism of the past half-century, the balance among these three elements — social, communal, and private — may sway sometimes one way, sometimes another. But short-term changes are less important than what the French *Annales* School calls the long wave: *la longue durée*. I am thinking, in particular, of what Owen Barfield and others describe as western humanity's gradual shift, over several millennia, toward greater self-consciousness, individuality, and subjectivity, in religion as in other matters.[5]

Confession and Social Control

Among the best places to look for objective evidence for internal states of mind over the past two millennia is the rite of penance or confession. Confession is especially useful to a cultural historian because it deals with the interface between objective actions and subjective thoughts, between social relationships, communal ties, and individual states of mind. Since most sins have an impact on the sinner's society and neighbors as well as on his inward mind and soul, confession as a cure for sins touches on the social, the communal, and the personal. Although through most, perhaps all, of its history the actual matter of confession was kept private, protected by the seal of the confessional, still it was often entangled in public life and politics. Even in unremarkable cases, confession was regulated and informed by bureaucratic institutions, written documents, and confessors' manuals. Through sermons, poems, and visual arts, tales of sin and penance proliferated, tales with a basis in experience — although the names were changed to protect the guilty or to increase wonder by appropriating a famous name.

As a useful analytical tool, confession appeals to cultural historians. But observers in a post-Protestant, post-Freudian America (including many practicing Catholics) commonly view it with jaundiced eyes. They regard it as a means of imposing rather than removing guilt; of inhibiting rather than freeing the spirit. Sin and guilt are presumed to be psychological categories rather than spiritual conditions, to represent neurotic repression rather than the practical results of wrong moral choices. Similarly the priestly power to excommunicate and readmit sinners into the Church has come to be regarded as a manifestation of social control rather than of charitable correction or of reconciliation to the community. Such attitudes go back to the Reformation, gain strength in the Enlightenment, and find new support in Postmodernism. In his important study, *Sin and Confession on the Eve of the Reformation*, Thomas Tentler argues that the public function of confession is "to insure discipline, to exercise control," and its private function is "reconciliation with the self and with those social norms that the penitent has internalized."[6] In other words, it provides social control externally and internally, through public sanctions and psychological manipulation. What earlier generations called "conscience" becomes introjection and internalization of social norms.

A brief example may suggest how such reductionist assumptions distort cultural analysis. Tentler takes the Church's decision at the time of Augustine to allow deathbed confessions to mark a significant turn from public to private understanding of the rite. He asserts that deathbed confession must be a pure instance of the individual's psychological need to feel good about himself, since it has no practical social purpose. Why readmit someone into the freedom of a society he is about to leave forever? He concludes: "In this ritual the function of giving psychological comfort is self-evident" (12–13). Tentler ignores the common belief of Christians that dying in a state of grace entails not only personal salvation but incorporation into the company of the blessed. The Apostles' Creed ends: "I believe . . . in the communion of saints, the forgiveness of sins, the resurrection of the body, and life everlasting." These articles of faith unfold a logic of belief as well as mere contiguity. According to an ancient commonplace: "What is the Church if not the assembly of all the saints?"[7] Shaped by modernity, we may see no immediate social purpose in the practice of deathbed confession, but people in earlier times thought differently. Moreover, deathbed confession resonates with further social consequences: it comforts family and friends; it provides virtuous examples for the living to imitate. Exemplary "last words" were immensely popular; last wills and testaments directed executors to settle all outstanding debts and quarrels and thus mend any persisting social breaches between the living and the dead. The late-modern imagination is inclined to see death as lonely annihilation, severing the individual's ties to the community. Earlier generations preferred to imagine dying in the company of family and friends, in good repute with neighbors, at peace with the world. Showing that deathbed confession has social and communal purposes does not, of course, invalidate the argument that penance could be used for social control, but it reveals the limitations to which such presuppositions are vulnerable.

Early Development of Confession and Penance: Public and Private

In the early Church penance was a serious business. Forgiveness of major sins that violated the fabric of the community, such as adultery, murder, and idolatry, could only be obtained through the canonical rite of public penance. The early Church distinguished between graver and lesser sins (see 1 John 5:16–17); a more precise line was later drawn by St. Augustine, and the full distinction is found in the *Summa* (1–2.88.2). Chaucer's Parson represents the high medieval consensus: "For sothe, synne is in two maneres; outher it is venial or deedly synne" (line 358).[8] In the early canonical rite, baptized Christians who confessed serious sins were publicly excommunicated by the bishop and forbidden the Eucharist on Ash Wednesday. They performed strenuous public penances all through Lent. On Holy Thursday they were readmitted to communion. Such public penance and absolution were permitted only once in a lifetime. Ambrose says: "There is only one penance, just as there is only one baptism."[9] Those who submitted to the rite, even after reconciliation with the Church, were permanently handicapped. They were forbidden to marry or, if married, to engage in sexual relations with their spouses, and they were not permitted to serve in the army or be ordained to the priesthood.

The first significant movement toward mitigating and privatizing canonical penance was the appearance in Ireland in the second half of the sixth century of the religious manuals called "penitentials," which codified practices more lenient and private than before.[10] Based originally on the practice and advice of holy saints and abbots, they were extra-canonical in origin and only gradually gained formal recognition.[11] The penitentials spread into England and Europe with the Irish and British missionaries. They codify and classify sins and sinners. By consulting them, a scrupulous confessor could ensure that sins were justly weighed and that penances were proportional. Typical of their specificity is a rule from the ninth century *Burgundian Penitential*: "If anyone has committed fornication with women who have fornicated with others and have lost their virginity, or with widows, he shall do penance for three years, but if a monk, seven."[12] The penitentials mark a shift toward privacy. At first, councils and popes resisted their use. In 829 The Council of Paris declared: "That the small codices that they call penitentials be completely abolished because they are opposed to canonical authority."[13] But the demand of working clerics for exact and convenient advice was too strong. By the early twelfth century, penitentials and canon laws were virtually indistinguishable.

A new period begins with Gratian's *Decretum*, which marks, in Pierre Payer's words, "the end of the long period of diverse collections of canon law and the beginning of a more sophisticated, scientific, and 'authorized' approach."[14] Gratian drew only sparingly on the penitentials themselves. But bishops still needed well-trained priests in the field to care for souls and keep the peace. Individual confessors still needed to consult practical guides. A new penitential genre appeared, the *summa confessorum* or summa for confessors. A key event in the development of penitential practice was the publication in 1215 of the bull *Omnis utriusque sexus*, in which Innocent III, following the Fourth Lateran Council, commanded all Christians who had reached the age of discretion to confess annually to their pastor. In practice, pastors used assistants, but hedge priests would not satisfy the requirement. Annual confession became known as the "Easter duty" because it normally took place at Eastertide.

The summas for confessors extended the movement from outward, public rites toward privacy and inwardness. In parallel with developments in theology, inward contrition is increasingly emphasized while harsh penalties are greatly reduced. Scholastic theologians debated the relative efficacy of outward rite and inward contrition, but by the fourteenth century a consensus had developed that both were needed, and the movement toward privatization continued. Among the more provocative and suggestive studies of penance in recent years is John Bossy's article, "Social History of Confession in the Age of the Reformation." Bossy argues that, at a moment of historical transformation, not only the Protestant Reformation but the Catholic Counter-Reformation "shifted the emphasis away from the field of objective social relations and into a field of interiorized discipline for the individual."[15] Although Tentler argues that the Fourth Lateran Council of 1215 and the papal bull *Omnis utriusque sexus* decisively privatized confession, Bossy points out that the notion of penance as a rite with social significance lingered on through the late middle ages into the Renaissance, at least up until the Council of Trent in 1551. He argues that the Council of Trent — a council that Protestants and Catholics alike immediately recognized as decisive for Catholicism in the early-modern era[16] — confirmed the dominance of a newly privatized view of confession as primarily the internal absolution of an individual's sins. But he points out that the older view — that its primary function should be to reconcile sinners to the Church and make peace in the community — was still sufficiently alive for the German theologian Johannes Gropper to urge it upon the council, "with great attention and applause" from those in attendance, although Bossy argues he did not prevail. In fact, the Council did not repudiate the social function of penance, even though it explicitly stressed its private function.[17] The essential change took place not in theology but in European culture. People were beginning to see things differently, to act on different assumptions, and to differ from their ancestors not so much in theory or in practice as in how they *saw* their practice.[18]

Practice of Confession in the Fourteenth Century

The practice of confession in late medieval Europe and England, as Bossy points out, "was a face-to-face encounter between two people who would probably have known each other pretty well,"[19] that is, between the parish priest (often aided by curates and visiting assistants) and his parishioners. The private confessional booth was not introduced until the sixteenth century, and did not come into general use until the seventeenth. The man chiefly responsible for spreading the technology of the confessional, as Bossy observes, was Cardinal Borromeo, the great Roman reformer.[20] His chief motive seems to have been to avoid the occasion or appearance of sexual scandal in connection with penance, an urgent issue because of Protestant accusations. A decision of the Roman Congregation of Bishops and Regulars in 1645 explicitly stipulates what was earlier assumed: that confessionals should be designed so that not even a little finger could be poked through the grill. Borromeo had said that the holes should be "about the size of a pea." He advised that men and women confess separately and that use of booths be obligatory for women. (In some countries, notably Spain, men rarely used the confessional; they thought it more manly to confess face-to-face.) Confessionals spread gradually, by local adoption rather than fiat, until they were regular parts of church architecture, first in Italy, then elsewhere. According to Bossy they were uncommon in France until after 1650.

In the fourteenth century, parochial confession took place

once a year, ordinarily on Maundy Thursday. Contemporary illustrations show lines of people waiting their turn to confess. A woodcut reproduced in Eamon Duffy's *Stripping of the Altars* portrays the pastor seated at the center of the picture on an elaborate chair, hearing a kneeling man's confession.[21] On his lap he holds a closed book, probably a manual for confessors ready to be consulted if an unusual case should arise. He presses his other hand against the side of his head, signifying that he is listening intently to the penitent's words and offering a degree of visual privacy. In an alcove to the right, another priest absolves a kneeling woman. He rests his hand on her wimpled head: in addition to verbal absolution in the name of the Trinity, priests traditionally signified pardon by the ritual laying-on of hands.[22] In a second alcove to the left, a hooded friar listens to another man's confession. The subordinate presence of the friar suggests peaceful cooperation in administering the annual rite between the pastor, a secular priest, and members of the mendicant orders, although, as we know from Chaucer and abundant historical evidence, there was sometimes fierce rivalry between parochial clergy and friars, as authority over administration of penance was disputed among diocesan bishops, priors, and abbots.[23] Indeed, such blurring of the lines of authority (which from one point of view might be thought scandalous but from another allowed salutary breathing room within the Church) go back to the founding of Christianity in England by St. Gregory the Great and St. Augustine when popes consistently let it be understood that the Archbishop of York (who bore the pallium) was at the same time subordinate and equal to the Archbishop of Canterbury.

In the woodcut, the lines look crowded, but the confessions, although still visible to those waiting their turn, are well spaced to preserve privacy. Another depiction, carved on a font in Walsoken, Norfolk, shows the line of waiting penitents pressing right up against the back of the person making his confession.²⁴ Probably the crowding reflects medieval artistic convention (which ignores perspective and distance) rather than actual practice. The artist needed to fit three kinds of representative figures — priest, penitent, and community — into a small panel on one face of the font. As for overhearing a penitent's words, confessional privacy was firmly established in theology and canon law. There was no canonical requirement for visual privacy, but custom recommended it. Jacobus de Clusa advises the priest to hide his face so he hears only the penitent's voice.²⁵ In a study of East Anglian font reliefs, Ann Nichols notes that the priest usually wears a hood "draped to veil his face."²⁶ Female penitents wear shielding headdresses. One male penitent wears a kind of hood turban, appropriately named a "chaperon." Still, especially in smaller churches, waiting parishioners could watch their friends (or enemies) confess. Given the nature of small communities, they would notice an absence. Whatever theologians and canonists might say, material circumstances made confession more communal than it was after enclosed confessional booths were installed.

Further to support his argument that medieval confession was predominantly social, Bossy claims that, according to many late-medieval manuals for confessors, "the average person was much more likely to tell the priest about the sins of his neighbors than about his own."²⁷ In one account, a man confesses his wife's sins to a priest, who gives him an absolution to carry back home to her. But this is clearly a shaggy-dog story. If it happened, it was retold because it was funny or scandalous.²⁸ The general topic of people who confess the sins of others, as Bossy admits, only appears in complaints about or warning against abuse of the sacrament. The frequency of these complaints and warnings testifies only to orthodox concern. Bossy adds that "the priest could not absolve a person from his sins if he proposed to remain in a state of social hostility with a neighbor: . . . it was the most frequent reason why people refused to go to confession, and the only one which received a certain degree of official tolerance. But abandoning such hostilities was not purely a matter of the heart; the commentators were clear that a man was required to show forgiveness by performing the social acts of recognition and salutation."[29] That is, he should clasp hands with his former enemy or give him the kiss of peace. This exception to the obligation, however, is explicable on two counts: first — as Bossy argues — for social reasons, namely that reconciliation with the community cannot be validly completed until serious breaches of the peace against family or neighbors have been healed; and second, for private reasons, that serious sins cannot be absolved until the individual has repented and confessed all of them without exception. Authorities agree that a confession in which the penitent holds back a mortal sin not previously confessed is invalid. According to St. Thomas, "It is irreverent and heretical to expect half a pardon from Him who is just and justice itself."[30] Refusal to repair a serious breach with a neighbor signifies a corresponding inward refusal to repent a serious sin against charity, sufficient reason to defer confession until the breach is mended.

In his metrical treatise *Handlyng Sinne*, Robert Mannyng addresses precisely this issue in his twelfth point of shrift:

> No poynte þou shalt wiþholde
> For al holy [wholly] hyt oweþ be tolde. . . .
> Telle alle þy synnes & wyþhold noun
> Or elles y seye shryft ys þer noun.
> (11,827–28, 11,843–44)[31]

"Wholeness" of confession is violated if the penitent withholds a serious sin, implying a lack of sincere contrition. It is also violated if he visits several priests and splits his sins among them.

> 3if þou þe shryue by parcelles,
> þe holy man seyþ þy shryfte þou steles.

> 3yf þou shewe one o party
> And a nouþer prest þou tellest a nouþer foly,
> þat shryfte ys noght: þy soule ys betrayd,
> And god almyghty ys myspayd.
> For to echoun þyn hert was stoken,
> A synne þou helde þeryn loken.
> þat þou wyþhelde was nat for3yve:
> þou shewedest hyt nat, hyt ys vnshryue.
> Body ne soule ys payd weyl
> Tyl þou haue told þy synne echedeyl.
>
> (ll. 1831–42)

The first error, "shriving by parcels," might arise from desire to avoid the embarrassment of doing one's Easter duty properly. Some sins are easier to confess to a stranger than to one's own pastor. It might be tempting to confess the worst of them away from home and reserve the lighter ones to satisfy the annual obligation. Chaucer's Parson confirms the point: "Also thou shalt shryve thee of alle thy synnes to o man, and nat a parcel to o man and a parcel to another ... as for shame or drede, for it nys but stranglynge of thy soule."[32]

There were, however, perfectly legitimate ways to evade the Easter duty. *Omnis utriusque sexus* requires all the faithful to confess annually to their pastors but does not discourage them from confessing oftener. Therefore in normal practice they could confess to whomever they chose as long as they did so more than once a year. The medieval Church was a scene of jurisdictional disputes among bishops, between secular and religious clergy, between pastors and friars. Lawrence Duggan argues that dissonance in regulating confession was the normal state of affairs, and that, unedifying as it may seem, these disputes give people plenty of room for maneuver. "In consequence of this disorder," Duggan says, "the average Christian could fairly well elect his confessor." Although in theory Rome demanded that all men should confess to their pastors, strict control was difficult. As Duggan argues, "If [in these matters] men of the Middle Ages knew Augustine's dictum, 'Roma dixit, causa finita est,' they paid it little heed." As Duggan, who provides plentiful documentation to support his thesis, also writes: "[P]arish discipline, however much the underlying ideal here [in the Fourth Lateran decree], remained only a dream until the modern era. This aspect of late medieval ecclesiastical organization and religious life had, like virtually every other, become highly fragmented and complex. Controversy reigned, confusion prospered, and, I deeply suspect, the harsh priests largely fell through the cracks"[33]

In fact, it was not clear, as Duggan's evidence further reveals, even what Rome wanted. The popes encouraged creative jurisdictional ambiguity. Although *Omnis utriusque sexus* demands annual confession of "omnia peccata" to the pastor, that may simply mean that all sins must be confessed to someone and annual confession made to the pastor. Pope Martin IV's bull *Ad fructus uberes* (1281) permits friars to shrive without episcopal license. It repeats the demand of Fourth Lateran for annual confession to the pastor but omits the phrase "omnia peccata." Pope Boniface VIII's *Super cathedram* (1300) requires that friars obtain the bishop's permission to shrive; this bull was vacated by Benedict XI (1304) and reinstated by Clement V and the Council of Vienne (1311). Popes John XXII (1321) and Nicholas V (1447–48) condemned John of Pouilly's thesis (1312) that all sins confessed to friars must be confessed again to the pastor. John of Pouilly, as one might expect, was a pastor. On the eve of the Reformation, the fifth Lateran Council (1516) confirmed the right of friars to shrive and neglected to mention the role of pastors at all.[34]

Thus — depending, of course, partly on one's suppositions — it may be easier to argue on the evidence that confession was efficacious as a sacrament that eased consciences and reconciled communities than that it was efficient as a means of social control. As Duggan suggests, the common people probably found it more consoling than terrifying. If they chose, they found various ways to evade the parish duty. This breakdown of the parochial system of supposed "social control" just one year before Luther posted his 95 theses undermines Steven Ozment's well-known thesis that intensifying anxiety resulting from fear of confession was an important cause of the Reformation, as well as Tentler's that the imposition of strict rules laid down by Lateran IV was being handled with increasing administrative efficiency.[35] For the most part, the sacrament was well administered for the cure of souls, but it was not well administered as a means of social control. True, Martin Luther complained that unnamed "decretals" required everyone to "make confession of all his sins once a year," which he calls "either a diabolical and murderous doctrine or . . . in need of a loose interpretation."[36] But as we have seen, by the time Luther wrote these words, *omnia peccata* had been loosely interpreted in general practice and in papal bulls for more than a century. We shall return to Luther's views on confession in the next chapter.

Social and Private Religion in the Fourteenth Century

The thirteenth and fourteenth centuries in England were a time of growing interest in religion among the laity. On the heterodox side, Wyclif and the Lollards witness to the thirst for spirituality among the gentry and common people, which arose not so much because elements in the government and clergy were corrupt and in need of reform, as some historians suggest, but because the Church successfully raised the expectations of the laity. Revolutions typically occur not at the moment of greatest oppression or corruption but in a time of rising expectations. The broadest and most obvious early modern movement toward a religion of the laity, the Protestant Reformation — as also the Counter-Reformation in certain of its aspects — evolved from earlier events and practices as well as revolting against others. The rise of lay piety within Catholicism is sometimes said to begin with the Christian humanists More and Erasmus in the sixteenth century, or with the spread of devout humanism among the followers of St. Francis de Sales and of humanitarianism among the followers of St. Vincent de Paul in the seventeenth century. But, although lay fervor was a prominent feature of the sixteenth century, it was not unprecedented. In the fourteenth century, the kind of fervent, popular religion that Scarisbrick and Duffy[37] sympathetically describe and mourn at its passing in the Reformation entered secular society both from the hierarchy above and from the laity below. As Jonathan Hughes argues in his impressive recent history of the Archdiocese of York, the period was marked both by strong Church administration and fervent piety. John Thoresby, archbishop of York (1353–73), owed his appointment to close connections with Edward III. A strong and loyal administrator, keeper of the Privy Seal and chancellor before his elevation to the pallium, Thoresby was at home in the Norman patronage system. He was trained in canon law, had served in the Papal Curia, and was a "friendly correspondent" with Pope Clement VI.[38]

Yet, if Thoresby was a loyal servant of the king, he was also admirably energetic in providing for the pastoral needs of his people during repeated visitations of the Black Death. In 1349 alone nearly half his clergy and laity died. In 1362–63, even greater numbers of benefices were vacated. In the face of such difficulties Thoresby devoted himself to building up the basics of the faith, especially to catechizing the laity. Much of this was accomplished through the annual rite of penance. Various manuals were pressed into service in York, including William of Pagula's *Oculus sacerdotis* (c. 1320), Ralph Fitz-Ralph's *Memoriale presbiterorum* (1344), William Nassyngton's *Speculum vitae*, and the anonymous *Pricke of Conscience*. Like *Handlying Sinne*, they were organized to emphasize catechetical topics: the Ten Commandments, the Seven Deadly Sins, the Seven Virtues, and the Seven Sacraments. Thus each year they provided the faithful with practical education in the basics of the faith.[39]

Thoresby and his fellow administrators may have viewed penance primarily as a social or even a legal function. Among offenses the Archbishop "reserved for his own absolution" were breaches of the social order such as "hostility toward clerics" and "all public offenses disturbing the peace of city, town, or countryside."[40] Yet this practical encouragement of lay religion fed a remarkable flowering of mystical spirituality in the archdiocese, coming not from the established religious orders but from an independent eremitical movement that arose mainly among the laity and was patronized by lay gentry. Richard Rolle, the Hermit of Hampole, was the first and most widely influential of these figures.[41] Others include the anonymous author of *The Cloud of Unknowing*, Margery Kempe, Julian of Norwich, Walter Hilton, and, later, Nicholas Love (a Carthusian with a lay following). These mystics preferred to treat sin as a spiritual, not a social, problem: as something to be cured in the depths of the soul. But to preserve good order and obedience in the Church they counseled their disciples to observe the annual obligation. Thus in the early fourteenth century, as later, two distinct approaches to the sacrament of penance coexisted in England. "Recluses were responsible for encouraging introspection in their clients, and they . . . [regarded] confession as an intimate disclosure to an understanding spiritual guide. Parish confessions were made in front of the congregation to a parish priest . . . they were public affairs, but confessions were made to anchorites through barred windows in what was the first step towards the development of the private confessional."[42] The great mystics of the fourteenth century still live on in their treatises, while the bishops and laymen have passed away. Yet one should credit Thoresby, who saw to it that squires and plowmen learned their paternosters, for preparing the ground for spiritual flowering. Bishops, charged with administering dioceses in which violence, murder, abduction of wards, and assaults on priests were common, naturally wanted to keep the peace. Anchorites were free to care for the inward soul. For the most part, these different personalities lived together in the same Church with mutual respect.

Handlyng Synne: *Individual and Communal Guilt*

Robert Mannyng's *Handlyng Synne*, a practical, representative penitential manual set in verse, takes a middle way. It respects the privacy of confession.

> Of pryvytees speke y nou3t:
> þe pryuetees wyle y nou3t name,
> For noun þarfore shuld me blame.
> leuer ys me þat þey be hydde
> þan for me oponly were kydde.
> Noþeles þey mote be shreuyn
> 3yf 3yfte of grace shal be 3euyn.
>
> (lines 30–36)

The "privities" of confession, the sins that the priest privately hears, must remain under seal. Yet the penitent sinner must confess them to the priest if he wishes to receive absolution, by the "gift of grace" conveyed through the sacrament. In his fifth point of shrift, Mannyng urges sinners not to let their fear that the priest may betray their secrets keep them from confession:

> And some lette here synne to seye
> For doute of prest þat wyl hem bewreye.
> No shame myghte to moche be
> To prest þat telþ þat pryuyte.
> Letteþ nat 3oure synne to telle:
> þenkeþ on þe peynes of helle.
>
> (lines 505–10)

Mannyng warns hesitant sinners, who fear that the priest might reveal their secret sins, that that would be less terrible than not to confess them, which would lead to the "pains of hell." A priest could commit no act more shameful than to break the seal of the confessional, for in doing so he would undermine a sacrament given by Christ to rescue sinners from hell. Mannyng's word to describe such an act is "betray."

Throughout *Handlyng Synne*, Mannyng also delineates the social consequences of sin. In his various tales, sin breaks the bonds of families and of communities. Sin leads to sin, and violence to violence. In one story (lines 1255–74), a woman who goes to the water to bathe gives her clothes to her daughter to hold, warning her not to sleep but to be ready to bring them instantly. When she calls for her clothes, the daughter fails to appear. The impatient mother curses her: "þe deuyl come on þe." Sure enough, the devil comes and strikes her mad where she stands. The story, which Mannyng tells under the fourth commandment, honor thy father and thy mother, warns against abusing parental authority as well as cursing. It pictures sin as personal but social in its consequences. Yet the individual's fate, salvation or damnation, is never far from Mannyng's mind. In other tales, hardened sinners sicken or drop dead on the spot, struck down by God for their wickedness but also as exemplary warnings to others not to sin or to repent, lest they suffer a similar penalty.

A good indication that sins thought to violate the communal good were more harshly judged than those of a more private nature is the different treatment of various sexual sins recommended by the manuals. Fornication, heterosexual intercourse between two unmarried lay persons, was always considered less grave than adultery, in which at least one party is married. Indeed, while the Church did not condone sexual relations outside of marriage, the penitentials seldom prescribe a specific penalty for relations between unmarried lay persons. St. Thomas distinguishes clearly between simple fornication and adultery in the *Summa*. His reasons are two, personal and social. First, fornication is a "carnal" sin but adultery a "spiritual" one, more damaging to the soul. Second, fornication is a sin against one's own body, adultery an injustice against others that violates the marriage vow and damages society.⁴³ So Mannyng is in the central tradition when he treats adultery as an especially wicked violation of the social bonds:

> 3yf þou fordost þe weyl fare
> Betwyxe þo þat weddyd are,
> þou synnyst certys wykkydly
> And brekst spousale and cumpany.
>
> (lines 1725-28)

Adultery "breaks marriage and community." Mannyng makes the same point in his discussion of lust or lechery:

> As wedded man takþ a nouþers wyf,
> þat ys more synful lyf.
> 3yf wedded man sengle womman takþ,
> For soþe spousebreche þer he makþ.
>
> (lines 7361-64)

According to Mannyng, wife stealing is even worse than consensual adultery, because it "raises strife." Offending God, it also offends the social order and "fills the world with great dread" (lines 7403-06).

Treatment of masturbation and bestiality in penitential texts measures how seriously sins were viewed that were predominantly, if not entirely, personal and carnal rather than social. The penitentials are relatively lenient with bestiality, by contrast with the Council of Ancyra and early authorities who advocated severe penalties. Theodulf of Orleans (late 8th century) writes: "[T]he law of Moses lays down the death sentence for those having sexual relations with a mule and with a male and with a blood relative." in contrast, the penitentials usually prescribe only a few months' penance for masturbation, rather than the year or more accorded fornication.⁴⁴ Bossy recounts an irresistible tale from Tuscany (c. 1515).

> A young peasant comes to confess at Easter, and after confessing a whole string of thefts, including that of a quantity of corn from the priest, pauses overcome by embarrassment.

>Encouraged to continue, he finally confesses that when he was 15 he used to go out in the meadows to masturbate, which gave him great pleasure. The priest told him to masturbate whenever he felt like it, but keep his hands off of other people's property, and above all give him back his corn.[45]

Charming as this is, I am sure Bossy knows that it, too, is a shaggy dog story.[46] Yet it is true that masturbation, though a violation of chastity and purity, was not taken as seriously as other sexual offenses. It was more embarrassing, not more serious. It hurt mainly the perpetrator.

I say "mainly," rather than entirely, as Bossy assumes, since, if indulgence of lust blinds the eye and darkens the soul, as tradition has taught since Plato and Aristotle, even private sexual sins have social consequences. A recent statement of Pope John Paul II to the Bishops offers a cogent summary of traditional wisdom concerning the connections between private sin and its social and communal consequences:

>To speak of social sin means in the first place to recognize that, by virtue of human solidarity which is as mysterious and intangible as it is real and concrete, each individual's sin in some way affects others. This is the other aspect of that solidarity which on the religious level is developed in the profound and magnificent mystery of the communion of saints, thanks to which it has been possible to say that "every soul that rises above itself, raises up the world" [Elisabeth Leseur, *Journal et Pensées de Chaque Jour* (Paris, 1918), p. 31]. To this law of ascent there unfortunately corresponds the law of descent. Consequently one can speak of a communion of sin, whereby a soul that lowers itself through sin drags down with itself the church and, in some way, the whole world. In other words, there is no sin, not even the most intimate and secret one, the most strictly individual one, that exclusively concerns the person committing it. With greater or lesser violence, with greater or lesser harm, every sin has repercussions on the entire ecclesial body and the whole human family. According to this first meaning of the term, every sin can undoubtedly be considered as social sin.[47]

Although for Mannyng the worst sexual sins destroy marriage and community, most of his lengthy discussion of the seventh deadly sin of lechery is given over not to the offenses themselves but to avoiding the occasions of sin: dwelling upon dreams, sinful imaginings, temptations of the eye, keeping private company with women, and so forth. If such temptations are welcomed and entertained, Mannyng asserts, they will become habitual and will lead inevitably to sinful and antisocial acts. For similar reasons, for fear of introducing penitents to tempting thoughts and images which might not otherwise have occurred to them, confessors were discouraged, sometimes by force of law, from questioning them too specifically about sexual matters. In the strict hierarchical order, pride was the first and deadliest of the seven deadly sins, and lust was among the least. Yet medieval spiritual advisers generally recognized that these two sins were the most troublesome, prevalent, and dangerous, both to individuals and to society as a whole.

Thus according to Mannyng's way of thinking, what is inward and spiritual cannot be altogether separated from what is outward and social. This is not, of course, the modern view of things, which reverses the connection. It prefers a psychological, sociological, and anthropological approach, asking not how inward habits lead to outward actions, but how impersonal cultural forces shape the subject inwardly. Thus a society might be clinically analyzed and categorized as a "shame culture" or a "guilt culture," depending on what methods it uses to impose social control on the individual. Guilt is merely the introjection of cultural and parental norms, a subtler means of social control than public shame. For example, Tentler writes: "From a penance of shame and expiation, the church, through centuries of development, had turned to a penance of guilt and remorse"[48] The modernist solution is for the free soul simply to shake guilt off. Doubtless western cultures have witnessed recurrent episodes of overly scrupulous or even pathological guilt about sexual matters, but that still does not render all guilt pathological. Some guilt is well-earned. It serves a beneficial, not a repressive, purpose, socially as well as spiritually. Jean Delumeau's massive, overwhelmingly documented study of guilt in Western culture, for all its admirable scholarship, fails to distinguish sufficiently between kinds of guilt, and in particular to ask whether guilt may not sometimes be appropriate. To suggest that internalized shame and guilt, like subjectivity, first emerge in Europe in the fourteenth century, in the Renaissance, or with Kierkegaard, is to ignore widespread manifestations of shame and guilt in classical writings, long before Christianity prevailed as a dominant cultural force.[49] The man entirely without guilt or shame has always been viewed — and rightly so — as a monster, as an object of horror. Paradoxically, even modern psychology, which declares guilt and shame to be neurotic, admits that their absence is psychotic.

The older view of these inward perturbations recognized the possibility of over-scrupulosity or false guilt but provided, in the rite of penance, an effective instrument to assuage shame and remove guilt. These were, however, only the proximate effects of penance's ultimate ends: to repair the soul and return it to the community of the just. According to Mannyng, there are eight "graces of shrift," or what we might call reasons or purposes for confessing:

1. "He makþ þy soule for to live."
2. "Hyt aleggeþ þe of heuy charge"
3. "A noynting ys gode for body sore / And shryfte ys a noynting for euermore."
4. "shryft shent þe fende of helle."
5. "Hyt makþ vs lefe þer we were loþe / Hyt peseþ god whan he ys wroþ."
6. "Hyt ioyeþ al þe court of heuene."
7. "þat oure shryfte þe deuel blyndeþ."
8. "Hyt makþ Ihu cryst to þe myke."[50]

These graces may conveniently be reduced to five: Penance relieves the sinner of a heavy internal burden; it protects him from the devil and the threat of hell; it cures and revivifies his soul eternally; it reconciles him with God through Christ; it brings him into the joyous company of the angels and saints. Some of these graces, especially inward relief and freedom from anxiety, were felt immediately in the natural order. They are social and psychological effects, about which modern scholars can agree to disagree. Some, if they are real at all, belong entirely to the supernatural order: salvation and eternal life in the communion of saints. They posit the existence of transcendent realities and therefore constitute a much greater stumbling block to modern views concerning the nature of things and of rational scholarly argument. Following a basically materialistic view of human affairs that can be traced back to Sir Francis Bacon and his contemporaries,[51] modernity has decided to concern itself only with what Bacon called "second causes," that is, natural effects in the material world, including such matters as psychological comfort and social control. The conventional boundaries of the debate allow us only to argue whether these effects — themselves only partly observable and subject by their nature to a range of interpretation — are predominantly beneficial or malevolent: whether they free the subject or increase his or her subjection. The problem, of course — the real chasm between cultures — is that Mannyng undoubtedly thought that the ultimate benefits of penance — salvation of the soul and reconciliation with God in the loving communion of the angels and saints — overshadows its immediate pragmatic ones, peace of mind in a reunified community. To understand the past, we need first to understand our own chosen or assumed cultural constraints. How to decide and what if anything to do about these matters, however, is beyond the scope of this study.

Confession in Sir Gawain: Isolation and Fellowship

To illustrate how confession in the later middle ages was thought to have a double effect — both to repair social breaches by reconciliation with the community and individual sins by the cleansing and renovation of the soul — we may turn to *Sir Gawain and the Green Knight*. If the following reading of the poem seems brief after the comparatively lengthy discussion of the historical and cultural background, that is partly because the background is unfamiliar to most readers, and partly because it gives us needed context for the following chapter, on the social, communal, and private significance of confession in *The Faerie Queene*.

The Sacrament of Penance seems to play only a small role in *Sir Gawain*, where it occupies part of a stanza. Yet, given the author's constant concern with religious matters, his unmatched "moral sensitiveness," as Tolkien and Gordon call it,[52] and the larger context in which he places Gawain's formal confession, this brief mention is highly significant. On the morning of his third temptation in the castle of Sir Bertilak, right after he accepts the lady's girdle as a supposed magical protection against injury, Gawain rises, dons his finest clothes, tucks the girdle away in a safe place, and goes to the chapel to confess his sins. The whole stanza deserves close attention:

> Thene lachchez ho hir leue, and leuez hym þere,
> For more myrþe of þat mon mo3t ho not gete.
> When ho watz gon, Sir Gawayn gerez hym sone,
> Rises and riches hym in araye noble,
> Lays vp þe luf-lace þe lady hym ra3t,
> Hid hit ful holdely, þer he hit eft fonde.
> Syþen cheuely to þe chapel choses he þe waye,
> Preuély aproched to a prest and prayed hym þere
> þat he wolde lyste his lyf and lern hym better
> How his sawle schulde be saued when he schuld seye heþen.
> þere he schrof hym schyrly and schewed his mysdedez,
> Of þe more and þe mynne, and merci besechez,

48 *Aspects of Subjectivity*

> And of absolucioun he on þe segge calles;
> And he asoyled hym surely, and sette hym so clene
> As domezday schulde haf ben diȝt on þe morn.
> And syþen he mace hym as mery among þe fre ladyes,
> With comlych caroles and alle kynnes ioye,
> As neuer he did bot þat daye, to þe derk nyȝt,
> > with blys.
> > Vche mon hade daynté þare
> > Of hym, and sayde, "Iwysse,
> > þus myry he watȝ neuer are,
> > Syn he com hider, er þis.
>
> > > (lines 1870–92)[53]

> Then the lady takes her leave, and leaves him there,
> For more mirth from that man she might not get.
> When she has gone, Sir Gawain dresses himself —
> Arises, and adorns him in noble array —
> Lays up the love-lace the lady had left him,
> Hid it full safely, where he found it again.
> Then quickly he finds his way to the chapel,
> Privately approached a priest, and prayed him there
> That he would listen to his life and teach him better,
> How his soul should be saved when he should go hence.
> There he shrove him surely, and showed his misdeeds,
> Of the largest and the least, and beseeches mercy,
> And he calls on the man for absolution;
> And he absolved him surely, and made him as clean
> As if Doomsday should have dawned the very next day.
> And then he made him as merry among the noble ladies
> With lovely carol-dancing and every kind of joy,
> As never he did till that day, till the dark night:
> > With bliss.
> > Everyone was delighted
> > With him, and said, "Certainly,
> > He never was this merry before,
> > Since he came here — till now."

Several points are noteworthy in this description of Gawain's confession and its aftermath. First, he makes a private, personal confession. Not only does he confess "Preuély," but he manages to visit the chapel and return without anyone suspecting what he is up to. This is not, plainly, anything like an Easter confession, witnessed by a congregation, nor does Gawain make it to his usual confessor or pastor. We are told that it is a full confession, which includes both serious and venial sins. It is the kind of confession in which the priest plays the role of a skillful catechist and spiritual director. Presumably he not only questions Gawain closely, according to fourteenth century practice, taking him through the traditional categories — the ten commandments, the seven deadly sins, and so forth — but also counsels him spiritually, teaching him better how to save his soul. In describing Gawain's confession, the poet noticeably observes the seal of the sacrament and refrains from telling us what his sins are. For the poet to allow an audience to overhear the confession would strike a false note. One vital point he leaves entirely dark is whether Gawain confesses that he accepted the girdle from Bertilak's wife. Arguably, he does not. If he had any idea that accepting the gift was sinful and tried to confess it, his absolution would surely be contingent on restitution. We know that he tucked the girdle away in his room before confessing and that he intends to reclaim and use it afterward. Yet the poet assures us that Gawain withholds nothing. He confesses "the largest and the least." The poet further tells us that Gawain is "surely" absolved, that he leaves the confessional spiritually clean and ready for judgment. We can only conclude that the poet considers Gawain's behavior in accepting and retaining the girdle not sinful but — as we shall see — shameful: an offence against chivalric honor, not against God or religion. We shall return to this point.

Despite the poet's reticence about details, Gawain's confession is clearly private. We are not told that he makes it to a hermit through the bars of a grill; otherwise it has all the marks that characterize private confession in the fourteenth century. Yet, as the stanza unfolds, a further immediate effect of his secret confession is plainly communal. Gawain emerges to become the very soul of joyful fellowship. Of course, his conduct testifies to his unpretentious courage, but primarily it testifies to the power of the sacrament to remove fear and anxiety and to reunite the individual with the community. Never is Gawain more the center of Christmas festivities than after he has cleansed his soul of sins. Gawain does not simply present an outward show of fortitude, a stiff upper lip. He truly becomes what he seems: a chief celebrant in the joyous singing and dancing, an exemplary model of communal love.

Like *The Wanderer*, *Sir Gawain and the Green Knight* achieves some of its strongest effects by contrasting communal joy and comradeship with loneliness, and it does so in similar ways. Arthur's court is the epitome of Christian community and good fellowship, as the opening feast reveals. Gawain's joyful mood a year later, amid the festive nobles and ladies at Bertilak's castle, plainly echoes the earlier passage in which the poet describes the holiday exuberance at Arthur's court after the celebration of New Year's mass:

> Wyle Nw 3er watz so 3ep þat hit watz nwe cummen,
> þat day doubble on þe dece watz þe douth serued.
> Fro þe kyng watz cummen with kny3tes into þe halle,
> þe chauntré of þe chapel cheued to an ende.
> Loude crye watz þer kest of clerkez and oþer
> Nowel nayted onewe, neuened ful ofte;
> And syþen riche forth runnen to reche hondeselle,
> 3e3ed 3eres-3iftes on hi3, 3elde him bi hond,
> Debated busyly aboute þo giftes;
> Ladies la3ed ful loude, þo3 þay lost haden
> And he þat wan watz not wroþe, þat may 3e wel trawe.
> (lines 60–69)

> While New Year was so fresh that it had just arrived,
> That day twice on the dais the company was served,
> When the King had come with his knights into the hall
> The sung mass in the chapel having come to an end.
> Loud was the cry of the priests and the others,
> Celebrated Noël anew, repeated it often,

> Then the nobles run forth to fetch hand-gifts,
> Cried "New-Year's gifts" aloud, and held them in hand,
> Debated busily about those gifts,
> Ladies laughed full loudly, even though they had lost,
> And he that won was not wroth, that you may well believe.

Modern readers may be puzzled at the way the Gawain poet runs the sacred and secular together. The chanting of Mass gives way to the shouting of gamesome courtiers, and the priests call out more loudly than anyone. Celebration of Mass gives way to celebration of banqueting, gift-giving, and kissing games, much as Gawain's sacramental confession changes his mood to pure joy, to the extent that he becomes the life of the party. Religion is not a separate category; it permeates life. Arthur's court rules as much by example as by the prowess of his knights, and the greatest example Camelot gives is joy of community, based on chivalric and religious ideals set in the kingdom's heart. Never is this more evident than on the festive occasion of the Christmas season. Recognizing the moral authority vested in the communal image of Arthur's court, which legitimates political authority, Morgan Le Fay aims to tarnish or destroy it, thus to undermine its civilizing influence in the hearts of observers. Indeed, although Gawain is welcomed into Bertilak's castle from the first as the best possible ambassador from Arthur's court — someone to be closely observed and imitated — not until after he has returned from making his confession does he shine with the irresistible joy and communal fellowship that such an ambassador should display.

In sharp contrast with the communal joy at Arthur's court that opens the poem is the bleak isolation of Gawain's quest for the Green Chapel at its center. The quest resembles an exile. It evokes strong emotions: forlornness, forsakenness, loneliness. The hero, deprived of the loving support of friends and companions, is driven into himself. In these circumstances, *Sir Gawain*, like *The Wanderer*, resorts to vivid natural description. The landscape of *Sir Gawain* (unlike the customary allegorical *paysage moralisé*) is almost unmatched in its detailed naturalism before the eighteenth century. The only poem that approaches it in this regard is Wyatt's *Mine Own John Poyns* — which also portrays isolation and exile. The detailed material vividness and the human loneliness of this landscape combine, for they are products of the same experience:

> For werre wrathed hym not so much, þat wynter nas wors,
> When þe colde cler water from þe cloudez schadde,
> And fres er hit falle my3t to þe fale erþe.
> Ner slayn wyth þe slete he sleped in his yrnes
> Mo ny3tez þen innoughe in naked rokkez
> þer as claterande fro þe crest þe colde borne rennez
> And henged he3e ouer his hede in hard iisseikkles. . . .
> Bi a mounte on þe morene meryly he rydes
> Into a forest ful dep þat ferly watz wylde,
> Hi3e hillez on vche a halue, and holtwodez vnder
> Of hore okez ful hoge a hundreth togeder;
> þe hasel and þe ha3þorne were harled al samen,
> With ro3e raged mosse rayled aywhere,
> With mony briddez vnblyþe vpon bare twyges,
> þat pitosly þer piped for pyne of þe colde.
> þe gome vpon Gryngolet glydez hem vnder,
> þur3 mony misy and myre, mon al hym one,
> Carande for his costes lest he ne keuer schulde
> To se þe seruyse of þat syre, þat on þat self ny3t
> Of a burde watz borne oure baret to quelle;
> And þerfore sykyng he sayde, "I beseche þe, Lorde,
> And Mary, þat is myldest moder so dere,
> Of sum herber þer he3ly I my3t here masse,
> Ande þy matynez tomorne, mekely I ask,
> And þerto prestly I pray my Pater and Aue
>   and Crede."
>   He rode in his prayere,
>   And cryed for his mysdede,
>   He sayned hym in syþes sere,
>   And sayde, "Cros Kryst me spede!"
>   (lines 726–32, 740–62)

> For war did not anger him so much, that winter was not worse,
> When the cold, clear rain shed from the clouds,
> And froze ere it might fall to the pale earth;
> Near slain with sleet he slept in his irons,
> More nights than enough in the naked rocks,
> Where clattering from the crest the cold brook runs,
> And hung high over his head in hard icicles. . . .
> Past a mount in the morning merrily he rides
> Into a forest full deep, that was fiercely wild,
> High hills on each half, and thick woods beneath,
> Of hoar oaks full huge, a hundred together,
> The hazel and the hawthorn were gnarled all together,
> With rough, ragged moss hung everywhere,
> With many birds, unhappy, perched on bare twigs,
> That piteously piped there, for pain of their cold.
> The man upon Gringolet glides underneath them,
> Through many a marsh and mire, a man all alone;
> He feared for the cost to him, lest he fail to attain
> To see the service of that Sire, who on that same night
> Of a maiden was born, our pain and strife to quell.
> And therefore sighing he said, "I beseech thee, Lord,
> Some harbor where haply I might hear mass,
> And Thy matins tomorrow, meekly I ask,
> And thereto promptly I pray my pater and ave
>   And creed."
>   He rode in his prayer,
>   And wept for his misdeeds,
>   He crosses himself several times
>   And said, "Cross of Christ, speed me!"

Gawain can face monsters and giants with equanimity but fears to be alone. He fears especially to be alone on Christmas day, when, of all days of the year, he should be in good Christian company, hearing mass and matins and celebrating the joyous feast in a civilized community.[54]

Christmas is, of course, a Holy Day of Obligation, according to the precepts of the Church, which (then as now) define the Third Commandment's obligation to "keep holy the Sabbath" as requiring attendance at Mass on Sundays and certain major holy days. Since Gawain is pledged by oath and duty to quest through the wilderness seeking the Green Chapel, he cannot reasonably be faulted for neglecting this grave obligation if unavoidable circumstances simply do not allow him to fulfill it — although the prospect of failure nonetheless troubles him. The poem is silent on whether Gawain has earlier been given the opportunity to attend Mass on any of the dozen or so Sundays that have passed during his travels through uncivilized regions. Unlike the wilderness portrayed in the *Quest del Saint Graal* (c. 1225), for example, which is dotted with Cistercian hermitages where wandering knights conveniently find the solace of Mass, confession, and good spiritual advice, what we see of the wilderness in *Sir Gawain* is dark, cold, savage, and lonely, populated mainly by beasts and monsters.

So presumably Gawain's long isolation and estrangement as well as the prospect of missed Christmas cause him to "weep for his misdeeds." They arouse contrition not only because he is about to miss a Holy Day of Obligation — for which he could hardly be blamed in the circumstances — but also because of all the unnamed sins he has committed during his wanderings far from Court, Chapel, and priests: those many sins, "largest" and "least," which he will later confess at Bertilak's castle. Next to the prospect of imminent death, which he will face in a short while, isolation is the most potent cause of his spiritual introspection and prayer for amendment. This inward crisis marks a turning point. Driven by deep anxiety that he may never complete his lonely quest, no sooner has Gawain signed himself for the third time than he sees a "won," a dwelling, in the midst of the woods, surrounded by lawns and civilized appurtenances. With this prompt answer to his prayers, he emerges safely from his long trial by isolation and confronts his next challenge.

When Gawain leaves Bertilak's castle for the pledged encounter at the Green Chapel, he reverts from company to loneliness. Again there are passages of vivid natural description.

þay bo3en bi bonkkez þere bo3ez are bare,
þay clomben bi clyffez þer clengez þe colde.
þe heuen watz vp halt bot vgly þer-vnder;
Mist muged on þe mor, malt on þe mountez,
Vch hille hade a hatte, a myst-hakel huge.

(lines 2077–81)

They ride by banks where the boughs are bare,
They climb by cliffs where the cold clings,
The clouds were high, but ugly beneath;
Mist drizzled on the moor, melted on the mountains,
Each hill had a hat, a huge cape of mist.

Gawain's guide leaves him to finish his quest alone. In parting, he urges Gawain to avoid the Green Knight, whose grisly strength he cannot possibly survive. Since Gawain will be alone, no one will know if he keeps tryst or not. If he chooses to avoid the meeting, the guide will keep his secret faithfully.[55] The guide's words parody the seal of confessional. They are parodic because the fault he offers to hide is against honor, not sin but shame, and because his role as a perverse spiritual advisor is to tempt rather than absolve. Gawain politely declines. He believes that the guide would keep his fearsome oath. But for Gawain honor is not just what others think of him. It is too thoroughly and willingly internalized for the promise of secrecy to tempt him.

Internalized shame is not quite the same as guilt. *Sir Gawain and the Green Knight* is consciously and centrally concerned with questions raised by two codes, not altogether congruous, the Christian and the chivalric. There are separate questions of virtue and honor, sin and dishonor, guilt and shame. Gawain's temptation by the lady is, of course, central to the poet's delicate and appreciative analysis of these matters. Should Gawain accede to her thinly veiled seductions and make love to her, he would commit the mortal sin of adultery and betray his host's hospitality — the latter offense both dishonorable *and* sinful. But he cannot flatly refuse her, for that too would be ungentle, a grievous offense against honor. Even to acknowledge that he suspects her of tempting him would be boorish. As many readers observe, Gawain treads a very delicate path, and does so with magnificent, goodnatured grace. His decision to keep tryst with the Green Knight is presented in a way that clearly indicates that for him honor is so thoroughly internalized that he will not deny it even when he finds himself utterly alone, isolated from all observers. Ironically, the guide's role, against his intention, is to emphasize that Gawain does not need the community's presence to bolster his inward sense of honor. Honor is not just a personal matter, any more than sin is. But Gawain is sufficiently at one with his community to bear its honor and trust within himself.

Gawain has committed a fault by accepting the girdle and concealing it from Bertilak, contrary to their agreement. The law of self-preservation mitigates his fault, while his trusting to supposed magic increases it. However that may be, the relative slightness of his fault is proportional to the small nick he receives at the third swing of the Green Knight's axe. He feels shamed only after Bertilak reveals who he is, and that he knows what Gawain has done. Bertilak's words simultaneously parody confession, mock Gawain's *untrawthe,* and offer a truce, or social reconciliation:

> þou art confessed so clene, beknowen of þy mysses,
> And hatz þe penaunce apert of þe poynt of myn egge,
> I halde þe polysed of þat ply3t and pured as clene
> As þou hadez neuer forfeted syþen þou watz fyrst borne.
> (lines 2391–94)

> Thou art confessed so clean, shriven of thy faults,
> And hast thy visible penance at the edge of my weapon,
> I hold thee cleansed of that offence and purified as clean
> As if thou hadst never transgressed since thou wast first born.

Since Gawain has offended against Bertilak, although his rebuke stings, it releases him from that aspect of his debt. At

Privacy and Community 57

the same time, Bertilak rubs it in that Gawain actually did not confess to him that he had kept the girdle, and certainly not wholly nor "cleanly." Thus he subjects him to ironic mockery, pretending to "shrive" him of a fault he tried to conceal.

After the explanations are done, Gawain rides home to Arthur's court. He wears the lady's girdle openly on his shoulder like a baldric, as a badge of dishonor for all to see. Bertilak has forgiven him personally for his breach of their agreement, but he has power to forgive only the offense against himself. Gawain has also offended against the honor of his community. As he tells the court his adventures, his heart burns inwardly with intense shame:

> He tened quen he schulde telle,
> He groned for gref and grame;
> þe blod in his face con melle
> When he hit schulde schewe, for schame.
>
> (lines 2501–04)

> He suffered torments when he spoke,
> He groaned for grief and mortification;
> The blood began to swirl in his face,
> When he revealed it, for shame.

Gawain concludes his tale by insisting that his shame is ineradicable, that his honor can never be restored to its former brightness.

> "þis is þe token of vntrawþe þat I am tan inne,
> And I mot nedez hit were wyle I may last;
> For non may hyden his harme, bot vnhap may hit,
> For þer hit onez is tachched twynne wil hit neuer."
>
> (lines 2509–12)

> "This is the token of falseness that I was caught in,
> And I must needs wear it as long as I live,
> For no one can conceal his fault, but bad luck may reveal it,
> For where it once sticks, it will never let go."

Like sin, shame can be hidden; but unlike sin, Gawain insists, it cannot be undone. Wherever it fastens, it sticks forever, within the mind if not to the outward reputation. Gawain felt no such compunction earlier about confessing his sins and putting them cheerfully behind him. As a good Christian, he knows that there is an established rite for absolving sins, the sacrament of penance, founded and authorized by Christ himself. Even a bad confession could subsequently be repaired by a good one. If that were his problem — that he should have confessed keeping the girdle to the priest rather than to Bertilak — his solution would be simple: confess again, to one of the priests at Arthur's court. But his problem is not sin; it is dishonor, an offense that renders him unworthy of association with his noble peers. An equivalent mechanism to repair honor is lacking.

Gawain's first act upon meeting his friends is, in fact, another kind of confession. Unlike confession of sins, he makes it to a court of honorable peers — knights and ladies — not to a priest, and he confesses openly, not secretly. In response to his anguished despair, King Arthur devises an impromptu chivalric rite, which removes his shame and readmits him to full membership in the court, just as the rite of penance absolves sin and readmits to full membership in the Church. Adopting the girdle as a badge of honor, Arthur and his knights hit on a method to repair the breach and restore Gawain fully to the community. In a gesture of remarkable courtesy, they bring the community to him, since he judges himself unworthy to rejoin them. *Hony soy qui mal pence* is their motto. No one is perfect, but Gawain is the best of knights, and Arthur's is the most Christian and chivalric of courts. Evil is he who thinks evil of it.

What *Sir Gawain and the Green Knight* tells us about the balance of public and private in the fourteenth century is not easily reconcilable with the modernist view that individual freedom is opposed to social participation and obligation, that society controls the individual by outward sanctions and inward guilt, and that Christian guilt is nothing but social control and discipline driven inward, where it festers as psychological neurosis and susceptibility to political mystification and domination. One of the essential marks of chivalry is honor; another is freedom. In Middle English, to be "free" is interchangeable with the qualities of gentility, nobility, and knighthood. Neither is possible without the other. Terrible as his predicament becomes, Gawain freely, even joyously, submits himself to the internal constraints of honor. He chooses freely and rationally to impose them on himself. His service is neither forced nor slavish. At any moment he could choose otherwise, but then he would cease to be himself — the best ambassador of what Arthur's court represents. The Gawain poet has a splendid grasp of the complexities of life in society, the making of civilization, and the subtlety of relations among individuals, cultures, and ideals of conduct. Like the Wanderer, Gawain displays interior depths and strong inner resources. They come to the fore especially when he is subjected to the psychological pressures of isolation. But he is capable of more quotidian introspection, as is shown by his confession, which he makes without fuss as a matter of course. His religious confession is not a public ritual but inward, private, and spiritual. Yet still it has power to knit him more closely to the community in which he finds himself. So too with his chivalric confession to his fellow knights and ladies of the court. In *Gawain*, forgiveness of guilt and forgiveness of shame have rich connections to the community and to the individual's inner life. They may be taken as synecdochic for the medieval balance in most areas of life among the social, the communal, and the private.

THREE

Sin and Penance at the Reformation

֎

Redcrosse, the Church, and Everyman

As Leo Miller has suggested, the Reformation put many basic theological and legal principles into a state of contention and uncertainty for as long as a hundred years, not only among the radical sects but within the major denominations. Countries did not, ordinarily, change their allegiance from Catholicism to Protestantism without open debate on many fundamentals of belief and culture, and authoritative resolution of those debates was not always immediately forthcoming or unquestioned.[1] Although Protestant leaders spoke with ringing certainty on some few points — notably on their opposition to the papacy — for the most part, after the authority of one universal Church came into question, everything — to use an apt late-modern phrase — was up for grabs. Recent historians remind us that the form that the Reformation eventually took in Europe and in England was not historically inevitable.² Many seemingly accidental contingencies were involved, including the notorious fact that when things settled down after the Thirty Years' War — as was also the case in England in the sixteenth century — most countries turned Protestant or Catholic according to the beliefs and political interests of their rulers. In England, there was a very complicated process of imposition from above meeting enthusiastic support from some below, as well as widespread popular resistance and even open revolt on the part of others. Altogether the process involved many economic, political and cultural forces as well as honest differences of religious opinion. Increasing interest among historians in the practices and beliefs of ordinary people has brought such issues to the fore, although sympathizers with the common people have often been reluctant to set aside long-established Whig views of progress and to reconsider the historical evidence impartially.³

In the previous chapter we looked at the rite of penance as a useful indicator of the relative balance among public, communal, and private concerns in the fifteen centuries leading to the Reformation, as exemplified by *Sir Gawain and the Green Knight*. In this chapter we shall consider what happened to the whole constellation of practices and beliefs that had been integrated into the single rite or sacrament of penance in the early and medieval Church — ideas of sin, reprobation, excommunication, repentance, reconciliation, forgiveness, and absolution — when they were cut loose from that rite. Over the years, many scholars have tried to explain to modern readers, to whom these religious concerns may seem like a foreign language, what Spenser and his contemporaries meant. What I should like to attempt, instead, involves a thought experiment of a different order. Namely, how might Spenser's resolutely Protestant treatment of these various topics, which had formerly been connected and subsumed under the rite or sacrament of penance, have looked to a late medieval observer or interpreter? How might they appear when viewed in terms of the cultural assumptions of the past instead of the future? This deliberate reversal of historical perspective may help us see more clearly how the balance between the social, the communal, and the private actually shifted in the English Reformation and Renaissance, and what may have been some of the causes and consequences of these changes. Having large territories yet to cover, we shall again concentrate in depth on a significant, representative literary exemplar: the tale of the Redcross Knight in book 1 of Spenser's *Faerie Queene*. But we shall also turn briefly to *Everyman* to help illuminate how attitudes changed as the late middle ages gave way to the Reformation.

Confession at the Birth of Protestantism

Martin Luther had a low opinion of the standard, late-medieval confessional manuals. He burned the *Angelica* and referred to another summa for confessors as "bilgewater."[4] Yet Luther was not averse to the idea of formal confession as a rite with social value. Between 1519 and 1520 he ceased to call it a sacrament, but he and the early Lutherans continued to regard it as "necessary."[5] Indeed, Bossy (who takes pleasure in turning conventional wisdom upside down) calls Luther, in this regard, a "utopian traditionalist rather than a revolutionary."[6] That is to say, while the Council of Trent newly emphasized the private aspects of confession, Luther emphasized its social function. He retained the practice of calling for annual formal confession, privately heard, to the pastor in church, provided that the sins in question were social, communal, or public rather than spiritual and private. Sins of hatred, public breaches, and offences against the community provided the matter for this confession. By retaining the practice of making formal, annual confessions, early Lutherans took a more "conservative" position than many other Protestants, who simply rejected auricular confession entirely. But over the course of time the practice of making an annual confession to a pastor came to have less significance for Lutherans than it had for Catholics. Since Lutherans were firmly committed to denying that confession had sacramental efficacy, a decline in significance is not surprising. "[A]s time went on it [annual confessing] clearly lost its social vitality; both in the private form which Luther had favoured himself, and in the collective form which tended to supplant it."[7] If salvation is given through faith alone — not by works, by sacraments, or by the other Pauline virtues of hope and charity — confessional rites could have only peripheral relevance in the all-important matter of the soul's eternal salvation. Confession might provide spiritual aid and psychological comfort as well as good social order and peace in the community, but it was no longer unavoidably necessary in the same way that the Catholic sacrament was necessary.

Still, Luther did not exactly return to the old emphasis on the social function of penance as the Church's sole, God-given means of reconciling serious sinners to itself and to the community, or to a new balance between the social and the private elements in a single rite. Instead, in practice and in attitude, he instituted a sharp split between secret, inward sins of the soul and outward transgressions against other individuals and against the community. As Bossy analyzes the matter, he "made a clear distinction between sins which upset the community — 'adultery, murder, fornication, theft, robbery, usury, slander, *etc.*' — and 'the secret sins of the heart', by which he seems chiefly to have meant interior sexual motions which had no overt consequences."[8] So Luther effectively separated internal sin and absolution from external peace-breaking and reconciliation. One kind of sin is deeply hidden within the soul; the other kind is an external act or an attitude publicly expressed. The line is not precisely drawn between the inward soul and the outward act, however, because Luther seems also to have considered some acts to be private and therefore not subject to confession. For example, he counts abortion — which, whatever one thinks of it, is surely an act with immediate material consequences — as a "secret sin." Thus he reveals that not all "private" sins are confined only to the inward mind. Also if, for example, a priest or a nun breaks a youthful vow of chastity by marrying, he or she commits no sin at all, because such public breaches only offend against the old order, from which Luther and his followers have separated themselves.[9]

The depth and importance of the distinction Luther draws between public sins and secret sins are confirmed by his explicit exclusion as appropriate matter for formal confession of all offenses against the ninth and tenth commandments. Luther generally disapproves of formal, objective examinations of conscience in connection with confession, of the kind commonly recommended by the penitential manuals and encouraged by pastors at annual confession, as the inventions of men. He writes with scorn: "The man about to make confession . . . should do away completely with the confusion of distinctions such as these: . . . what against the three theological virtues of faith, hope, and love, and against the four cardinal virtues; what through the five senses, through the seven mortal sins, against the seven sacraments, against the seven gifts of the Holy Spirit, against the eight Beatitudes, against the nine alien sins, against the twelve articles of faith." Against the fabricated schemes of confessors and ecclesiastics, Luther sets the commandments of Moses, which he regards not as inventions of men but as "God's commandments themselves."[10] Yet, even from this seemingly unexceptionable list, he makes a further, extraordinary exception. "[T]he last two [commandments] are to be completely excluded from confession. For the confession must be brief and above all a confession of those sins which hurt immediately" (39:37). In other words, a formal confession to the pastor cannot include any violations of the ninth and tenth commandments, since, Luther argues, these commandments are concerned not with public but with private sins, which if they hurt others, do so indirectly. It may be hard at first to see why confessing sins against the first eight commandments could be more than, say, twenty percent "briefer" than confessing sins against all ten. But there are many indications in all three discussions of confession that Luther found the sins of the heart to be virtually numberless, and therefore in practice unconfessable. He remarks, immediately following his exclusion of the last two commandments: "The sacrament of confession is instituted to appease rather than perturb the conscience" (39:37). But confessing "private" sins would only make the sinner feel guiltier rather than easier. It would involve him in endless scruples and doubts. It would weigh down his conscience instead of freeing it. The *Augsburg Confession* (1530) and other early Lutheran documents closely accord with Luther in dividing moral offenses into public sins, which should be confessed, and private sins, which are too vague and numerous to allow confession.[11]

Somewhat like Thomas Cranmer in England, who allowed confession for those who simply could not do without it, Luther is willing to allow scrupulous individuals "oppressed by secret sins" to confess them privately to another member of their Church, "'a brother or a neighbour, at any time or in any place, in the house or in the fields.'"[12] That he allows any member of the Church to play the part of a confessor in these transactions indicates that he does not view the confession of private sins in the same light as the confession of public sins, or as an action even faintly corresponding in purpose to the old sacramental confession. Moreover, he is at pains to insist that no penance should be attached to such confessions, for that might suggest that works, rather than faith, can free the individual from his burden of sin. The purpose of such confessions can only have been psychological, since God forgives the sins of the truly penitent man, if He chooses to do so, through the direct action of free grace in the individual soul. Confessing to a brother or a neighbor can be useful only if it helps make the repentant sinner feel better, relieving him of false feelings of guilt that may in turn lead to despair. Since guilt itself can only be absolved by faith, and faith requires belief, and bad feelings can diminish or extinguish belief, false guilt-feelings can come between a despairing sinner and God's forgiveness of his real guilt. Here, although there is a transcendental theological element, there is also so strong a natural psychological element that Luther comes close to anticipating Freud and late modernism on the nature of guilt.

Still Luther is adamant against confessing private sins formally to the pastor, for any attempt to do so will almost inevitably produce further guilt in the sinner's heart, rather than relief from its burden. "Here is where this whole sea of laws and impossible questions about 'cases of sins', etc., comes up, since it is impossible for a man to know when he was mortally proud, or lustful, or envious in his heart. . . . Meanwhile, they do not see that if this has to be brought before man, all of life would consist of nothing but confessing; and even the confession itself would have to be confessed in another confession by the man afraid of guilt where there is no guilt. . . . Therefore, let someone else explain it. I am content with the fact that not all sins of the heart have to be confessed."[13] Social sins are the proper business of the Church. Private sins are a matter to be settled between the individual and his God.

Luther's view was by no means the only, or perhaps even the standard, Protestant response to questions of sin and forgiveness. It was certainly influential, especially in the Lutheran and Anglican communions. Like Lutherans, early Anglicans retained auricular confession on the books, although it is unlikely that it was commonly used among them except on the deathbed. The first and second versions of the Book of

Common Prayer have rubrics in the Communion Office to the effect that anyone who is "troubled and grieved" in conscience may confess his sins to a priest and be absolved before receiving communion. The wording is permissive, not obligatory; private or General Confession is equally efficacious. As in early Lutheranism the decisive emphasis is on the sinner's inward psychological state, on guilt feelings rather than objective guilt. In the Order for Visitation of the Sick, a similar rubric permits auricular confession and absolution to the ill or dying. Later editions of the Book of Common Prayer preserve these rubrics essentially unchanged.[14] Anecdotal records describe English Protestants like Sir Philip Sidney seeking pastoral help to ease the burden of sin before dying, but regular use of formal confession to prepare for communion was probably rare until the Anglo-Catholic revival of the nineteenth century.

Luther's division of sins into the public and the private or personal, which resonates through early Lutheran and Anglican confessional documents, was, I think, symptomatic of a larger split that took place in the early formation of modernism between private guilt and disruption of the social order, or — to put the matter in other terms — between private morality and public law. Ecclesiastical courts continued to operate in England through the sixteenth and early seventeenth centuries, ensuring good public order in the diocese and the parish.[15] But the reformers were unable to impose Geneva-style discipline widely in England, and the ecclesiastical courts, which were run by the bishops, were disliked by the Puritans and abolished in 1640. Even in their heyday these courts were primarily concerned to keep moral and economic order in the community, not to absolve individual sins or cure souls. Gradually the medieval idea that the laws of men should imitate the laws of God, however imperfectly, was displaced by the Hobbesian model of law as pure sovereignty, a necessary but arbitrary means by which rulers keep the peace and protect citizens from one another.[16] In this view, the individualistic war of "all against all" would break out if there were any weakening in the preventive sanctions of centralized power. The Hobbesian view of power as divorced in practice from traditional moral and spiritual considerations is recognizably a predecessor of modernist politics, the politics of sheer power and the separation of law from inward morality.

Likewise, Luther's views led inevitably to the separation of public morality from secret sin that characterizes most modern cultures. Hawthorne later portrays the results vividly in *The Scarlet Letter*, which looks back on the seventeenth century from the nineteenth. Hester Prynne sins publicly by giving birth to a child whose very existence proves her adultery. Therefore she is publicly punished. But what is necessarily public for the woman remains private for the man, Reverend Arthur Dimmesdale. The quintessentially secret sin of sexual transgression, always threatening to become disruptively public, haunts English literature from Defoe and Richardson to George Eliot, Charles Dickens, Henry James, and Edith Wharton.[17] In Hawthorne's probing treatment of this novelistic theme, Hester Prynne's lover Dimmesdale suffers the pangs of guilt concealed within the heart. Puritan Massachusetts has no established means for the confession and forgiveness of such "private" guilt — or for the reconciliation of such a sinner with his God and his community — short of making his sin public by a confession that will at the same time relieve his conscience and destroy him. Dimmesdale can, of course, confess his sins directly to God and pray for justification, but that conduct fails to assuage his guilt. He continues to feel intense remorse at having escaped the punishment and the public scorn inflicted on Hester and at the hypocrisy forced on him by the seemingly arbitrary distinction between his secret and her public forms of guilt. The distinction is more than incidentally entangled in gender differences. Although seemingly identical, sins in a man which belong to Luther's category of "secret sins of the heart" can, in a woman, easily move into the category of "obvious mortal sins."¹⁸ So strong is Dimmesdale's need to confess his sins publicly and make himself right with his community as well as his God, yet so unbreakable are the cultural barriers against formal auricular confession, that no constructive solution is possible. Hawthorne memorably depicts Dimmesdale's attempt to relieve himself of his psychological and spiritual burdens — fruitlessly, of course — in the paradoxical scene of his midnight confession upon the scaffold where Hester had suffered public shame. At the end of the novel, he makes a second, public appearance on the scaffold with Hester and their child: but, apparently, only because he is about to solve his dilemma (in this world at least) by dying.

Although Luther saw great usefulness in the rite of confession, and even the most reform-minded Anglican bishops proved unwilling to remove it from the Book of Common Prayer, most Protestants simply and forcefully repudiated the whole idea of priestly auricular confession. Spenser, for example, can think of no more damning way of portraying the superstitious ignorance of blind Abessa and her simpleminded mother Corceca than to show them at their penance. When — aided by the lion, who breaks down their door — the wandering Una enters their cramped and dismal cottage, the episode strangely resembles a well-meaning Anglican lady's visit to an Irish peasant's hut, under the protective escort of an English soldier:

> She found them both in darkesome corner pent;
> Where that old woman day and night did pray
> Vpon her beades deuoutly penitent;
> Nine hundred *Pater nosters* euery day,
> And thrise nine hundred *Aues* she was wont to say.
>
> And to augment her painefull pennance more,
>   Thrise euery weeke in ashes she did sit,
>   And next her wrinkled skin rough sackcloth wore,
>   And thrise three times did fast from any bit.
>   (1.3.13–14)¹⁹

For readers willing to think about *The Faerie Queene* in its relationship to *A View of the Present State of Ireland* — which it often echoes — passages like this mark a troubling dissonance between Spenser's expansive, quintessentially poetic, idealism and what can only be called intrusions of sectarian hatred. To hate the sin has been thought justifiable, but sometimes Spenser slips into hating the sinner. Una is one of English literature's most admirable and memorable heroines. An old-fashioned admirer cited in the *Spenser Variorum* writes of her: "Where else is woman, in her pure ideal, still so humanly beautiful?"[20] It would be regrettable if admiration for Una should be abandoned altogether because it no longer suits our postmodern sensibility — or (more aptly) because it is undermined by Spenser's moral blindness at such moments in the poem. Yet it would be misleading to lay all the burden of dissonance on the difficulties of satisfying the complex requirements of "allegory." There is an artistic problem here too.

For, however we explain it, clearly we cannot expect Una to feel any sympathy or understanding for this old peasant woman, forced to give shelter to these abrupt intruders into her home, or expect her to find beneath Corceca's ugly sackcloth and her wrinkled skin the revelation of an inward spiritual beauty that resembles her own cloaked radiance. The traditional rite of penance, like the crone herself and her expiatory beads, has become entirely foreign and "other" to Una, as to Spenser. In its traditional form penance is simply unavailable to a true Protestant believer or to Una in her person as the Church of England. It has dwindled to a superstitious caricature, hateful because it is ugly and ridiculous.

Spenser and the Medieval Heritage

Spenser was unquestionably familiar with traditional ideas about sin, virtue, moral choice, repentance, and forgiveness, as these matters were understood in the Middle Ages and earlier. His poem, which belongs to the chivalric revival of the Tudor period, uses language and imagery that are deliberately archaic. The action of book 1, "the Legende . . . of Holinesse," though greatly complicated by its use of many sources and its movement among many levels of meaning, nevertheless is based chiefly on the chivalric quest, and especially on the popular medieval legend of St. George, the Lady, and the dragon. St. George's feast day, which falls on April 23, was widely celebrated in festive pageants around England until past the middle of the sixteenth century, when reform-minded local officials acted to suppress it. As David Cressy remarks, celebration of St. George's day continued at Norwich, in one instance, as late as the reign of James I. In that city a curious compromise was effected between the disparate motives of purifying religion and propitiating popular custom. In 1559, the mayor banned the appearance of St. George and Lady Margaret in the annual procession, as remnants of idolatrous superstition, but permitted the dragon to keep his traditional place as entertainment.[21]

Spenser's familiarity with medieval treatments of sin and virtue is abundantly evident in his gruesome and elaborate procession of the Seven Deadly Sins at the House of Pride. Hitched to Lucifera's triumphal chariot, six mounted counselors represent the six other deadly sins: "sluggish *Idlenesse*" riding a "slouthfull Asse," "loathsome *Gluttony*" on a "filthie swyne," "lustfull *Lechery*" on a "bearded Goat," "greedy *Auarice*" on a "Camell loaden all with gold," "malicious *Enuie*" on a "rauenous wolfe," and "reuenging *Wrath*" on a "Lion, loth for to be led." Sitting on the "wagon beame," lashing this grotesquely ill-matched and "lasie" team with his "smarting whip," is Satan. Duessa, the Whore of Babylon, rides alongside Lucifera herself (1.4.16–36). In painting this vivid pageant Spenser incorporates familiar materials found in dozens of medieval allegories, virtually without change.[22] His figures resemble characteristically medieval versions of evil — ugly, diseased, debilitated, defined by what they lack, according to Augustine's influential definition of evil as a lack, a refusal, an absence, a deprivation of goodness. There is little of the fallacious energy and demonic vitality that characterize typical Renaissance versions of evil — powerful, ambitious, and overreaching — which we see in Marlowe, Shakespeare, and Milton.[23] In Spenser's procession of the Seven Deadly Sins we find iconic materials drawn not only from medieval poetry but from the confessional manuals, to whole sections of which they give shape, order, and liveliness. These are, moreover, the same vivid images on which medieval pastors and pardoners drew to illustrate and enliven their sermons at Eastertide, when the season came round again to exhort their parishioners to repent, confess their sins, and be relieved of their burdens of guilt.

Although Spenser was deeply influenced by Neoplatonism, which was in vogue among Renaissance humanists, Catholic and Protestant alike, he also drew deeply on that favorite moral philosopher of the late Middle Ages, Aristotle, as he explicitly reveals in his letter to Ralegh and — more tellingly — by his heavy reliance on the *Nicomachean Ethics* throughout book 2 of *The Faerie Queene*.[24] Furthermore, as Gerald Morgan persuasively argues, Spenser drew on Aristotle largely through the intervening treatises and interpretations of the scholastic theologians, especially St. Thomas Aquinas. Aquinas reached his highest and widest measure of influence among Protestants as well as Catholics in the sixteenth and seventeenth centuries.[25] That Spenser derived some of his basic thinking about the virtues from Aquinas, as well as directly from Aristotle, becomes evident with the appearance of the first of his "Aristotelian" virtues: Holiness. As many readers have remarked, holiness is not one of the original Aristotelian virtues. In reaction to the apparent discrepancy, some of Spenser's critics have dismissed the letter to Ralegh as an annoying distraction from what the poem actually embodies.[26] But according to the scholastic philosophers holiness *is* a moral virtue. As Morgan points out, "holiness" or "sanctity" is for all practical purposes identical with "religion." According to Aquinas: "[It] is by sanctity that the human mind applies itself and its acts to God: so that it differs from religion not essentially but only logically."[27] In light of this equivalence, it is not surprising that the learned John Selden remarks of the Redcross Knight, that "our admired *Spencer* hath made him an emblem of religion." Although the final end of Redcross's quest is Holiness, to reach that end he must first, in Donne's phrase, "Seeke true religion" as the proximate means.[28] Before he can achieve his quest, he must discriminate truly between Una and Duessa.

Although religion is not counted as one of the three theological virtues (faith, hope, and charity) or as one of the four cardinal or primary moral virtues (prudence, justice, temperance, and fortitude), nevertheless it has special importance because of the high end toward which it is directed. Aquinas approvingly cites Cicero's influential words: "[R]eligion consists in offering service and ceremonial rites to a superior nature that men call divine."[29] Aquinas is uncertain whether *religio* derives etymologically from careful study and re-reading (*relegere*) of "the things that pertain to the worship of God" or from binding together (*religare*), as St. Augustine had punningly suggested: "May religion bind us to the one Almighty God."[30] But he is certain that religion is a "special" virtue and that it should be preferred above all other moral virtues. "[R]eligion approaches nearer to God than the other moral virtues, in so far as its actions are directly and immediately ordered to the honor of God. Hence religion excels among the moral virtues."[31] That explains why Spenser puts Holiness first, although it is not to be found among the better-known cardinal virtues and seems to disrupt his "Aristotelian" scheme. Clearly it does not belong originally to the ranks of Aristotle's virtues, among which (depending on the interpreter)

Magnanimity or Justice has the highest place. Yet as Morgan (succinctly summarizing Aquinas) explains, religion as a virtue is surpassed only by the three theological virtues: "Religion is thus a moral and not a theological virtue; the object of religion is worship, but the object of faith is God. Whereas the object of the theological virtues is the last end, the object of the moral virtues is the means to the last end."[32]

Since religion is directed toward man's proper worship of God, it is characterized by certain acts, external and internal. The two characteristic internal acts of religion are devotion and prayer. The three external acts are adoration, sacrifice, and the proper use of "divine things." Two of these divine things are properly available for human use: the sacraments and the name of God. There are seven sacraments (baptism, confirmation, holy orders, marriage, penance, last rites, and the Eucharist) and three legitimate ways to use the name of God (oaths, adjurations, and invocations).[33] Much of this scholastic thinking remained current in Protestant England, although there were notable changes too, such as the reduction of the sacraments in the Church of England from seven to two: Baptism and the Lord's Supper. At least, that was the official compromise hammered out in the Thirty-nine Articles, to which all Anglican clergy pledged their adherence. Still, covertly or overtly, many more zealous reformers preferred to reduce the role of the sacraments even further.[34] Moreover, where it was retained, the term did not have quite the same meaning or importance it had previously had.

Some groups also repudiated what had traditionally been thought to be legitimate uses of the divine name, uses widely codified in law and ritual. Seekers, Quakers and others refused to take oaths. The author of the *Christian Doctrine* forbade invoking the Holy Spirit.[35] Other aids to religion formerly thought legitimate, visual representations of God and the saints, were smashed, defaced, or removed from churches. Bacon first taught a rising generation influenced by the New

Science that only theologians and clergymen should properly talk about God, and that spiritual matters should be rigorously eliminated from the quest to control nature. As if they were imaging the new technology in a mirror, fervent Reformers grew increasingly reluctant to invoke the sacred in the world. In the seventeenth century sacred and secular poetry went separate ways, and sacred poets felt obliged to repudiate their secular writings. Of the major poets, only Milton and Marvell followed Spenser's example of mingling the sacred with the secular in the same poem. But in Spenser the relationship between the sacred and the secular — and between the religious and the political — had already changed from what it had been in *Sir Gawain and the Green Knight* or in Chaucer. As relations between Church and state — between religion and nationalism — changed in England, so they changed in English literature.

Guilt and Penance in The Faerie Queene

In canto 3, Spenser despises Corceca for spending long hours telling her beads: "Where that old woman day and night did pray / Vpon her beades deuoutly penitent" (1.3.13). His readers have already learned from Archimago's sinister example that beads are an ominous sign. Yet in canto 10 Spenser tells us with warm approval that Caelia prays in almost the same way as Corceca: "All night she spent in bidding of her bedes, / And all the day in doing good and godly deedes" (1.10.3). The balance between Caelia's contemplative prayer-life and her charitable deeds, which Spenser clearly approves, contrasts with Corceca's useless idleness, yet is insufficient to explain why long, devout prayer should issue in virtuous action in her case, but not in Corceca's. True, the narrator describes Corceca's penance as excessive: she recites fully 900 "*Pater nosters*" and 2,700 "*Aues*" every day, presumably in Latin, a grotesque feat. But since Celia likewise "bid[s] her bedes" all night, every night, the distinction grows less clear. The difference seems to be that (on the level of the allegory) Corceca's beads, sackcloth, and penance are outward and literal but Caelia's are inward and spiritual. Corceca is capable only of superstitious gestures and meaningless repetitions. By internalizing and spiritualizing these same gestures, Celia transforms them into a nourishing life of prayer.

Spenser borrows more of the trappings of medieval spirituality in the House of Holiness. Critics have called attention to his use of monastic imagery throughout the canto. Just outside the House of Holiness, seven Beadsmen keep the "holy Hospitall" (1.10.36) that houses the corporal works of mercy. At this point Spenser's imagery recalls chantries, hospitals, and free colleges founded to pray for the souls in Purgatory, administer the sacraments, and care for the poor. All of these institutions were abolished by 1547, as we shall note in the next chapter. Spenser's Beadsmen comfort the dying and provide them with proper burials, almost to the verge of falling into forbidden medieval practices — confession, absolution, and praying for the dead — which good Protestants rejected as Romish superstitions. Contemplation, Redcross's last and highest guide, has even retired from the world into a "litle Hermitage," where he prays "day and night" just like Corceca (1.10.46) — and just as did Richard Rolle and the other hermits who transformed the spiritual culture of England in the fourteenth century and became stock characters in Middle English chivalric romances. Contrary to usual Protestant practice, Contemplation also fasts and neglects his body. Once again it seems insufficient to say that contemplation must issue in virtuous action to gain Spenser's approval. The difference is in the kind of contemplation, as of retirement from the world, fasting, and abstinence. One kind results in a fruitfully balanced life; the other cannot have good issue. So once again, the good exemplar is figurative, the bad literal.

Admittedly the point is difficult to prove, given the degree to which Corceca and Caelia, Archimago, the Beadsmen, and Contemplation, are all allegorical. Emile Legouis finds the House of Holiness episode strangely and inappropriately Catholic. Padelford responds that "The establishment has, to be sure, the character of a medieval religious house, but Spenser was thereby merely making use of pictorial machinery long familiar through the morality plays and the moral poems." The justice of Padelford's remark is not in the similarity he points out between Spenser's episode and the works he cites, which are late medieval and Catholic in spirit. Rather it is in his appeal to a "pictorial" method. Spenser's use of images drawn from monasteries — and from hermitages, hospitals, and chantries — in connection with Caelia, the Beadsmen, and Contemplation, is simply more metaphorical than are his depictions of Corceca and Archimago. Through his villains, Spenser attacks the medieval "machinery" of which Padelford speaks. In his House of Holiness and its outbuildings, he adapts the same medieval machinery as a trope for the inner life. As a further point in response to Legouis, Padelford insists that there is nothing in Spenser's "program of discipline" that cannot be found in Calvin's *Institutes*.[36] That may be true — if we are persuaded that Spenser, like Calvin, advocates inward discipline, not literal beads, penance, prayers for the dead, hair shirts, and flagellation. (Calvin's inward discipline may become public, subject to outward enforcement by the magistrates, if it is openly breached, but that is a different matter.) With Corceca and her superstitious kind, however, Spenser presumes it to be all outward show, empty of inward, spiritual meaning.

If Spenser repudiates traditional Catholic modes of penance in the figure of Corceca with her sackcloth and ashes, then how do we explain his introduction of Penance as a key figure in the Redcross Knight's renewal at the House of Holiness? "Penance" is itself a suspect term for early Protestants, who usually prefer the word "repentance," and prefer inward contrition to outward rites and acts of reparation. The particular punishments that Penance and his fellows inflict on Redcross look suspiciously like those that might be inflicted in the severest of Catholic rituals. Indeed, they may better be described as a Protestant nightmare of Catholic penance, since by the late middle ages penance had, both in theory and in practice, grown increasingly lenient. Hair shirts were not unknown, and extreme fasting and flagellation were sometimes practiced, but voluntarily and normally by those who took religious vows. Although groups of flagellants appeared in parts of Europe, usually in response to terrible crises like the plague, the practice was scarcely known in England. Religious superiors, confessors, and other authoritative writers regularly warn their readers against such extreme practices, which they are likely to find misguided and dangerous. Still less did any responsible authorities demand them or impose them forcibly on lay penitents as conditions for the forgiveness of sins.

The figure who supervises the process of relieving Redcross of his burden of sin is Patience, aided by various figures who appear to represent the stages or parts of the old rite of penance. Among them is Penance himself:

> But yet the cause and root of all his ill,
>   Inward corruption, and infected sin,
> Not purg'd nor heald, behind remained still,
> And festring sore did rankle yet within,
> Close creeping twixt the marrow and the skin.
> Which to extirpe, he [Patience] laid him priuily
> Downe in a darkesome lowly place farre in,
> Whereas he meant his corrosiues to apply,
> And with streight diet tame his stubborne malady.
>
>   In ashes and sackcloth he did array
>   His daintie corse, proud humors to abate,
>   And dieted with fasting euery day,
>   The swelling of his wounds to mitigate,
>   And made him pray both earely and eke late:
>   And euer as superfluous flesh did rot

>   *Amendment* readie still at hand did wayt,
>   To pluck it out with pincers firie whot,
>   That soone in him was left no one corrupted iot.
>
>   And bitter *Penance* with an yron whip,
>   Was wont him once to disple euery day:
>   And sharpe *Remorse* his hart did pricke and nip,
>   That drops of bloud thence like a well did play;
>   And sad *Repentance* vsed to embay,
>   His bodie in salt water smarting sore,
>   The filthy blots of sinne to wash away.
>   So in short space they did to health restore
>   The man that would not liue, but earst lay at deathes dore.
>
>   In which his torment often was so great,
>   That like a Lyon he would cry and rore,
>   And rend his flesh, and his owne synewes eat.
>   His owne deare *Vna* hearing euermore
>   His ruefull shriekes and gronings, often tore
>   Her guiltlesse garments, and her golden heare,
>   For pitty of his paine and anguish sore;
>   Yet all with patience wisely she did beare;
>   For well she wist, his crime could else be neuer cleare.
>   (1.10.25–28)

Spenser has given an unusual, if not a misleading, name to the supervisor of Redcross's punishment for sin and renovation from guilt. Ordinarily, patience is the virtue that willingly suffers adversity through faith in God's goodness and loving-kindness. It has no essential connection with the integrated process of repentance, forgiveness of sin, cleansing from guilt, and renewal of grace. Redcross needs patience to provide him with fortitude under suffering; but in that sense patience plays an auxiliary, not the leading, role. Spenser's Patience guiding the grisly allegorical torture of the body to root out sin and cleanse and save the soul appears to be a euphemism for penance in its more general sense, as it has been traditionally used to refer to the whole process and not just to the penalty stage.

Several of the indispensable parts of the rite of penance in its larger sense are found in Patience's treatment of Redcross's "inward corruption, and infected sin." There is Penance in its more specific sense, as punishment, who scourges him with an iron whip. There is Remorse or guilt, who pricks and nips at his heart until it bleeds like a fountain. There is Repentance or contrition, which bathes his body in the salt tears of sorrow. Spenser also clothes Redcross in sackcloth and ashes, the ancient traditional garments of penance. He draws on the conventional imagery of sin and guilt as disease and of penance as medicine, used by the penitential manuals to describe the cure of souls. There are, however, significant differences between Spenser's allegory and traditional pre-Reformation practices. Above all, no figure is here to represent Confession. And, although penance originated in the early Church as a means of reconciling sinners with the community, Una as Church plays no active part in supervising the administration of Redcross's cure. She knows he must suffer if he is to be healed. But her role is reduced to that of a friend or a loved one, kept in the waiting room, while the real physicians — or torturers — administer their treatment elsewhere, in the hospital or dungeon chamber of the soul.

The end result of their curative treatment is to heal Redcross and restore him to Una as the true Church, healed of sin, cleansed of filth, and freed from suicidal guilt:

> Whom thus recouer'd by wise Patience,
>   And trew *Repentance* they to *Vna* brought:
>   Who ioyous of his cured conscience,
>   Him dearely kist, and fairely eke besought
>   Himselfe to chearish, and consuming thought
>   To put away out of his carefull brest.
>
> (1.10.29)

Assisted by Arthur, Una has brought Redcross to the House of Holiness and introduced him to the allegorized interior faculties who effect his cure. She herself does not participate in the cure but must stand idly by until her cured knight is restored to her.

Una's supportive but distant role in the Redcross Knight's regeneration is a useful indicator of how far the balance between social or communal and private notions of sin and forgiveness has tipped toward the private, in the relatively short time since the birth of Protestantism. After the Council of Trent, Catholics retained, but significantly privatized, auricular confession. The material evidence for this privatization is the spreading use of the enclosed confessional booth. Nevertheless, retention of the sacramental aspect ensured that confession would also retain, at least implicitly, its ancient communal function of reconciliation with the Church and the local parish community. Protestants went much further than Catholics. They largely discarded formal auricular confession. With the formal ritual of confession (as opposed to private prayer directly to God) went the practical means developed over the millennia to provide a way of balancing the communal and the spiritual functions of penance, as a rite capable both of forgiving sins and of reconciling sinners to the Church.

In *The Faerie Queene* confession has disappeared altogether from the penitential process, along with the presence of the officiating priest or confessor. The Church and its ministers no longer actively intercede to reconcile the sinner to the community. God provides the grace Redcross needs for forgiveness, not through a human agent or a sacrament but through direct action within his individual soul. As instrumental aids the Protestant God uses not priests and ministers but the mind's internal faculties and virtues. Spenser's whole theatrical spectacle of torture and healing is — as it must be — an interior drama. It takes place within Redcross's soul. In *The Faerie Queene*, the Church, having relinquished the practical instrumentality of priests and sacraments to forgive sin, necessarily plays a more passive role than it would have done in an earlier work. Instead, Una waits anxiously at a distance, watching and praying, as Redcross undergoes a wholly internalized and individualized process of contrition, remorse, inward torment, spiritual healing, and rebirth.

By way of comparison to a work on which Spenser probably drew, confession plays a pivotal role in *Everyman*, written about a hundred years earlier than *The Faerie Queene*. After Everyman has been abandoned by his former friends and is faced unaided with the prospect of imminent death and judgment, his one remaining friend, Good Deeds, though unable to assist Everyman with his own powers,[37] introduces him to a new guide, Knowledge. Pledging, "Everyman, I will go with the[e], and be thy g[u]ide, / In thy moost nede to go by thy side," Knowledge immediately leads Everyman to the House of Salvation. There he introduces him to Confession. "Lo, this is Confession. Knele downe and aske mercy; / For he is in good conceite with God Almighty" (lines 522–23, 543–44).[38]

Following Knowledge's advice, Everyman kneels and begs Confession to help him:

> O glorious fountaine, that all unclennes doth clarify,
> Wasshe fro me the spottes of vice unclene,
> That on me no sinne may be sene.
> I come, with Knowledge, for my redempcion,
> Redempte with herte and full contricion;
> For I am commaunded a pilgrimage to take,
> And grete accountes before God to make.
>
> (lines 545–51)

Comforting Everyman with assurance that he will be saved if he throws himself on God's mercy, Confession assigns him his penance:

> Here shall you receive that scourge of me,
> Whiche is penaunce strong that ye must endure,
> To remember thy Saviour was scourged for the[e]
> With sharpe scourges, and suffred it paciently. . . .
> But in ony wise be seker of mercy,
> For your time draweth fast. And ye will saved be,

> Aske God mercy, and he will graunte truely.
> Whan with the scourge of penaunce man doth him binde,
> The oile of forgivenes than shall he finde.
>
> (lines 561–64, 568–72)

Everyman's decisive turn from despair to hope comes at the dramatic moment he performs his penance:

> In the name of the holy Trinité
> My body sore punisshed shall be.
> *[Scourges himself.]*
> Take this, body, for the sinne of the flesshe!
> Also thou deli[gh]test to go gay and fresshe,
> And in the way of dampnacion thou did me bringe;
> Therfore suffre now strokes of punisshinge.
> Now of penaunce I will wade the water clere,
> To save me from purgatory, that sharpe fire.
>
> (lines 611–18)

From the moment he accepts and performs his penance, Everyman's journey is increasingly dominated by the joy reflected back from his anticipated end. Penance frees and empowers Good Deeds to walk by Everyman's side to the judgment. As his end comes nearer, Everyman receives Communion and last rites from Priesthood. Five Wits repeats Christ's authorizing words: "The preest bindeth and unbindeth all bandes." The strong curse of God is on any wicked priest who sells the sacraments, for his is a heavy responsibility. The priest alone is the "surgyon that cureth sinne deedly; / No remedy we finde under God / But all onely preesthode" (lines 740, 744–46). When he goes down to the grave, deserted at the end even by his own inner faculties, Everyman is quietly hopeful that, as Confession has promised, God will receive him with mercy:

> Into thy handes, Lorde, my soule I commende.
> Receive it, Lorde, that it be not lost....
> *In manus tuas,* of mightes moost
> Forever, *commendo spiritum meum.*
>
> (lines 880–81, 886–87)

Confession and Penance have set Everyman's feet on the right path toward this last end.

Spenser's House of Holiness closely resembles *Everyman*'s House of Salvation, which may, as Padelford's remark suggests, have been one of Spenser's sources. But there are obvious differences. Spenser reduces the importance of Penance and omits Confession and Priesthood. On at least one level of the allegory, it is possible to take Everyman's House of Salvation to represent an actual church, to which he is led by Knowledge (probably *cognitio peccati* gained through catechesis but also through acknowledgment or experiential "conviction" of sin), and to take Priesthood to represent an actual priest who, somewhere offstage, administers the sacraments of Penance, Communion, and Last Rites to him. Although Everyman's self-administered scourging is probably allegorical, it represents real penance of some kind. It would be ludicrous, however, to imagine that Redcross's stay in the House of Holiness could in any way represent a visit to an actual church where he would be thrown to the floor of an inner dungeon and operated on by surgeons and torturers, while scourging himself with an iron whip. The Anglican Church and its ministers in Spenser's day did not perform such operations on penitents even metaphorically. Spenser's Patience is not a priest, but an internal virtue. His House of Holiness is not a church, but a site of inward regeneration.

The hero of *Everyman* is already strongly individualized, in a manner typical of the late middle ages. He represents not all people but each individual person, who must die alone and face judgment alone. The play makes it clear that no one else can do it for him. The use of intercessory prayer, so basic to the medieval sense of community, seems not to occur to any of Everyman's kindred or neighbors, as they abandon him to his lonely fate. After his confession, Everyman fervently but briefly pleads for Mary to intercede for him; otherwise he is nearly as much on his own, as an individual alone with his

God, as any Protestant might wish. Yet, unlike Redcross, Everyman is not deprived of outward helps or thrown altogether on his own inner resources. He has Confession and Priesthood to aid him. Here we find a significant difference between individuality as it was conceived in the late middle ages and as it was further developed in the Protestant Renaissance. The late medieval rite of confession, though privatized, keeps open a practical link between Everyman and the Church. Still, the resemblances in attitude between *Everyman* and *The Faerie Queene* are substantial. Although *Everyman* retains the old sacramental vision, it strongly emphasizes the individual, not the communal. It treats sin and salvation mainly as personal matters. It sharpens the hero's isolation by dramatizing his desertion by all his kindred and friends. It neglects opportunities to treat sin as separation, and forgiveness as reconciliation, both in its depiction of Everyman's confession and in his final reception into Heaven. When Everyman goes into the hands of God at his death, he is compared to a bride coming home to her bridegroom. He is greeted on the far side of death by an angel. But there is no explicit mention of his incorporation into the heavenly community or communion of saints.

Perhaps the only clear reference in *Everyman* to the communion of saints, or to any kind of supportive family or ecclesial community, is found in one or two suggestive lines in God's opening speech, which deplores the behavior of men:

> They use the seven deedly sinnes dampnable,
> As pride, coveitise, wrath, and lechery
> Now in the worlde be made commendable;
> And thus they leve of aungelles the hevenly company.
> Every man liveth so after his owne pleasure.
>
> (lines 36–40)

God characterizes sin as separation from the community into a kind of perverse individuality. It is a departure from the "hevenly company" of the angels, a fall into selfish pleasure and self-regard, with each sinner going his own separate way. But this theme of evil as social rupture does not explicitly recur again: not in Everyman's confession and absolution, where one might expect to find it, not even in the closing celebration of his reception "into the hevenly sp[h]ere," where "Hye in heven he shall be crounde" (lines 899, 917). Thus, although it is still possible in *Everyman* to regard sin as separation from the community, the play throws all its skillful emphasis on the individual and the spiritual, not on the social and corporate. Similarly, *Everyman* does not value confession as a sacrament of reconciliation, but as a sovereign means of personal salvation. For the Catholic Everyman, confession continues to point the individual sinner back into the Church by a kind of practical necessity, since no other institution or community can provide him with the cure he needs. "No remedy we finde under God / But all onely preesthode." Nonetheless, the communal meaning of sin and confession is deeply hidden, obscured by the playwright's deliberate and highly dramatic isolation of his protagonist. So we may reasonably conclude that in matters of sin, confession, and salvation, the emphasis on the internal and individual at the expense of the public and communal, which distinguishes the early modern from the feudal, was already well developed in 1485, before the Reformation in England was imaginable.

Spenser's Church

Una's inability to assist Redcross actively in freeing himself from the burden of his guilt is symptomatic of the relationship Spenser adumbrates in book 1 between the individual and the English Church. For Spenser, as for Aquinas, religion is a proximate means toward sanctification. Therefore Spenser's true Church can lead the individual Christian to his inner House of Holiness, and she can joyfully reunite herself with him after he has been cured. But when it comes to the actual transformative process of repentance and regeneration that he must undergo to be saved, she can do no more than stand by as an anxious and prayerful onlooker. Further examination of Una's role in *The Faerie Queene* may suggest why her actions are limited in this way.

Unquestionably Una is one of Spenser's most memorable creations. As many critics have argued, Spenser's allegory is too complicated for us to reduce her to a simple figure. Still, there are recurrent difficulties whenever Spenser uses Una to represent Truth or the True Church, a role she plays in opposition to Duessa as falsehood, the Whore of Babylon, and the false (that is, Catholic) Church.[39] In an essay written early in this century, Padelford suggests what may be the nature of some of these difficulties, although he attempts to explain them away:

> On first acquaintance Una is a rather disappointing character. Frail and dependent, she seems a sorry representative of Truth, which we would fain conceive as regal, self-sufficient, serenely enthroned in her own cloudless light, far removed from all passion and turmoil, remotely accessible alone, and revealing herself only now and again to a favored mortal, and then only in part.... Una, on the other hand, is a profoundly social conception, and a profoundly Christian and compassionate one. Truth is here conceived as having assumed the garments of human frailty, as making herself dependent upon the services of man, that, through his chivalric service in her behalf, man might grow in grace, might attain the full measure of Christian knightliness.... To Una the knight is at last wed, as the Christian, following the customary terminology, is made one forever with Christ.[40]

It is unclear what Padelford means in this context by "profoundly social," since Una manifests and engages herself not to a community but to an individual, representative though he may be of other individuals. Moreover, although Padelford also speaks of Una as "profoundly Christian," his own tone and expectations may better be described as — for his time —

profoundly American: that is, individualistic and invincibly romantic. His interpretive stance is not inappropriate, since Una works better as a romance invention than as a traditional figure of Christian allegory. If it is difficult at first for a romantic idealist to see the "frail" Una as Truth, it may be even more difficult to see her as a theologically appropriate model for the Anglican Church, still less for the universal Church. And as we shall remark, there are further difficulties with what Padelford too easily takes to be Spenser's use of "customary terminology" for the wedding between Una and her knight, which Padelford takes to represent the wedding of the individual Christian to Christ. Not only is the marriage endlessly deferred, as more recent critics delight in pointing out,[41] but it is by no means simply "customary" or conventional in its implications.

Spenser modifies the basic story line of St. George and Lady Margaret (which in turn had been influenced by the tale of Perseus and Andromeda) in a way that diminishes the passivity of the heroine's role. He makes Una more than a passive victim tied to a tree or a post, needing to be saved by the hero. He allows her to rescue her rescuer several times. Still, her basic role is to serve as the quest-object whom the hero seeks to free, as the beautiful lady whom he wins by defeating her oppressor. Unlike St. George's lady, however, Una is in distress not because her people have offered her up to the dragon, but mainly because, misled by Archimago and Duessa, Redcross abandons her in the wilderness. Spenser's chief source for the theme of Una's abandonment in the wilderness, to which he alludes in a way that he would have expected contemporary readers immediately to recognize and correctly interpret, is Revelation 12:6: "And the woman fled into the wilderness, where she hath a place prepared of God, that they should feed her there a thousand two hundred and threescore days."

Early Protestants commonly took this text to be a prophecy of the fate of the true Church, which would be displaced from the world through most of Christian history by a false, idolatrous Church ruled over by the popes. This true but hidden Church was destined to suffer in exile from the time of Constantine or even earlier, until the Reformation restored her again to the sight of the world.[42] The underlying importance to Protestantism (and modernity) of the displacement of the "true" Church by a false one through most of Christian history is well argued by Anthony Kemp. Although Protestants usually insisted that the origins of Protestantism were prior to those of Catholicism, and therefore Spenser presents the lineage of Una as more ancient than that of Duessa, originating with Adam and Eve, there is still a troubling discontinuity to be accounted for. Wisdom or Prudence is conventionally depicted with three faces, looking toward the past, the present, and the future; remembering, anticipating, and thereby rightly knowing and choosing in the present. Spenser reveals Duessa's shortcomings by having her look only to the past, to false tradition and illusory continuity. She is blind to the future. Yet Una reveals comparable shortcomings: she is capable of looking to the future but forgets the past.[43] If Una is to act wisely in the present, one would expect her to remember the past as well as foresee the future. Presumably her odd limitation reflects in some way Spenser's reaction to the question of historical continuity in the Church of England.

In England, the true Church had to await its restoration by Henry VIII, a restoration that Spenser and his fellow Protestant nationalists hoped would be completed by Queen Elizabeth. In this scenario raw politics played a considerable part, since the English Church is, in a practical sense, subordinate to the ruler who claims to rescue her from exile and restore her to her proper place in the eyes of the world. Indeed, Henry VIII claimed to be head of the Church, a title which theologians had previously reserved for Christ alone and which not even the boldest of Renaissance popes had ventured to appropriate. In *The Faerie Queene* numerous interlocking characters take on aspects of this key role as the Church's imperial savior. They include Prince Arthur, Artegall, Britomart, the Fairy Queen Gloriana, Oberon, Queen Elizabeth, and the Redcross Knight himself as St. George, the patron saint of England. Probably Spenser deliberately blurs and complicates the religio-political typology that underlies this touchy issue of church-state relations. It was deeply in his interest to do so, for the relation between the British monarch and the Church lies at the dangerous heart of the self-aggrandizing Tudor myth yet is (to say the least) theologically problematic — for fervent Protestants as well as for Catholics, as the Stuart kings were to learn to their sorrow in the next century.

Although Spenser takes the fundamental Protestant theme of a Church long hidden in exile then revealed to the world at the Reformation by a Protestant Defender of the Faith, and closely links it to the fundamental romance theme of a maiden lost in the wilderness and rescued by her questing knight, this powerful combination may be judged to be more successful esthetically than theologically. And this is so even though Spenser clearly intended that *The Faerie Queene* should speak to both esthetic and moral concerns — should please and instruct — and that it should have real-world political and religious consequences. The root of the difficulty is evident if we look again at Padelford's solution to the problem he senses in Una. "To Una the knight is at last wed," he concludes, "as the Christian, following the customary terminology, is made one forever with Christ." But this statement raises obvious complications with gender and identity. In the "customary terminology" to which Padelford refers, there are two ways of reading the Song of Songs and other biblical passages that concern the divine marriage. One is to speak of a marriage between God and Israel or Christ and his Church; the other is to speak of a marriage between God and the individual soul, as the playwright does toward the end of *Everyman*.[44]

Both readings were traditional and familiar to anyone in Spenser's time.

Which of these two traditional sacred marriages does Spenser represent in the betrothal of Redcross and Una? What does it mean for the knight who has discovered himself to be George, the patron saint of England, to marry Una, the "one, true, catholic and apostolic" Church of England (according to the creedal formula in the Book of Common Prayer)? It cannot be the marriage of the soul to Christ, as Padelford suggests, because the sexes are wrong. Una is not Christ, and cannot be said to play the traditional role of bridegroom to the soul as bride. Nor can it be the marriage between Christ and his Church, because Redcross is not Christ any more than Una is, although at times he imitates Christ (especially in his battle with the dragon). A closer analogy to the engagement that concludes book 1 is the "marriage" of Henry VIII to the Church of England. That marriage or political maneuver tacitly displaces Christ from his conventional role of Bridegroom and Head of the Church and establishes Anglicanism, headed by the king, as the one true religion. It is exceedingly doubtful that even the most crassly political Protestant nationalist would have dared to affirm all of the theological and political implications that such an imagery implies, however, especially the displacement of Christ (rather than the pope) by England's monarch. Yet there is no doubt that, in its earliest years, English Protestant apocalyptic fervor focused its hopes not in Parliament but in the figure of the monarch as savior, until James I (who seems at times really to have thought he *was* Christ) unwisely overstepped the bounds. As William Lamont argues, Anglicanism was originally founded on the apocalyptic vision of a restored Christian empire. All of its greatest early apologists, including Jewel, Tyndale, Grindal, Bale, and Foxe, enthusiastically supported the formulation first offered in the preamble to the Act in Restraint of Appeals (1533): namely, that there is "one Supreme Head and King having the dignity and royal estate of the imperial crown."⁴⁵ There could be no higher authority than that royal head of Church and state.

Still, it is one thing to say that Henry VIII or Queen Elizabeth should be honored as supreme Head of the Church and Defender of the Faith, and another to insert them, or their allegorical surrogates, into the tropology of divine marriage, as Spenser seems to do. Several recent feminist critics, noting that the precise title of "Head" was discontinued with Queen Elizabeth and not resumed, attribute this change to a patriarchal unwillingness to grant the title to a woman. It is doubtful, however, that Elizabeth, so fiercely protective of her royal prerogatives, would have acceded to substituting "Supreme Governor" for "Head" had she suspected her advisors of harboring any such view. More likely, she was persuaded of the inherent danger in using a title previously reserved for Christ alone, familiar to everyone from its repetition as the central trope or mystery in each celebration of the rite of matrimony. Although she relinquished the title, she did not relinquish the office it signified or her "heart and stomach of a man." McCabe remarks that "There can be little doubt that Una's union with George 'shadows' Elizabeth's celebrated 'marriage' with her kingdom."⁴⁶ I argue that more immediately it shadows her marriage, like her father's earlier, to the English Church, from which, in the eyes of Protestant nationalists, the imperial kingdom was now inseparable. Thus the questions we have raised suggest that, on the level of religious allegory, something new and different — something by no means traditional or conventional — occurs at the betrothal of Redcross and Una. If their marriage is to be deferred, the most likely reason is precisely the one Spenser offers: that there is still work to be done before it can take place. This marriage represents an event so apocalyptic that it will resolve all prior history since the exile of the hidden Church — or, as the last cantos suggest, since the fall of Adam. It cannot properly take place until the whole poem and the history it unfolds reach their fulfillment. Nevertheless, a formal betrothal is a serious commitment, not merely a means of avoiding closure or asserting indeterminacy. Betrothals were generally considered to be as firm and unbreakable as marriage itself. To plight one's troth is precisely to pledge unending loyalty. Redcross has pledged six years' service to Gloriana before he returns to wed Una, the hexameral number representing all historical time, until time ends at the Last Judgment in the last, eternal Sabbath.[47]

In practical terms, national and political, Protestantism was the establishment of religion by monarchs, according to the principle formalized after the Thirty Years' War: *cuius regio eius religio*. The Church of England was an established fact, and the will of a Tudor king or queen was not lightly to be questioned. In more personal terms, however, cultural and spiritual, Protestantism was the quest of separate individuals for religious truth. It is no coincidence that, although we usually think of Spenser as confident and optimistic in his religious beliefs and of Donne as doubtful and pessimistic, of Spenser as a national poet and of Donne as a private one, nevertheless they converge in a remarkable way on this particular point. Spenser's Redcross, who must go on a quest in order to find and establish true religion, whose identity is by no means obvious, in the event must choose between two ladies, two religions, and two Churches. In that, he is much like the seeker in Donne's Satire III, who also must distinguish and choose between true and false Churches, although for him Spenser's two alternatives have become three.

There is an even closer convergence between the situation in book 1 of *The Faerie Queene* and that in Donne's late sonnet, "Show me deare Christ, thy spouse, so bright and cleare."[48] Although Donne starts his sonnet by evoking the traditional Christian marriage trope and distinguishing between the true bride of Christ and the false mistresses, he soon veers into the same strange territory first entered by Spenser. Donne's speaker turns into a questing knight, who seeks to find, woo, and marry the true Church. "Dwells she with us, or like adventuring knights / First travaile we to seeke and then make love?" Moreover, in Donne the confusion of genders implicit in Spenser's ultimate wedding becomes explicit, as the sonnet ends with the deliberately shocking image of God as a complacent husband, eager to share his wife, the Church, with anyone who seeks her, so she will be "embrac'd and open to most men." The image of the Church as a bride, who must be sought by questing individuals, works in its own peculiar way. But it conflicts with the conventional imagery, deriving from the Bible, of the Church as the bride of Christ, which derives in its turn from the old image of Israel as the bride of God.

Donne's sonnet renders the conflict, which is still implicit in Spenser — if not deliberately obfuscated — clear and explicit. Like Spenser, Donne sees the Church in a way fundamentally different from the way earlier Catholic generations had seen her. She is no longer easily to be visualized as a holy and nurturing Mother, who brings all Christians together in communal brotherhood. She has instead become a longed-for bride, who must be sought by individual questers, searched for through a world where nothing is what it seems. These seekers must choose, woo, and wed any of several competing ladies who offer themselves up to them. They can expect no help from anyone, indeed they must weigh carefully and often reject proffered advice. This is a strong tenet of early Protestantism, although it may seem to have been contradicted by outpourings of religious advice from the presses: no one can find your religion for you; you must find it yourself. Thus Donne writes in Satire III: "At the last day? Oh, will it then boot thee / To say a Philip, or a Gregory, / A Harry, or a Martin taught thee this?"; and Milton affirms in *Areopagitica* that "A man may be a heretick in the truth . . . if he beleeve things only because his Pastor sayes so."[49] Protestants must accomplish the quest for themselves individually, relying only on their own inward discernment and calling, guided by a grace that is parceled out to each soul separately. They do not begin *within* a Church or a Community; they begin as exiles in the wilderness, seeking a wife, a Church, a Truth, and a home. Calvin employs the same metaphor as Spenser to invoke the gravity of the individual quest for salvation: until they are called, even the elect "wander scattered in the wilderness common to all; and they do not differ at all from others except that they are protected by God's especial mercy from rushing headlong into the final ruin of death."[50]

The spiritual life of the individual was by no means neglected in the middle ages. But it was balanced against the life of the community. The state of that balance between the public and private can, with considerable accuracy, be measured by the rite of penance. In *Everyman* the emphasis has already gone a long way toward the private and personal and away from the social. But a practical link still remains between sin, guilt, forgiveness, the life of the soul, and participation in the community. That practical link *Everyman* evokes first as Confession, then as the other sacraments, all of which are dependent on and only available through Priesthood, and therefore also dependent on membership in the Church. The link between the private and the public provided by formal confession broke down at the Reformation. Private morality split off from public law, and private conscience no longer found ready support from the mothering culture of the Church.

What was cause and what was effect in this transformation of religion and culture is hard to say — perhaps impossible to prove. The death of Everyman is noticeably isolated and lonely, suggesting that the psychological or cultural shift toward religious individualism may have preceded the institutional shift represented by the Reformation. What the example of confession suggests, however, is that, as long as the institutional practice remained, there was a certain elasticity in the cultural shift toward individual, private spirituality, which was already well developed in the fourteenth century, if not earlier. There might be some degree of dissonance and contradiction, as there usually is in human experience, but no break. But when the sacramental rite of penance, though still widely popular according to recently adduced evidence, was rejected by the Reformers as an unwanted and outmoded imposition, cultural change in this critical area where the public meets the private and the social meets the psychological had no remaining external restraint. The departure of early modern culture from the assumptions of the middle ages concerning the place of the individual in society and community grew more distinct, more nearly absolute, and possibly irrevocable.

Although Donne's "Show me deare Christ" may well have been directly influenced by *The Faerie Queene*, as one poet influences another, it is more likely that the primary link was cultural rather than literary. In Reformation culture, although old formulations linger, attitudes toward the Church begin to change. The nurturing mother becomes more like a bride; the son becomes more like a questing suitor. Spenser and Donne inhabit a transformed culture, which assumes increasingly different notions about the nature of religion and truth, community and privacy. The old, traditional marriage tropes persist, and are still entirely familiar to Spenser and Donne, who use them elsewhere in their writings,[51] but they no longer fit their lived experience in the same way. Neither religion nor truth belongs any more to an unbroken tradition or a stable community that can be taken for granted. Both must be endlessly sought after and rediscovered.

If, as Donne anxiously protests, the Church sleeps for a thousand years, then "peepes up" one; is "selfe truth," yet "errs" (ll. 5–6), then anything is possible, and each individual, alone or working alongside other like-minded individuals, must rebuild his own religion from the ground up. Like Spenser's knights they may meet occasionally and work cooperatively, yet their quests are separate. In *Sir Gawain and the Green Knight*, the court of Arthur is visibly present from first to last, human and substantial, the center of government and religion. In *The Faerie Queene* as we have it, the court of Gloriana is quite different, resembling the fundamental Tudor and Anglo-Protestant concept of a regenerate empire knit with a "Church Invisible." The new empire and Church, although everywhere mystically present, are not yet fully realized or visible to mortal sight. Prince Arthur has yet to found his kingdom. Queen Elizabeth has yet to be persuaded to become what she might be, to assume the full role that providence, in the eyes of the poet, has assigned to her. Truth itself, represented by Una, is changing into what it will seem to be for Milton, and after him for the Enlightenment: something perpetually to be sought for, ever to be pieced together, but never again to be seen whole until the end of time. The prospect of endless quest and deferral gives Spenser and Donne something in common that sets them apart from their ancestors. It gives a new, far more individualistic, meaning to the old idea of life in the world as a pilgrimage and a new twist to the theme of exile in the wilderness.

Four

Hamlet and the Ghost of Purgatory

☙

Intimations of Killing the Father

> Once an angry man dragged his father along the ground through his own orchard. "Stop!" cried the groaning old man at last, "Stop! I did not drag my father beyond this tree."[1]

Shakespeare's Hamlet and Milton's Satan are two pivotal figures born out of the imaginative stirrings in early modern culture that led to the rise of Enlightenment, Romantic, modernist, and postmodernist individualism — all arguably beads in the chain of a single, sinuous, long-wave development toward liberal autonomy.[2] Great literary inventions, Hamlet and Satan are also grand portents of subsequent cultural change. Moreover, buried deep in the tragedy of *Hamlet*, as I shall argue in this chapter, are intimations of what may be called a transformative event that led to still another essential paradigm of modernity, a necessary adjunct to autonomous individualism, for which the brutally appropriate name is *killing the father*. With the rise of postmodernism (and as emphasis has shifted further from the warfare between generations to that between genders), it is even more evident than it was earlier in this century that the Reformation, Enlightenment, Romantic, modernist, and postmodernist projects (all of which may be included under the umbrella term of modernism) require an attack on patriarchal tradition. As Freud's writings often suggest, killing the father is not a new idea. But unlike earlier generations, the modernists did not stop at what Gertrude Stein calls the customary tree.

In another typical passage, Gertrude Stein writes: "I have been much interested in watching several families here in Belley that have lost their fathers and it is interesting to me because I was not grown when we lost our father. As I say fathers are depressing any father who is a father or any one who is a father and there are far too many fathers now existing. The periods of the world's history that have always been most dismal are the ones where fathers were looming and filling up everything. I had a father, I have told lots about him in *Making of Americans* but I did not tell about the difference before and after having him. . . . Then our life without a father began a very pleasant one." Similarly, Virginia Woolf writes in her diary for 28 November 1928: "Father's birthday. He would have been . . . 96, yes, today; & could have been 96, like other people one has known; but mercifully was not. His life would have entirely ended mine. What would have happened? No writing, no books; — inconceivable." To bring us into the attitudes which typify postmodernism, we may cite J. Hillis Miller's deliberate provocation: "a deconstructionist is not a parasite but a parricide. He is a bad son demolishing beyond hope of repair the machine of Western metaphysics."[3]

"As If a Man Were Author of Himself"

The transformative event I have mentioned, which made it more easily possible to repudiate tradition and kill the father in early modern English and European culture — an event successfully obliterated from modern memory by early, deliberate acts of forgetting and by the decision of Renaissance politicians and gentry to rewrite history — was the abolition of purgatory. If modernism is largely a process of desecularization (an analysis which discomfits both secularists and Christians, yet which is virtually unavoidable),[4] then crucial, irreversible steps in that direction were taken by the Chantries Act and Royal Injunctions of 1547 and by the Church of England's declaration, in the Edwardian Prayerbook of 1549, that purgatory had never existed and therefore that Christians should cease mourning and praying for their dead. The issue is far too large to be conclusively demonstrated in a single chapter, or even a book, but I put it forward as a hypothesis, and as a way of making better sense of certain speeches and events in *Hamlet*.

Before the modern autonomous individual can step forth in all his glory, he must first free himself — and increasingly herself — from the past, from tradition, from ancestral piety, and especially from the father and the paternal lineage. We find exactly this gesture of repudiation in several of Shakespeare's heroes and villains. Coriolanus most explicitly embodies the modernist desire for total autonomy. In the pivotal scene in which Shakespeare has him deny his family and his country in the face of three generations of that family — mother, wife, and son — who beg him not to destroy Rome, he utters these ominous words:

> I'll never
> Be such a gosling to obey instinct, but stand
> As if a man were author of himself
> And knew no other kin.
>
> (5.3.34–37)[5]

Since the nineteenth century the word "instinct" has had a particular scientific meaning, but for Coriolanus it means to be bound by an unselfconscious inward stain or tincture to the obligations of family, culture, citizenship, duty, and tradition. Now Coriolanus will throw off all these instinctive restraints that make him a true Roman. He will become the "author of himself," forget all other ties, and act from unnameable internal principles, all of which we now recognize as the underlying axioms of autonomous individualism. Even at this tragic stage of extreme hubris, since he is a man of his own time or rather of Shakespeare's, Coriolanus implicitly recognizes that he cannot actually *be* the "author of himself"; yet he is determined to act *"as if"* he were. The arc of the play's action reveals this gesture to be an act of hubris for which he will be tragically punished. Yet we know that such acts of self-fashioning, although they begin as role-playing, can issue in authentic change, first in the individual, then in the culture.

Similarly Shakespeare's Edmund, that enterprising bastard whom most modern readers and playgoers instinctively admire — because they are themselves the children of modernist egalitarianism and self-assertion — repudiates what he calls "the plague of custom" (*Lear*, 1.2.3), which in its context is much the same thing as Coriolanus' "instinct," in favor of a proto-Darwinian version of "Nature" — a Nature virtually "red in tooth and claw," according to whose laws it is every man, beast, and monster of the deep for himself. After he comes to this resolve, Edmund determines to displace his brother and betray his natural father, Gloucester, as well as his feudal father, King Lear. Above all, he is determined to stand on his own, to deny the influence of stars, gods, custom, or natural law (Nature in her older sense), and to be the final arbiter of his own free will. Here again the first prerequisite of self-conscious autonomy is killing the father. The self-declared iron law of Edmund's brave new world is: "The younger rises when the old doth fall" (3.3.26). In the older natural order sons replaced fathers in the ripeness of time, but in *King Lear* sons and daughters, who have become "monsters of the deep" (4.2.50), devour their fathers before their time. Patricide has happened before, but what Gloucester and Lear instinctively feel to be unnatural Edmund finds natural. His view is the more modern.

As Ulysses tells Agamemnon, in his ironically placed speech on order and degree in *Troilus and Cressida*, "Take but degree away, untune that string . . . / And the rude son should strike his father dead" (1.3.109, 115). In recent years, E. M. W. Tillyard has been much pilloried for interpreting this seminal speech at face value. Yet, however much we enclose it in nesting boxes of subversion and containment, recognize the irony of speech and speaker, and understand that the words should be read in a cultural as well as a literary framework, Ulysses' speech still tells us much about how the Elizabethans feared such subversive notions.[6] After all the political deconstructions Ulysses' troubling question still remains: what can possibly prevent the son from striking his father dead — literally, psychologically, or culturally — once the civilizing achievements of the past — what Ulysses calls "degree," Milton and Chapman "discipline," others tradition, custom, ancestry, patrimony — once those achievements, the lineage that bears them, and the culture that provides their matrix, have been destroyed and forgotten?

Buried deeply in *Hamlet*, in the relationship between the prince and his father, is a source tale, an unspoken acknowledgment that the modernist project of achieving complete autonomy from the past rests (at least for the great majority of Shakespeare's contemporaries who are still Christian) on the denial and forgetting of purgatory. Shakespeare's personal religious beliefs are notoriously difficult to pin down.[7] For every place in the plays that a critic has identified an outpouring of Protestant nationalism, another has found covert Catholicism, and a third has found skeptical agnosticism. Not coincidentally, these findings tend to chime with the critics' own beliefs. What we know, however, is that whatever Shakespeare personally believed about religious matters, whether his deepest allegiances were national or universal, Protestant or Catholic, nostalgic or progressive, spiritual or agnostic (all positions for which critics have found at least some evidence) he knew his audience and knew how to play on their expectations. Given the difficulty of extracting "Shakespeare" from his plays, I shall not consider the question of whether he personally believed in the existence of purgatory or regretted its disappearance from English life not long before he was born. But there is ample, only partly covert, evidence in the play that he understood very well that the abrupt and, to a large degree, forcible dismantling of purgatory at mid century, together with its deep psychic resonances among the common people, its elaborate cultural associations, and its extensive institutional supports, had drastic consequences for society and for the individuals who formed and were formed by society. Before the Reformation, few countries had a deeper investment (financial, cultural, and spiritual) in purgatory and in commemoration of the dead than England. After the Reformation, few countries turned their backs more abruptly on purgatory and, with it, on their own dead.

Purgatory at the Eve of the Reformation

The early history of the development of the doctrine of purgatory is too long and complicated to outline here.[8] Most modern readers, if they think about purgatory at all, are likely to think of it in terms of its notorious abuses, publicized and disparaged by Luther and the first Reformers (and by loyal Catholics such as Chaucer as well). But recent studies suggest that purgatory was not just a hierarchical imposition on the laity, a means of social control, or a way to raise money for the popes' building projects and art collections. In England at the eve of the Reformation it was a thriving and popular institution, whose social and material framework was likelier to well up spontaneously from the laity than to be imposed calculatingly downward by the bishops. The chief interest that most people had in purgatory was concern for their souls and those of their ancestors, together with a strong sense of communal solidarity between the living and the dead. Praying for the dead and provision for one's own soul after death were central to late medieval religion. Commemoration might be accomplished by individuals by paying for special Masses, giving alms to the poor, or praying at shrines. But satisfactory commemoration could more safely and efficiently be accomplished through a variety of institutions, foundations, and voluntary fraternities. A king, a queen, or a rich noble might ensure sufficient prayers for him- or herself and family after death by founding a contemplative or charitable nunnery, or a monastery whose grateful monks would return the gift by chanting perpetual masses and offices for their souls, or a religious hospital, which might combine prayers, charity, and almsgiving on their behalf.

People of the middling and poorer sort could band together in voluntary fraternities, confraternities, guilds, burial societies, and the like. Far from taking their instructions from the hierarchy of bishops and priests, these lay groups customarily took the initiative in hiring priests to say masses on their behalf and for their dead, presumptively in purgatory. Through most of the later middle ages in England there was a surplus of clerics, which, in effect, created a buyer's market when lay trustees sought to staff a chantry or a chapel.[9] Thus, for example, "the guild of the Virgin in the church of St. Giles Cripplegate [later Milton's parish church] had, by 1388, acquired sufficient lands to employ a perpetual fraternity chaplain to celebrate mass every day. The chaplain was to be chosen by the vicar of the church (if he were a member of the guild), the two wardens and twelve of the best men of the guild. The chaplain was to be provided with a house, he was to be attentive to all brothers and sisters, poor as well as rich, sick and healthy."[10] Although the chaplain could not be dismissed except for cause and with consent of the directors, the guild was financed and controlled by its lay members, gathered in voluntary association. Thus the priest had the faculties provided by ordination to say mass, hear confessions, and absolve from sins, but the laity took the initiative and controlled the funds. In this regard the system was closer to Congregationalism than anything available to ordinary people in the Church of England after the Reformation. Such a dispersal of authority and initiative among the laity would not flourish in the same way under the Catholic Counter-Reformation, which in its struggle against Protestantism likewise tightened clerical and hierarchical control.

Corpus Christi fraternities were founded by the laity for the purpose of honoring the Real Presence of Christ in the Eucharist. Nevertheless, as Miri Rubin remarks, these fraternities too were routinely preoccupied with proper burials and regular prayers for the dead. "Thus, all Corpus Christi fraternities made provisions for commemoration, 32 out of 42 employed a chaplain for regular daily or annual celebration of masses for the dead, and half of the fraternities provided for burial of their poorer members at the gild's expense." As J. J. Scarisbrick puts it, "What was a fraternity? It was an association of layfolk who, under the patronage of a particular saint, the Trinity, Blessed Virgin Mary, Corpus Christi or similar, undertook to provide the individual member of the brotherhood with a good funeral — as solemn and well-attended a 'send-off' as possible — together with regular prayer and mass-saying thereafter for the repose of the dead person's soul. . . . In their most modest form, therefore, fraternities were simply poor men's chantries. They were inseparably connected with the doctrine of Purgatory. . . . The humblest village fraternity might aspire to no more than the individual funeral mass for every deceased member, for which all the living members had to subscribe a 'mass penny', plus an annual mass and audit. . . . Many guilds undertook to bring back for decent burial a brother's body from wherever he happened to die."[11]

Wealthier founders of chantries and other institutions connected with purgatory by no means acted only from self-interest. The usual formula was to offer prayers "for n. and n., and for all who suffer the pains of Purgatory."[12] Colin Richmond describes the elaborate and (to the modern sensibility) amazing benefactions that Geoffrey Downes specified in his Last Will and Testament of 1492. Together with Joan Ingoldsthorpe, Downes founded and endowed a chapel in Cheshire, with two priests to say daily masses. In addition, he established a trust for the purchase of a hundred cows, to be "individually rented to the poor of Pott Shrigley," the rent being "'oonly to pray for the sowle of Jane and Geffrey and for all the sowlles in the paynes of purgatory.'" Downes appointed lay trustees to hire and (if necessary) fire the priests, who are to live devoutly and "not to keep horses, hawks or hounds." They are "to burn candles before the Images of Mary and Jesus on their feast days." In addition, they are to teach local children, tell their beads, say their offices, and run a small lending library of devotional books, which may be borrowed "for the space of 13 weeks" by members of the fraternity "or any other Gentleman."[13] Downes's device of endowing a herd of cows to be lent to the poor in return for their prayers is especially ingenious, thus neatly combining as it does almsgiving and prayers, to most efficiently benefit the living and the dead. In the coming age of Reformation, and later age of capital, such ingenuity will be turned in other directions.

The Abolition of Purgatory

Many things were repudiated at the English Reformation, including transubstantiation, confession as a sacrament, the monasteries, and the primacy of Peter. But the Church of England retained the Lord's Supper, claimed apostolic succession for its bishops, and permitted (although it did not encourage) auricular confession. Few things were ended so absolutely as purgatory. W. K. Jordan, no apologist for the old religion, nevertheless recognizes that "the most shattering and irreversible action of the Reformation in England was the proscription of prayers for the repose of the souls of the dead."[14] In the Book of Common Prayer as published under Elizabeth, article 22 reads: "The Romish Doctrine concerning Purgatory, Pardons, Worshipping and Adoration, as well of Images as of Relics, and also Invocation of Saints, is a fond thing, vainly invented, and grounded upon no warranty of Scripture, but rather repugnant to the Word of God." Also relevant is part of article 19: "As the Church of Jerusalem, Alexandria, and Antioch, have erred, so also the Church of Rome hath erred, not only in their living and manner of Ceremonies, but also in matters of Faith." In his fascinating study of the psychic and social effects of the abolition of Purgatory, Theo Brown suggests that when the Anglican Church promulgated its repudiation of "The Romish Doctrine concerning Purgatory" in the first Book of Common Prayer (1549), the bishops did not intend to dispose of purgatory altogether, but only to correct well-known abuses.[15] I find this interpretation of the historical event unpersuasively sanguine. Just as the English government used particular abuses in some monasteries as excuses to do away with the monastic life, root and branch, and to sell off or confiscate the monastic properties, so it used abuses in the administration of indulgences to do away with purgatory, root and branch, and to loot and sell off the chantries, free chapels, and other properties by which that doctrine and associated practices were supported. Even the colleges at Oxford and Cambridge barely escaped, by distancing themselves from the terms of their foundation. Both abolitions took place in the earliest phases of the English Reformation. Moreover, the abolition of purgatory occurred for most of the same combination of reasons as the abolition of monasteries. Reformist mistrust of Rome and her institutions and zealous indignation against real abuses combined with weariness at paying old spiritual debts inherited from the past, but above all with greed to confiscate wealth that pious ancestral donors had given over the preceding centuries to chantries, free chapels, fraternal endowments, guilds, poorhouses, hospitals, dependent colleges, and many other institutions.[16]

The effect of these events may be read in the wills of ordinary people. In the late Middle Ages, last wills and testaments were as concerned with ensuring proper prayers for the deceased as for ensuring proper disposal of their goods. Indeed, the obligation to pray for the deceased was legally attached to accepting or inheriting property. Beginning in the late 1530s, however, wills began to change. "[M]oney for prayers, masses and anniversaries was entrusted to families or executors in preference to public bodies such as gild or parish, presumably due to fear of confiscation." By the mid 1540s, "testators requested elaborate funerals and commemoration only 'if it be lawful.'" By 1547, under Edward VI, "all this was absent from the will and the testator's personal tastes were marked by opaque phrases 'at the discretion of myne executors', 'according to the laudable custome of the realm.'"[17] Presumably the writers of these wills did not fear political retribution after death. Rather, they did not venture to ask their heirs to pray for their souls explicitly, because they feared confiscation of any goods associated with memorial purposes, even within the family. Thus, in marked contrast to earlier wills, after 1647 children inherited goods and estates from their parents but inherited no explicit, legal obligation to pray for them in return. Insofar as these heirs were in tune with the times, they felt no spiritual or moral obligation either. This does not necessarily imply that children loved their parents less than formerly; but as attitudes changed they no longer thought it useful to remember formally or to pray for them. The money saved could be used for more practical purposes.

Material evidence of changing attitudes toward remembering the dead is provided by graves and monuments as well. Edward Bonahue finds it significant that John Stow, author of the *Survey of London* (1598), is "aghast at the confused jumble of church graves and monuments inside Aldmarie Church in Cordwainer Street Ward, where men have bought and sold the holy tombs intended for others." Stow laments that "Sir *William Laxton* Grocer, Maior, deceased 1556. and *Thomas Lodge* Grocer, Maior, 1563, were buried in the Vault of Henry Keble," the church's original founder. Keble's bones "were unkindly cast out, and his monument pulled downe, in place whereof monuments are set up of the later buried." Doubtless Stow was disturbed because he interpreted this incident as the displacement of respectful religious piety by newfangled commercial ambition. Bonahue calls it "the commodification of graves,"[18] and his use of the Marxist term rightly evokes the displacement of aristocratic traditions by new, middle-class money. But we may also see it as the displacement of one kind of religious memorial, intended to remind churchgoers and passersby to pray for the soul of the deceased founder, in favor of another kind of memorial, meant to remind them of the names and the worldly successes of two wealthy donors. The change occurred just at a time when internal church architecture was undergoing iconoclastic adjustments. Although it was not unusual in the middle ages as well as the Renaissance to dig up the bones of ordinary folk for the practical and sufficient reason that more room was needed for new burials, as illustrated by the gravediggers' scene in *Hamlet*, there were few legitimate medieval precedents for the kind of monument defacement and expropriation that Stow describes. Such open and flagrant replacement of an undecayed monument by another became possible after 1547 only because by then Protestant leaders had rejected the pious intentions of the medieval founders for the commemoration of their souls as the true impiety, and therefore as superstitious, papistical relics of the dead past.

Not only dispossessed Catholic layfolk of the common sort, but some of the more conscientious reformers such as Latimer,[19] Crowley, and Hutchinson agreed that the peculiar path taken in England by the Reformation "turned the English into a nation of looters."[20] In the course of a generation the gentry who ran the Church and the state simply decided that it would be convenient to cease remembering their dead and spend the money left by ancestral donors on themselves. Funds used to endow fraternities and other practices of popular piety, which the Crown had once been content merely to license and tax, now were confiscated altogether. Those sweeping alterations, in which Reformist zeal competed with greed and guilt, must have had on their perpetrators some of the same combination of effects that Satan mentions in his first soliloquy in *Paradise Lost*. By abruptly ceasing to pray for the dead, to borrow Satan's words, the first generation of English Protestants "in a moment quit / The debt immense of endless gratitude, / So burthensome still paying, still to ow" (4.51–53). Yet like Satan, one of the original arch-individualists, they were left with a question. What does one do when the past has been erased and forgotten, and with it one's very origins? Satan's is the defiant modernist response: "We know no time when we were not as now; / Know none before us, self-begot, self-rais'd" (5.859–60).[21] With this utterance, Satan shares with Coriolanus the novel illusion that the creature can create himself, beget himself, and shape himself as he will, illusions from which Prince Hamlet, although less designedly, is not altogether free.

The Ghost from Purgatory

Much has been written concerning who the Ghost is and where he comes from. Although they recognize that, as Hamlet's friends warn him (1.5.69–78), he must be cautious not to be lured to destruction by a demon in disguise, most critics have nonetheless concluded by taking the Ghost at his word. He is the Ghost of Hamlet's father, come from the next world to tell his son the story of a brother's treacherous murder and to demand vengeance. Where, then, does he come from? Let the Ghost tell his own story:

> I am thy father's spirit
> Doom'd for a certain term to walk the night,
> And for the day confin'd to fast in fires,
> Till the foul crimes done in my days of nature
> Are burnt and purg'd away. But that I am forbid
> To tell the secrets of my prison-house,
> I could a tale unfold whose lightest word
> Would harrow up thy soul, freeze thy young blood,
> Make thy two eyes like stars start from their spheres....
> (1.5.9–17)[22]

Clearly this Ghost has not come from heaven. Nor can he have come from hell, since he has been "doomed" to remain in his "prison-house" only for a "certain term," after which he will be released from confinement. In Shakespeare's day, as earlier, all major churches and denominations agreed that damnation was eternal, and that there was no escape from hell. The only remaining alternative, as most Shakespeare critics agree, is purgatory.[23] Also consistent with purgatory is the Ghost's mention of "foul crimes" and "imperfections" committed while he was still alive (in his "days of nature"), which are in the process of being "burnt and purg'd away." As Harold Jenkins remarks, "We need not suppose that 'crimes' implies offences of great gravity."[24] Since the Ghost has not been condemned to hell, we may safely conclude that they are venial rather than mortal sins.

No distinctively Catholic bishops or priests appear in *Hamlet* (as in many of Shakespeare's other plays), only the nondescript "Doctor [of Divinity]" who supervises Ophelia's burial rites.²⁵ Nonetheless it is evident that King Hamlet was a Catholic. The religion of Prince Hamlet and of Denmark at that time is, as we shall see, much more ambiguous and diminished. Still it is significant that, unlike France and Italy, where Shakespeare set other contemporary or near-contemporary plays, Denmark in his day was Lutheran. Moreover, as Brian Gerald Murphy points out, Shakespeare repeatedly emphasizes (1.2.87–167) that Hamlet and his friends of the younger generation, Horatio, Marcellus, and Barnardo, are all students at Wittenberg, famous in his day as the intellectual headquarters of Melancthon, Luther, and the Protestant Reformation.²⁶ Nevertheless Shakespeare obscures the date, so we cannot be sure whether the action of *Hamlet* takes place before or after the Reformation. In Shakespeare's sources, Saxo Grammaticus and Belleforest, the events take place much earlier. Claudius's scornful reference to English tribute (the Danegeld) also would put us somewhere before the Conquest. But an early dating is sharply contradicted by the noise of cannons, instruments of modernity. In any case, Shakespeare often engages with contemporary events and controversies even when, as in the Roman plays, his chosen period is distant and distinct.

Further to establish King Hamlet's religion, the Ghost tells his son that when Claudius murdered him in his sleep he gave him no chance to prepare himself as a Catholic should for death:

> Cut off even in the blossoms of my sin,
> Unhousel'd, disappointed, unanel'd,
> No reck'ning made, but sent to my account
> With all my imperfections on my head.
> O horrible! O horrible! most horrible!
>
> (1.5.77–80)

In other words, the Ghost was deprived of his chance to receive three of the Sacraments that would have prepared him to face death and individual judgment. The Ghost's "housel" is an old-fashioned word that suggests the Catholic Eucharist. Becon contrasts Anglican celebration of "the Lordes Supper" with, "as the Papistes terme it, . . . their Hushel."[27] "[U]nanel'd" refers to oil of extreme unction, no longer in use among Anglicans, and "disappointed" refers to missed preparations for confession and absolution.[28] We may further speculate that Hamlet Senior would have made use of the sacraments of penance and Communion at least once yearly at Eastertide prior to his unexpected death, since that was the accepted late-medieval practice, still known to the generation that preceded Shakespeare's. That would help explain his not having been in a state of mortal sin. Although the King must have died in a state of grace, with unconfessed venial rather than mortal sins "on his head" — otherwise he would not be in purgatory — Claudius had no way of knowing that when he killed him, nor did he evidently care. According to the indignant Ghost, this callousness to a brother's eternal fate in the next world more than anything else — including fratricide, regicide, possible adultery, and incest — renders his deed triply and superlatively "horrible." Through most of the middle ages, marriage to a brother's wife was technically incestuous, as Hamlet repeatedly complains. In the Renaissance dispensation was possible and presumably granted to Claudius and Gertrude. The issue was made familiar by Henry VIII's "great matter." He had a papal dispensation to marry his dead brother's wife, Katherine of Aragon, on the grounds that their marriage had not been consummated. After failing to produce a male heir and wishing to marry Anne Boleyn, he claimed that his conscience told him his marriage was incestuous after all, and sought annulment. The king's ministers solicited favorable opinions from canon lawyers all over Europe, and the details were widely discussed.[29]

Before the Reformation it was common belief among everyone from theologians to peasants that if ghosts appeared to the living they came from purgatory, not from heaven or hell. In his magisterial book *The Birth of Purgatory*, Jacques Le Goff puts the general case wryly but clearly: "Purgatory would become the prison in which ghosts were normally incarcerated, though they might be allowed to escape now and then to briefly haunt those of the living whose zeal in their behalf was insufficient."[30] That, of course, is precisely what happens in *Hamlet*. After the English Reformers dispensed with purgatory, however, it was no longer clear to anyone where ghosts came from.[31] Educated people began to doubt their existence, or to think that they were demons in disguise. There was, nevertheless, a great popular outburst of superstitious ghost lore among the common people beginning at midcentury. Theo Brown amply documents this outbreak and associates it with the sudden abolition of purgatory. Instead of doing away with ghosts, the abolition caused them to flourish at the same time that they became theologically inexplicable, vaguer, more sinister, more demonic and menacing. The result is not altogether surprising since, as Norman Cohn has argued in another connection, the weakening of institutional religion by changes, doubts, and internecine conflicts often results in an increase in superstition, as it did about the same time in the better-known case of witchcraft.[32] Thus a reader or a playgoer familiar with purgatory would recognize at once where King Hamlet's Ghost comes from; but Horatio, Marcellus, the guards, and Prince Hamlet have all forgotten, or prefer not to acknowledge, that once-common lore belonging to their fathers' generation. Horatio, a modern skeptic, has heard tales about ghosts, and does in part believe them — indeed he must believe them on the pragmatic evidence of his own eyes. But for him and his friends ghost lore lingers on obscurely as remembered folktales and superstitions rather than present and authoritative knowledge.

"Remember Me"

The Ghost calls on Hamlet to avenge him against Claudius for his foul murder. But his last command to Hamlet is significantly broader. It is: "Adieu, adieu, adieu. Remember me" (1.5.91). These words touch Hamlet most deeply and linger longest in his memory:

> Remember thee?
> Ay, thou poor ghost, whiles memory holds a seat
> In this distracted globe. Remember thee?
> Yea, from the table of my memory
> I'll wipe away all trivial fond records,
> All saws of books, all forms, all pressures past
> That youth and observation copied there,
> And thy commandment all alone shall live
> Within the book and volume of my brain,
> Unmix'd with baser matter. . . .
>   Now to my word.
> It is 'Adieu, adieu, remember me.'
> I have sworn't.
>   (1.5.95–112)

But Hamlet takes his oath to "remember" with reference only to vengeance. He never remarks on the old understanding that to remember the dead in purgatory means chiefly to pray for them, especially by offering masses for their souls. The last of his words when the Ghost has departed and Hamlet's friends approach opens a cryptic possibility: "For every man hath business and desire, / Such as it is — and for my own poor part, / I will go pray" (1.5.136–38). But, as Horatio says, this promise is spoken amid "wild and whirling words." Its import is far from clear, perhaps even to their speaker. Jenkins speculates on "pray": "Perhaps for strength to carry out his task. But perhaps because 'it behoveth them which are vexed with spirits, to pray especially.'"[33] If we consider Hamlet's behavior in this scene and after, the least likely reading of his words is that he firmly resolves to pray for his father's soul.

He loves his father, but he recognizes no special obligation to pray for him.

Among the first of the Church Fathers to write more than briefly concerning this obligation was St. Augustine. In the *Confessions* he remembers his mother Monica, whose last request to her son was that he should remember her in his prayers:

> All she wanted was that we should remember her at your altar, where she had been your servant day after day, without fail.... [I]nspire those of them who read this book to remember Monica, your servant, at your altar and with her Patricius, her husband, who died before her, by whose bodies you brought me into this life, though how it was I do not know. With pious hearts let them remember those who were not only my parents in this light that fails, but were also my brother and sister, subject to you, our Father, in our Catholic mother the Church, and will be my fellow citizens in the eternal Jerusalem for which your people sigh throughout their pilgrimage, from the time when they set out until the time when they return to you. So it shall be that the last request that my mother made to me shall be granted in the prayers of the many who read my confessions more fully than in mine alone.[34]

Remembering his mother and father with love and affection, yet regarding them as his sister and brother in religion, Augustine incidentally renders them less threatening than if he had tried to "kill" or "forget" them. Modern experience has been that a dead father can be much more burdensome than a living one, as Donald Barthelme suggests in *The Dead Father*. And we need not limit the case to fathers. A dead mother is likewise more oppressive than a living one, as D. H. Lawrence finds in *Sons and Lovers* (not to forget that Paul Morel kills his mother with sedatives). So too Stephen Dedalus's neglected mother troubles his conscience in *Ulysses* after death as she never did while she lived. The efflorescence of ghost stories at the abolition of Purgatory manifests similar anxieties. In many traditional non-Christian cultures — ancient Greek, Roman, and Chinese for example — the dead do not rest or cease from troubling the living until proper rites have been performed.

Although (as Le Goff shows) the doctrine of purgatory unfolded gradually and was not fully formed until the high middle ages, Augustine already distinguished in many of his works between *poenae purgatoriae, tormenta purgatoria, ignis purgatorius*, or *poenae temporariae* (purgatorial punishments, purgatorial torments, purgatorial fires, or temporary punishments) and *poenae sempiternae* (eternal punishments, that is, the fires of Hell).[35] Much earlier than Augustine, however, "at a very early date," possibly in Apostolic times, Christians were already remembering and praying for their dead. Indeed, to pray for the dead was a distinctively Christian custom from the beginning. According to Le Goff: "This was an innovation, as Solomon Reinach nicely observes: 'Pagans prayed to the dead, Christians prayed for the dead.'"[36] To represent the contrasting pagan view, we may recall the Sibyl's stern rebuke of Palinurus, when he begs permission to cross over the Styx: "unde haec, o Palinure, tibi tam dira cupido? . . . desine fata deum flecti sperare precando" [Whence, O Palinurus, this dire longing of yours? . . . Cease to dream that prayer can turn aside the decrees of Fate].[37]

As we are reminded by Augustine's reaction to the death of his mother, it was especially the duty of family members — husbands, wives, sons, daughters, servants, clients — to remember and to pray for their dead. A son might, like Augustine, also ask others, friends and fellow parishioners, to pray for his dead parents, since he assures us that in the light of eternity all Christians, living and dead, are brothers and sisters "in our one Catholic mother the Church," and that one day they will all be "fellow citizens in the eternal Jerusalem." Like receiving the Eucharist and the sacrament of penance, to which the Ghost of Hamlet's father specifically refers, prayers for the dead were, until the Reformation, related to a sense of family and of the community between the living and the dead. The ancient creedal phrase is "the Communion of Saints."

Notably, when Hamlet's father asks his son to "remember" him, he asks for something more than vengeance but couches his request in terms less explicit than to ask him to lighten his burdens through prayer. It is perilous to argue from absence, but the ambiguity in the Ghost's solemn request may be explained, at least in part, by two considerations. First, Shakespeare may have judged that his mostly Protestant audience would take it amiss if the Ghost were to ask Hamlet explicitly for prayers and masses. It is all very well for a dead king from out of the past to express belief in what most of the audience would take to be Catholic superstitions — confession, absolution, "housel" — but it would be another matter altogether, much more likely to offend, if Prince Hamlet were to be implicated in those superstitions, which are now safely relegated to the dead past for most of the audience and perhaps for Hamlet as well. Conversely, if Hamlet were to deny an explicit request by the Ghost to pray for him, that would strike a false note too. Second, throughout the play it appears that Hamlet and his friends, as members of the younger generation, simply are not prepared to hear such a request. The Ghost can only ask what Hamlet is ready, psychologically, culturally, and perhaps also politically, to hear and respond to. As we have seen, after 1547 English fathers who wished their sons to inherit safely put aside old ritual formulas and prudently evoked no more than the "discretion" of the executors or "the laudable custome of the realm." If the heirs were prepared to understand these hints, so much the better; if not, no harm was done. These explanations are speculative. What we can say with greater certainty is that even though the Ghost plainly comes from purgatory, and says so in terms as explicit as may be, short of an open declaration, neither Hamlet nor any of the younger Danes ever directly reveals that he has heard of such a place. As was the case in England, so in Hamlet's Denmark. Purgatory is not just abolished but effectively forgotten, as if it never were.

Forgetting the Dead

Nowhere in the play does anyone mention purgatory or pray for the dead. Although the word "pray" occurs often, it appears mainly as a fossilized part of polite clichés: "I pray you now receive them" (3.1.95), for example. But if there is no mention of purgatory, in several places there are significant absences, where the word would seem to be appropriate. In one of the play's most memorable sayings, for example, Hamlet declares: "There are more things in heaven and earth, Horatio, / Than are dreamed of in your philosophy" (1.5.74–75). Heaven can be taken as synecdochic for everything otherworldly, as in one part of the creedal phrase "visible and invisible." Still the words fall aslant when speaking about a Ghost who brings news from purgatory. It is still odder when Hamlet says that he is "Prompted to my revenge by heaven and hell" (2.2.580), as if he is repressing the real source of his prompting. Similarly, he refrains from killing Claudius at his prayer (which is not a prayer), because he interprets his father's triple condemnation of his uncle's "horrible" deed as a demand for reciprocal vengeance and not as a plea for filial prayer to ease or shorten his purgatorial torments. He vows to imitate that horrible deed and, worse, deliberately do to his uncle what his outraged father accuses his brother of nearly doing to him only through negligence, namely, to "trip him that his heels may kick at heaven / And that his soul may be as damn'd and black / As hell, whereto it goes" (3.3.93–95). In each instance, Hamlet conceives of only two states or places, with nothing in between. Nor does he consider the third place when he answers Claudius's question, "Where is Polonius?" Hamlet mockingly replies: "In heaven, send thither to see. If your messenger find him not there, seek him i'th'other place yourself" (4.3.32–35). There is no doubt where the "other place" is, or that he thinks Claudius properly belongs there. The best evidence of omission, however, may be Hamlet's outcry immediately after the ghost vanishes: "O all you host of heaven! O earth! *What else?* / And shall I couple Hell? O fie! Hold, hold my heart" (1.5.92–93; italics added). As Dover Wilson acutely remarks: "Heaven, earth — and what? Purgatory? He knows nothing of Purgatory." Wilson also notices Hamlet's odd oath, "by Saint Patrick" (1.5.142), which, he conjectures, is spoken in a low voice to Horatio.[38] St. Patrick was traditionally associated with purgatory. According to a thirteenth century account by an English Cistercian who visited Ireland, "St. Patrick's Purgatory" was an opening to that realm. Le Goff reports that the ancient account was reprinted in 1624, but a printed source need not be hypothesized since the place and tale were still notorious.[39] If his curious oath indicates that Hamlet's thoughts stray momentarily into territories forbidden by Elizabethan official culture, he does not follow them up.

In the same way, the closest anyone in the play comes to suggesting that it would be good to pray for the dead is negatively, when the Doctor of Divinity declares that there must be no official prayers or rites for Ophelia. "We should profane the service of the dead / To sing sage requiem and such rest to her / As to peace-parted souls" (5.1.229–30). This can be read as a Catholic's statement that no Requiem Mass may be offered for the soul of a presumed suicide, but a Protestant clergyman would say much the same thing about the service for "The Burial of the Dead."[40] Scholarly opinion has leaned toward identifying the Doctor of Divinity as a Protestant cleric. Martin Holmes, recognizing that the Ghost is "unquestionably in Purgatory" and therefore that Catholicism is in the air, proposes that a "copyist" or "type-setter" might have inserted the Protestant title, so there is no need to play him as "an aggressively post-Reformation Doctor of Divinity."⁴¹ Another explanation is that King Hamlet and Prince Hamlet belong to different generations and possibly different religions. "Requiem" is not an exclusively Catholic term, as witnessed by Spenser's complaint that no one offers a *"Requiem"* for the reformist Earl of Leicester.⁴² Shakespeare neglects an opportunity to make a Catholic priest look villainous to a Protestant audience sympathetic to Ophelia. Instead, he leaves the present state of religion in Denmark ambiguous, as he does everywhere else.

Laertes naturally takes violent exception to the Doctor's words. So does Hamlet, as soon as he hears the name "Ophelia" and understands who is being buried. Both leap into her grave together, wrestle and choke each other as they trample on the corpse. Although Shakespeare is reticent, we may guess from the bones thrown up earlier by the grave diggers that Ophelia is unceremoniously buried in a winding-sheet, not a coffin, and that in due course her bones will likewise go to the charnel-house.⁴³ It never occurs to either of the rival mourners to pray for their beloved Ophelia's soul. Hamlet shouts at Laertes, whose hand is at his throat, words of extreme irony: "Thou pray'st not well." In fact, neither of them prays at all, unless we count Laertes' curse, "The devil take thy soul!" or Hamlet's rejoinder, "I *prithee* take thy fingers from my throat" (5.1.251–53; italics added). It is hard to think that this cluster of mock prayers appears here accidentally. Whatever Laertes offers to do for Ophelia, Hamlet boasts he can do better: "Woo't weep, woo't fight, woo't fast, woo't tear thyself? / Woo't drink up eisel, eat a crocodile?" (5.1.270–71). The Doctor of Divinity has provoked their wild and extravagant boasts by forbidding their prayers for the wretched Ophelia. His grim stricture is scarcely needed, however, since praying for her soul is the last thing to occur to anyone attending the funeral.

"Remember me," the Ghost pleads. Toward the beginning of the play, Hamlet is the only person at the Court of Denmark who remembers his dead father. His "inky cloak" and "customary suits of solemn black" (1.2.77–78) cause him to stand out dramatically against the colorful costumes worn by everyone else on stage. They have put off black, according to the times, to celebrate the royal wedding. If it seems odd that everyone in Denmark has forgotten or cannot speak about purgatory in just the six months which have passed since the old king's death, it is surely no odder than that they have forgotten the old king, too. At this juncture, at the sight of Hamlet's visual stubbornness, King Claudius gives him good Reformist advice, such as was often heard in sermons preached in England in the latter part of the sixteenth century:[44]

> But to persever
> In obstinate condolement is a course
> Of impious stubbornness, 'tis unmanly grief,
> It shows a will most incorrect to heaven,
> A heart unfortified, a mind impatient . . .
> Fie, 'tis a fault to nature,
> To reason most absurd, whose common theme
> Is death of fathers.
> (1.2.92–104)

Claudius' words may sound heartless and self-serving to us, but they might have sounded all the more ironic to Shakespeare's auditors because they parody the rigorist language of sixteenth century sermons. For example, at the funeral of Martin Bucer in 1551, Matthew Parker, future archbishop of Canterbury, forbids all mourning: "Moreover, it agreeth not with the rules of faith, for a christian man to bewayle the dead. For, who can deny that to be against faith, which is flatly forbidden by the scriptures? And how can that be sayed to agree with the rule of fayth, whiche the scriptures most evidentlye proove to be done by those that have no hope?"[45] When Claudius scolds Hamlet for displaying excessive and therefore impious grief, implying that further persistence would be a mark of reprobation, he says no more than Parker does. Only "those that have no hope," that is, the reprobate, are guilty of such conduct. At bottom, of course, it is the absence of purgatory that renders grief and prayers inadmissible. As Augustine recognized, although one may pray for the most wicked of sinners while they are still in life, hoping for their conversion, there is no point in praying for those already in heaven or hell. "And likewise there is the same reason for praying at this time for human beings who are infidel and irreligious, and yet refusing to pray for them when they are departed. For the prayer of the Church itself, or even the prayer of devout individuals, is heard and answered on behalf of some of the departed, but only on behalf of those who have been reborn in Christ and whose life in the body has not been so evil that they are judged unworthy of such mercy, and yet not so good that they are seen to have no need of it."[46] By this logic, once purgatory is excluded, commemoration has no purpose.

Yet if Hamlet loves and remembers his father while everyone else forgets him in their eagerness to get on with their lives and to pursue the devouring business of preferment, Hamlet does not really remember *why* or *how* he should remember his father. He cannot swallow Claudius's advice not to mourn the dead, except by concealing his discontent and outwardly deferring to him. Yet like most English of the late sixteenth century, he has forgotten the old way to pray for the dead, that is, how to "remember" them: *memorare* and *commemorare*. The ancient liturgical formula, from the canon of the Mass, is *Memento, Domine, famulorum famularumque tuaram [nn.] qui nos praecesserunt cum signo fidei, et dormiunt in somno pacis* [Remember, O Lord, thy servants [names] who have gone before us with the sign of faith and sleep in the sleep of peace]. In his *Comparison of the Lord's Supper and Mass*, Thomas Becon mocks the practice: "for Philip and Cheny, more than a good meany, for the souls of your great grand Sir and of your old beldam Hurre, for the souls of father Princhard and of mother Puddingwright, for the souls of goodman Rinsepitcher and goodwife Pintpot, for the souls of Sir John Husslegoose and Sir Simon Sweetlips, for the souls of your benefactors, founders, patrons, friends and well-willers, which have given you either dirge-groats, confessional-pence, trentals, year-services, dinner or supper, or anything else that may maintain you."[47] Becon allows Sir John Husslegoose much the same contemptuous godspeed that Prince Hal gives old Sir John Falstaff.

When Hamlet's mother as well as his uncle accuses him of unusual excess in his grief, and therefore of dangerous impiety, Hamlet cannot grapple with the theological questions implied. Instead, he is driven inward, into the most famous of all early modern gestures of radical individualist subjectivity: "But I have that within which passes show, / These but the trappings and the suits of woe" (1.2.85–86). His assertion would not really be to the point, if Hamlet did not so forcefully make it so, turning the discussion momentarily away from Protestant suspicion of excessive mourning to the question of where true authenticity lies. What his plangent words reveal is that his deepest concern is not only for his lost father but for himself and for his innermost identity. So it is hardly surprising that, as the play progresses, the only way that he — and in response Laertes — can conceive of to "remember" his father is by resorting to vengeance. Although he cannot respond to his father's implicit plea to pray for him, he can respond to his call for vengeance and kill for him. As the play ends, Hamlet and Laertes repent and generously forgive each other. That is as close as they come to formal confession and absolution. Nor does Hamlet die asking his friends to pray for his soul, as he follows his father into the next world — perhaps into Purgatory. Rather, his penultimate words reveal his dutiful anxiety to settle the royal succession. His last words preserve, and take to a higher level, Shakespeare's refusal to define Hamlet's religion and Hamlet's earlier uncertainty about what lies beyond death: "the rest is silence" (5.2.363).

In spite of Hamlet's notable last omissions, the skeptical Horatio, left to do the private honors as Fortinbras enters to make the public arrangements, is prompted to spontaneous words of prayer: "Good night, sweet prince, / And flights of angels sing thee to thy rest" (5.2.341–42). Horatio's prayer is all the more moving in that it is so clearly spontaneous and heartfelt. As is everywhere the case with the younger generation of Prince Hamlet's friends, it is also theologically naive. It could be nothing else, if we imagine the alternatives. If Horatio had said, "And may the Lord have mercy on your soul," he would have stepped out of character. His oxymoronic combination of "flights of angels" — a flight of fancy which rises to the occasion — with the religiously neutral yet deeply satisfying "rest" (satisfying to Catholics, Protestants, and doubters alike) is precisely right. If he had been still more specific, and said, "And may your stay in Purgat'ry be short," he would probably have provoked a riot, both in Elsinore and at the Globe, followed by an official inquiry.

"The Time Is Out of Joint"

Audiences have always responded strongly to the moment of Horatio's prayer. Well they might, since it is the first and last time in the play that anyone finally breaks through into even a short, nondenominational prayer, unless it be Hamlet's notable displaced prayer to Ophelia: "Nymph, in thy orisons / Be all my sins remember'd" (3.1.89–90). In his notorious prayer scene (3.3), Claudius suffers from a blocked psyche and consequent inability to pray. All of Denmark — perhaps by implication all of England — suffers from a seemingly similar affliction. But it is not the same. Because he belongs to the older generation of King Hamlet, Claudius understands that if only he were to consent to give up his ill-gotten gains — his queen and his kingdom — he could repent, confess his sins, and receive absolution. Restitution is the necessary prior condition, and he will not make restitution. In contrast, Hamlet and Horatio, although their spiritual state is not depraved like Claudius's, have forgotten what even the self-damned Claudius knows but cannot put to use. Perhaps Shakespeare alludes to this strange forgetting in Hamlet's extreme decision to wipe the slate of his mind clean of everything but vengeance: "all trivial fond records, / All saws of books, all forms, all pressures past / That youth and observation copied there" (1.5.99–101). Alastair Fowler comments, "This must have been deeply shocking to a generation for whom the book was a symbol of devout Protestantism."[48] Perhaps Hamlet wiped away or repressed an underlayer of Catholic lore too. Claudius's older generation threw the times out of joint by committing an unnameable deed involving more than a single act of murder and usurpation. Prince Hamlet belongs to the next generation. He and his friends have forgotten (or dare not name) what went wrong, because their predecessors have taken that knowledge and thrown it down Orwell's "memory hole."

Hamlet does not kill his father, he avenges him. He does not forget his father, he remembers him — insofar as he is capable. But there are different sorts of memory. The abolished rite was: *Memento, Domine, famulorum famularumque tuaram.* Unwittingly Hamlet implicates himself, as all the younger generation are unwittingly implicated, in the hidden crime committed by the fathers. That crime, paradoxically, was to kill the fathers, those prior benefactors of whom Becon speaks with such unmerited scorn: "Sir John Husslegoose and Sir Simon Sweetlips . . . your benefactors, founders, patrons, friends and well-willers, which have given you either dirge-groats, confessional-pence, trentals, year-services, dinner or supper, or anything else that may maintain you."[49] Presumably, the persons responsible for abolishing remembrance of the dead in purgatory were Claudius and his chief ministers and advisers on high policy — including Polonius. If so, it is the greater irony that Polonius's daughter Ophelia is denied "sage requiem," a peaceful departure, and prayers for her soul. Hamlet and Laertes would surely have defied the Doctor of Divinity's ban against praying for her soul had they not forgotten the old assumption that such prayers are efficacious.

Probably some of Shakespeare's audience would have noticed that Claudius has it in common with Henry VIII that he married his dead brother's wife — as we have remarked, it was a very famous case — although Claudius far exceeds Henry by murdering his brother first. Moreover, an overwhelming burden of restitution lies on both kings' consciences. It would not be unprecedented to find covert political reference in these resemblances, but one cannot press the point too far. Whatever he thought, Shakespeare could not afford to risk drawing an explicit connection. A Catholic in his audience might have imagined that Claudius combines elements of several kings. Henry VII usurped the throne, Henry VIII had marriage troubles and, by confiscating the monasteries and passing the Chantries Act of 1545, showed the way for the stewards of Edward VI to abolish purgatory altogether, in the Chantries Act of 1547 and the Prayerbook of 1549.[50] As a crowning irony, Henry VIII's last will and testament, which took effect at his death in 1547, left a huge sum, over £1,200, for Masses to be said for his soul.[51] He was one of the last important men in England who dared risk confiscation by providing for memorial Masses in his will. Having made it impossible for anyone else to do so, however, by setting in motion the abolition of the chantries, the monastic orders, the religious guilds, and purgatory itself — and having enriched himself by confiscating the funds that had been left to support these institutions — his deeds redounded on his head. There was no longer any will or way among his successors to honor his last intentions. Thus was "the enginer / Hoist with his own petard" (3.4.208–09).

The abolition of purgatory was only one change among many, but it was perhaps the most sweeping and uncompromising of all those changes. It was deeply traumatic at the time, and its effects have lingered long after the event itself has been forgotten. As Virginia Bainbridge sums up these large cultural transformations: "The tearing apart of death and charity, the reciprocity between the living and the dead, and the poor, their substitutes, struck a blow at the very core of medieval concepts of community."[52] The focus turned from community and solidarity, with the dead and with the poor, toward self-concern and individual self-sufficiency. If, as Hamlet fears, "the time is out of joint," and if according to his lineage he is "born to set it right" (1.5.196–97), unfortunately he cannot know how to do so, because he cannot or will not remember what went wrong in the first place. Instead, his ironic legacy is to add to the original, unspoken crime the powerful seal of his own fall into the depths of interior subjectivity, thus completing, by driving further inward, that earlier self-regarding assertion of progressive, autonomous individualism by his predecessors, who in a moment struck out ruthlessly against the communal past and against the generous benefactions and the crying needs of the dead.

FIVE

"Umpire Conscience"

❦

Freedom and Obedience in *Paradise Lost*

Contrary to what some Renaissance scholars have argued in recent years, there is considerable evidence that, well before the Renaissance, people had a sense of an inner self something like ours — that they were just as conscious as we are that they were individuals, distinct from society and from all other individuals. However, some 300 or 400 years ago, there was a historic turn in the nature and perception of our individuality. The person perhaps most responsible for that historic turn is René Descartes, with his revolutionary dictum, "I think, therefore I am." But so large a cultural shift was not the work of one person. We have glanced at the contribution made by Shakespeare's *Hamlet*. The subject of this chapter is Milton's contribution, mainly through *Paradise Lost*, to the way we have grown accustomed to think about ourselves as free, autonomous individuals.

Freedom and Obedience

For a modern reader, there is a paradox at the heart of *Paradise Lost*. Anyone who reads much Milton, especially *Of Education*, *Areopagitica*, and *Paradise Lost*, quickly realizes that he put the highest value on freedom: freedom of the will and freedom to choose whatever the individual judges best. In *Of Education*, whether Milton speaks about one of the proximate ends of learning, such as good citizenship in private and in public, in peace and in war, or whether he speaks about humanity's ultimate end, "to repair the ruins of our first parents by regaining to know God aright, and out of that knowledge to love him," the necessary means is freedom of the will. As Milton explains, free will is "that act of reason which in ethics is called Proairesis," which Merritt Hughes glosses as "intelligent choice between good and evil."[1] In *Areopagitica*, Milton writes that "God uses not to captivate under a perpetual childhood of prescription, but trusts him with the gift of reason to be his own chooser" (727). In the *Second Defense*, looking back on his polemical career, Milton explains that the purpose of all his prose writings was "the promotion of real and substantial liberty, which is rather to be sought from within than from without" (830). Putting the case most strongly in *Areopagitica*, he declares simply that "reason is but choosing" (733). For Milton, conditions in the fallen world often raise the revolutionary imperative to defend the individual's exercise of free will by deposing usurping kings and bishops who interfere with it. Yet even in this case although the proper exercise of freedom entails the overthrow of authority, Milton everywhere insists that freedom is not something that the individual seizes in rebellion against the natural order, but a free gift to all persons from God himself. In short, freedom to choose comes directly from God and belongs to the order of the universe as He created it from the beginning.

Although Milton believed that human beings lost their original freedom in the Fall, there are no signs in his writings that he ever subscribed to anything even approaching the Calvinist doctrine of total depravity. Through the Son's act of atonement, each individual human being has been given back freedom to choose. Grace, flowing from the atonement, restores fallen human nature sufficiently to recover free will and the ability to choose wisely, so that, as the Father puts it in *Paradise Lost*, man once more stands "On even ground against his mortal foe" (3.179). Yet not for nothing did Milton seize on Aristotle's term "Proairesis" to describe the faculty of choosing, since he does not expect God's grace to work in a vacuum. What Aristotle and those who work in the Aristotelian tradition describe is a long and arduous training process, in which individuals are educated in virtue by the wisest and best teachers that society can offer, and in which both the individual and society as a whole strive continually and cooperatively toward greater excellence.[2] As *Of Education* reveals — and as the repentance, regeneration, and education of Adam and Eve at the end of *Paradise Lost* confirm — the ability to make right choices depends on a strenuous process of learning, on difficult but successful resistance to temptation, and, if necessary, on successful recovery from failure to resist temptation. After Adam and Eve fall, they need "Prevenient Grace" to remove "The stony from thir hearts" and make "new flesh / Regenerate grow instead" (10.3–5),[3] but they also need inner, heartfelt contrition and patient determination to repent, to learn, and to continue along the path of choosing wisely. The term "prevenient grace," which Milton employs, was used both by those theologians of his time who believed that grace perfects nature and by others who believed that grace radically overturns or replaces nature. The phrase appears not only in many Protestant treatises but also in the documents of the Council of Trent. Milton was among those who thought that grace perfects nature. Unlike Calvin, he believed that grace could either be willingly accepted or wilfully resisted. That is why he portrays Adam and Eve working through their problems in book 10 in purely human fashion, using their hearts and their heads, before he afterward informs us, at the beginning of book 11, that God already gave them "prevenient" grace, which enabled them to act as they did.

This cooperation of nature with grace accords with Milton's educational theories. Whether from teachers or from books, Milton would have his students learn, not only through grace and from Scripture, but also, to quote again from *Of Education*, from "those people who have at any time been most industrious after wisdom" (p. 631), including especially the pagan Greeks and Romans. Right choosing, which for a student involves "the knowledge of virtue and the hatred of vice" (p. 635), is both gracious and industrious.

All this is clear, and for the most part congenial to a modern reader. Even purely secular readers have shown themselves willing to put up with Milton's insertion of God into the equation, as long as He is an authorizing God, who gives human beings the gift of freedom. Much less congenial, however, is another, seemingly opposite term, which Milton seldom forgets to mention whenever he speaks of freedom and free will: namely, obedience. Just as nothing could be more important to the Milton who wrote *Paradise Lost* than freedom, so — in what seems to us a puzzling contradiction — nothing could be more important than obedience. Freedom (we think) we easily understand; obedience is harder to accept. C. S. Lewis comments on modern resistance or obtuseness to the centrality of obedience: "'The great moral which reigns in Milton,' said Addison, 'is the most universal and most useful that can be imagined, that Obedience to the will of God makes men happy and that Disobedience makes them miserable.' Dr. Tillyard amazes me by calling this a 'rather vague explanation'.... Dull, if you will, or platitudinous, or harsh, or jejune: but vague? . . . [T]he real moral of the poem involve[s] an idea so uninteresting or so intensely disagreeable to them that they have been under a sort of psychological necessity of passing it over and hushing it up."[4]

Moreover, what Milton advocates is not grudging but "willing obedience." According to *Of Education*, ideal teachers should *educate* their pupils. As Milton puts it, tacitly playing (with false etymology) on the Latin roots, *educare*, to teach, and *educere*, to lead out or educe, teachers should "lead and draw" their pupils "in willing obedience, inflamed with the study of learning and the admiration of virtue" (633). Nor is such willing obedience just an essential *desideratum* for the reformist education of children; it is what God requires at all times of all human beings. In *Areopagitica*, Milton exclaims: "Many there be that complain of divine providence for suffering Adam to transgress. Foolish tongues! when God gave him reason, he gave him freedom to choose, for reason is but choosing; he had been else a mere artificial Adam, such an Adam as he is in the motions" (733). In other words, Adam is given complete freedom to choose, but, of course, if he wants to be happy and attain the end for which he was created, he must choose correctly, that is, he must exercise his God-given freedom within certain God-given parameters of obedience. Although Adam's fall incorporates pride, envy, greed, anger, lust, curiosity, and the rest, his fundamental sin is disobedience. So Milton tells us in the opening lines of *Paradise Lost*, where he proposes to deal with "Man's First Disobedience, and the Fruit / Of that Forbidden Tree, whose mortal taste / Brought Death into the World, and all our woe" (1.1–3). So too toward the end of *Paradise Lost*, Adam, "greatly instructed" by his education at the hands of the Archangel Michael, sums up all the lessons he has learned: "Henceforth I learn, that to obey is best" (12.557, 561). Thus, paradoxically, for Milton, if man is to realize his nature fully, he must be free; yet, if he is to realize his nature fully, he must also obey. Which of these two ultimate but apparently contradictory imperatives is the more basic it would be hard to say. For Milton, both are fundamental.

So, in the midst of his long speech on free will at the Heavenly Council in the third book of *Paradise Lost*, the Father returns several times to the theme of obedience. Indeed, free will and obedience are inseparable, for the proper end of the gift of freedom is to exercise true obedience to God:

> Not free, what proof could they have giv'n sincere
> Of true allegiance, constant Faith or Love,
> Where only what they needs must do appear'd,
> Not what they would? what praise could they receive?
> What pleasure I from such obedience paid,
> When Will and Reason (Reason also is choice)
> Useless and vain, of freedom both despoil'd,
> Made passive both, had serv'd necessity,
> Not mee.
>
> (3.103–11)

The Father echoes and authorizes Milton's key phrase in *Areopagitica*: "reason is but choosing"; here, "Reason also is choice." In doing so, he likewise evokes the substantial meaning of that key phrase in *Of Education*: "willing obedience."

The paradox is difficult. It grates upon the modern — or, if you prefer, the postmodern — mentality. How can we be truly free if we must remain under obligation to obey someone more powerful than we are? Surely to be free means to do or think whatever we choose to do or think, rather than to order our actions and our thoughts in accordance with someone else's instructions. The simple answer, of course, is that God is all-good and all-loving, as well as all-powerful. What He wills is best for his creatures and for their happiness. Therefore, the orthodox Christian position is well expressed by St. Augustine, in *The Enchiridion*: "For only he is free in service who gladly does the will of his Lord. And consequently he who is the servant of sin is free only for sinning.... This is the true liberty, because of joy for the upright act; and no less is it pious servitude, because of obedience to the commandment. But whence shall a man declared a bondman, and sold, obtain that liberty for well-doing, except he be redeemed by him who says, *If the Son shall make you free, then shall ye be free indeed?*"⁵ In the Anglican Book of Common Prayer, which Milton knew well and often echoed — much as he objected to its forced imposition on free Christians by the State — "A Collect for Peace" phrases the Christian paradox succinctly. The prayer begins: "O God . . . whose service is perfect freedom." Of course, the Scots Presbyterians and some dissenters in England took the Book of Common Prayer to be a political as well as a religious document, reminding us that obedience to God may also be taken, and sometimes mistaken, to require obedience to kings and bishops.

Love and Servility

In regard to church governance, Milton was a radical Protestant. He had no great use for churches of any kind. His position was to reject that sort of willing obedience to the State, which in this context we may loosely call Anglican,⁶ or to the Church, which we may call Catholic, but not to reject willing obedience to God. Adam instinctively recognizes that his true end in life is to know God and to worship him (8.280). Raphael's parting advice to Adam is:

> Be strong, live happy, and love, but first of all
> Him whom to love is to obey, and keep
> His great command; take heed lest Passion sway
> Thy Judgment to do aught, which else free Will
> Would not admit.
>
> (8.633–37)

To adore or to worship is only another name for that kind of highest love which is properly directed toward God alone. Since

God *is* who he is, "to love is to obey." Raphael puts the matter simply, succinctly, and powerfully when he describes himself and the good angels:

> Freely we serve,
> Because we freely love, as in our will
> To love or not; in this we stand or fall.
>
> (5.538–40)

Only love can make such service palatable. Without love, service to God becomes nothing but empty knee-worship, "warbl'd Hymns" and "Forc't Hallelujahs" in Mammon's vivid words (2.242–43).

Love makes the difference. In this particular sense, love is different from desire. Desire craves its object, as does love; but love also wishes the good for its object, even if that should conflict with the immediate cravings of desire. As Augustine, Aquinas, and others indicate, such love or *caritas* comes from the heart and is partly a matter of feeling but is primarily a matter of will. God gives man free will originally, and (according to Milton's theology in *Paradise Lost*) restores his freedom after the Fall, because he wishes freely to be loved in return, reciprocating his great gift of the creation of man-in-freedom by love freely offered, not by constrained service. Only love understands or responds to love. We see this more clearly in its absence, as in Satan's first soliloquy. Examining the reasons for his fall, Satan is forced to admit to himself:

> whom hast thou then or what to accuse,
> But Heav'n's free Love dealt equally to all?
> Be then his Love accurst, since love or hate,
> To me alike, it deals eternal woe.
>
> (4.67–70)

We may see with equal clarity the difference between love and desire in Satan's reaction to the sight of Adam and Eve unselfconsciously expressing their love for each other:

> Sight hateful, sight tormenting! thus these two
> Imparadis't in one another's arms,
> The happier *Eden*, shall enjoy thir fill
> Of bliss on bliss, while I to Hell am thrust,
> Where neither joy nor love, but fierce desire,
> Among our other torments not the least,
> Still unfulfill'd with pain of longing pines.
>
> (4.505–11)

Without love, God is merely "the Thunderer," as Satan characteristically refers to him (2.28; 6.491), or the "great Forbidder, safe with all his Spies / About him" (9.815–16), as Eve calls him just after she has fallen. In later centuries, this tyrant God, seen through the eyes of hate and rejection rather than love, will become Blake's Nobodaddy and Shelley's Zeus, the old usurping God of the Gnostics.

Seen from outside, unless it is freely willed and inwardly felt, love appears either as sheer madness or as abject servility. Most of us have enough of the rebellious streak in us to understand and sympathize when Mammon complains at the Council in Hell:

> with what eyes could we
> Stand in his presence humble, and receive
> Strict Laws impos'd, to celebrate his Throne
> With warbl'd Hymns, and to his Godhead sing
> Forc't Halleluiahs; while he Lordly sits
> Our envied Sovran, and his Altar breathes
> Ambrosial Odors and Ambrosial Flowers,
> Our servile offerings. This must be our task
> In Heav'n, this our delight; how wearisome
> Eternity so spent in worship paid
> To whom we hate.
>
> (2.239–49)

What Mammon cannot admit is that God no more wants to receive such empty lip service and knee service than Mammon wants to give it. When love turns to hate, all perspectives change and all relationships are turned upside down. What had been a willing community or a loving family becomes brutal tyranny or abject slavery. Once you see things as Mammon and Satan do, then of course you will feel as they do. For all practical purposes, love and hate become indistinguishable.

For Milton and others in his time, the place where free will and obedience — the inward choice and the outward imperative — converge is in the faculty of conscience. The key passage describing conscience in *Paradise Lost* is dense and complicated. It is introduced by a discussion of human will and divine grace. In response to the Son's offer to sacrifice himself for man, the Father responds that the Son's offer accords with his own eternal decree:

> Man shall not quite be lost, but sav'd who will,
> Yet not of will in him, but grace in me
> Freely voutsaf't; once more I will renew
> His lapsed powers, though forfeit and enthrall'd
> By sin to foul exorbitant desires;
> Upheld by me, yet once more he shall stand
> On even ground against his mortal foe. . . .
>
> (3.173–79)

This passage incorporates the same basic contradiction we have so often seen, between freedom and service. Man will stand, but only because God invisibly upholds him. He will be saved if he so wills — or chooses — not through his own will but by God's unmerited grace. Thus he owes everything to grace; yet that grace gives him the further power to accept or reject grace itself. *If* he chooses to cooperate with grace, sincerely witnessing his "true allegiance, constant Faith or Love" (3.104), then he will stand once more on even ground, in the unavoidable confrontation with Satan and his terrible progeny, Sin and Death, just as he did before the fall.

Many Miltonists have taken the next part of this passage to be a restatement of the Calvinist doctrine of election:

> Some I have chosen of peculiar grace
> Elect above the rest; so is my will:
> The rest shall hear me call, and oft be warn'd
> Thir sinful state, and to appease betimes
> Th' incensed Deity while offer'd grace
> Invites....
>
> (3.183–89)

Careful reading, however, shows that Milton's position is distinctly *not* Calvinist.[7] According to Milton's God, some people are specially elect — perhaps, we may speculate, such people as St. Paul's heroes of faith, Gideon, Barak, Samson, Jephtha, David, Samuel, and the prophets (Heb. 11:32–38) — but, contrary to Calvin, all people are called, and all may choose or refuse to respond to that call. As we have remarked, all those who called themselves Christian, whether Catholic or Protestant, agreed that prevenient grace was necessary first. To argue otherwise was to fall into Pelagianism. But Milton's God so dearly wishes man to be free and "sincere" (3.103) that he gives him the grace freely to reject even the grace that enables his freedom, just as he earlier so dearly wished Adam and Eve to be free — to love him with no touch of constraint — that he gave them the power to reject even his gift of freedom, and thereby freely to fall.

"Umpire Conscience"

To help them renew their freedom, to reempower their rational faculties, crippled by the fall, God promises to give Adam, Eve, and their descendants another gift, closely associated with grace. This gift he names "My Umpire *Conscience*."

> And I will place within them as a guide
> My Umpire *Conscience*, whom if they will hear,
> Light after light well us'd they shall attain,
> And to the end persisting, safe arrive.
> This my long sufferance and my day of grace
> They who neglect and scorn, shall never taste;

> But hard be harden'd, blind be blinded more,
> That they may stumble on, and deeper fall;
> And none but such from mercy I exclude.
>
> (3.194–202)

The dark fate of those who reject grace and close their ears to the voice of conscience throws a contrasting light on those who accept them, much as Satan's resentful hatred and burning desire throw light on the true love between Adam and Eve. But, although Milton has his elect and his reprobate, his reprobate are those who "neglect and scorn" God's "long sufferance" and his "day of grace," and thus freely choose to embrace their unhappy state.

In the seventeenth century, conscience was a pivotal concept. On the one hand, it was objective: Milton tellingly calls it God's umpire, like an external judge whose authority the players may question only at the cost of a complete breakdown of the game. Conscience is a reliable voice, put into the soul by God himself. Except in the case of those who deliberately close their ears and harden their hearts, conscience can be counted on not only to reveal God's objective rules of morality but to point toward the application of those general rules in any particular case. Furthermore, conscience is related both to grace, because it is a gift of God, and to natural law, because it is given to all, even pagans and unbelievers. In Romans 2:14–15, St. Paul says that even the gentiles, "which have not the law, do by nature the things contained in the law," because they have "the law written in their hearts, their conscience also bearing witness." This is a key text both for theories of conscience and for theories of natural law. God gives his laws not only to the Jews through the commandments of Moses, and to Christians through the fulfillment of the gospels, but to all, even those who have never heard of Moses or Jesus, through the law written in their hearts. That was the traditional Christian belief, but it gained new importance after the Reformation, when authority shifted from the teachings of the Church and the authority of the magisterium to the internal deliberations of the individual in his private relation to Scripture and the Holy Spirit. Conscience has always been thought to be individual and interior. It is what *I* believe to be right, not what someone tells me to do. It has also usually been thought to be universal and objective. It is God's voice speaking internally; it is a reliable umpire. But in the further growth of modernism since Milton, as belief in individual autonomy has led to increasing mistrust of tradition and authority, one of these two aspects of conscience has obviously grown at the expense of the other. Even the veriest neopagans among us still retain some of the old double sense, however, just as St. Paul might have predicted. Conscience is the bedrock of the self; it will not bow to outward authority. Yet, in the popular phrase, conscience "lays a guilt trip" on us, insists on telling us things we would rather not hear. So at the same time that conscience authorizes our freedom, it guides and inhibits that freedom. Milton would say that, if we listen to conscience, it will teach us how to serve freely.

So far Milton's double treatment of conscience appears to be fundamentally traditional, yet here too he reveals himself to be among the more radical Protestants. Although his conscience is double in nature — at once both personal and objective — Milton's particular version of objectivity rests only on the direct inspiration of God to the individual, not on custom, tradition, Church teachings, ministerial authority, consensus among a congregation, or instruction within a family. God the Father simply inserts His "Umpire conscience" directly into the individual soul, and nothing more is needed. In contrast, the traditional Catholic teaching is that each individual has a strong obligation to "form" his conscience, by learning his catechism, reading scriptures, heeding authority, and the like. Most traditional Protestants would say something similar: the individual has a duty to read scriptures, attend church, heed sermons, obey his parents and teachers, seek advice from wise neighbors. Thus, for example although Bunyan's Pilgrim undergoes much of his journey toward the Heavenly City alone and is elected and guided primarily by interior grace, nevertheless he finds companions along the way and is vitally helped by his conversations with them and by the teachings of the hosts in various stopping places along the way, such as the House of the Interpreter.[8]

Although Milton declares in various writings his belief in a community of the wise and, as we have seen, in the importance of an arduous process of education, when we think further about these passages, his community and his arduous education are seen to be mostly imaginary. They represent Milton's conviction of the way things ought to be, not the way they normally are. Milton tells us that he belongs to an invisible company of the wise from all ages — Homer, Virgil, Horace, Moses, Isaiah, and the rest — but Milton chooses them all and subjects them to his own interpretive strategies, without any possibility that they might talk back and contradict him. Except when he is imagining a visionary future, Milton rarely belongs to a real community, a Church, a congregation, an elect nation, and probably he never really opened his soul to anyone for spiritual advice, with the exception of his friend Charles Diodati. Certainly Milton had an unerring instinct for choosing the best possible imaginary guides and companions — and as written books these advisers and friends are not simply imaginary. Still books are something very different from real conversations with living people, and in Milton's case they are subject always to his bedrock conviction that the reader must always control the book, never the book the reader. So the objectivity of Milton's version of conscience rests finally on the authority of God alone and not on human conversation, formation, or consensus. In a sense, one could demand no higher authority to validate conscience than Omnipotence Himself. It remains, however, that such an objectivity depends not only on God's existence but on His willingness to instruct, personally and directly, the interior souls of strongminded individuals such as Milton, who refuse the usual obligation to form their consciences by listening to custom, tradition, their Church, their minister, their families, and their neighbors.

Moreover, there are further complications that suggest a still more radical Milton yet. *Paradise Lost* is always more subtle and more complicated than we might first think it to be. The passage on conscience that we have just been examining represents Milton's explicit explanation of the workings of free will under obedience. Yet, in the figure of Satan, Milton provides his readers not only with a contrast to heroic behavior, a negative exemplar, an instance of conduct and attitudes we should avoid, but also with what amounts to almost the invention and embodiment of modern autonomous individuality. Not for nothing do Blake, Shelley, Byron, and the rest of the Romantic-modernist line take Satan as their hero. Whether we call their appropriation and recasting of Milton's Satan as a flawed but gigantic hero misinterpretation or, in Harold Bloom's phrase, creative misreading, it remains that, by writing *Paradise Lost,* Milton gave the inventors of Romanticism and of modernity the gift of an irresistibly powerful figure to work with.

The Cartesian Flight from Calvin

Toward the middle of the seventeenth century, Descartes reordered philosophy and with it the whole development of western thought by shifting its basis from what had been presumed to be its objective foundations — that is, arguing downward from God — to subjective foundations — that is, arguing outward from the self. According to the famous phrase, *cogito, ergo sum;* I think, therefore I am. Shakespeare and Milton, with their figures of Hamlet and Satan, provided universal armatures that gave body and life to Descartes's shift in thought and perception.

Here I enter on speculative ground. What I think Milton and Descartes had in common, which in part impelled their visions literary and philosophical, was what I would call the deep fear of the shadow of Calvin.[9] Calvin was immensely influential in early modern England and France, not only among British Presbyterians, French Huguenots, and others who openly proclaimed themselves his disciples and dissented from the majority, but among mainstream Anglicans (including King James and his bishops) and French Catholics (including Port Royal and the Jansenists). Even those, Protestant and Catholic, who were alarmed and distressed by Calvin's theology, recognized its force and found it difficult to refute his arguments without falling into the trap of putting human limitations on God or belittling His overwhelming power and might, His ability to do whatever He pleased. As is sometimes said, Calvin was the deep organ note of Reformation theology, impossible to ignore and, for many, impossible to escape.

I shall begin this latter inquiry with a simpleminded question. Who — or what — is the real enemy in *Paradise Lost*? Milton, a masterly debater and rhetorician as well as a poet, habitually works by opposites: light against darkness, harmony against discord, standing against falling, expansiveness against contraction, love against hatred. As we have seen in one instance, the love of Adam and Eve emerges in bright relief by contrast with Satan's dark resentment. Similarly, Raphael's willing service gains clarity by contrast with Mammon's grudging refusal. It follows that we may better understand what *Paradise Lost* ultimately advocates if we ask what it most deeply fears, rejects, and refuses. A few preliminary answers are evident: Milton chooses light and rejects darkness, chooses harmony and rejects discord, chooses good and rejects evil, chooses God and rejects Satan. But he employs darkness, discord, evil, and Satan as ingredients in his poem, and sometimes readers find that these elements have gotten out of hand. Most significantly, Milton chooses freedom and rejects slavery, but as we have seen, that basic, underlying choice is intrinsically problematic. Moreover his choice of freedom severely problematizes the rest of his choices because the modern reader — and perhaps Milton already anticipates us by thinking this way — devoutly believes that the freedom to choose trumps everything else.

Let us try the further step of rephrasing our question in political and historical terms. Who was Milton's enemy in the context of his times? Politically, the usual response is that Milton hated kings, bishops, and tyrants. He hated Archbishop Laud, the Stuart kings, and the architects of the Restoration. In *The Ready and Easy Way*, he suggests that the Restoration was fully as bad as if the Jews, in the very midst of their Exodus, had given up God's great project and returned to the fleshpots of Egypt (898–99). Yet, as Robert Fallon has argued, it is not easy to explain how Milton actually embodies the expected political views in *Paradise Lost*, since God presides over the poem as an absolute monarch while Satan consults with parliament and gains the consent of the governed.[10] These discrepancies do not prevent radical-minded Miltonists, whose chief interest in the poem is as a political document, from spinning their theories. Still, a more defensible view is that in *Paradise Lost* Stuart kings and Restoration society make their appearances as enemies, but only episodically. Milton's deepest and most abiding concerns lie elsewhere.

If not politics, perhaps religion. As we might expect, one of the announced enemies in *Paradise Lost* is the Catholic Church. Milton agreed, with most English Protestants of his time, that the Catholic Church is the Whore of Babylon and that the Pope is Antichrist. In book 3 he suggests that after their deaths, St. Peter will mockingly consign most Catholics, especially friars, monks, and nuns, to a limbo called the Paradise of Fools. In addition, many Miltonists suspect, though without having definite proof, that Satan's headquarters,

Pandemonium, is modeled after St. Peter's Basilica in Rome. Finally, toward the end of *Paradise Lost*, Milton declares that after the death of the last apostles, "Wolves . . . grievous Wolves" (12.508) will shepherd the Church. They will prey upon their flocks instead of guiding them. But this last denunciation, the fiercest of the three, is antiecclesial more than anti-Catholic. Critics note that Milton's historical survey never even mentions Luther, Calvin, or the Reformation. The Church in any form will continue to go from bad to worse right up to the Last Judgment. Sensible Christians will fend for themselves. When all is said and done, even Catholicism is a subsidiary enemy in *Paradise Lost*. We notice that Milton's God spends no time in his speeches condemning popes or bishops. They are beneath his notice. Rather, he is obsessively concerned with free will, love, and service. In our paradoxical phrase, he is obsessed with willing obedience. Apart from the necessary business of forwarding the plot by explaining his redemptive plans, all of God's speeches, including his praise of Abdiel beginning "Servant of God, well done" (6.29), return persistently to that phrase in *Of Education*: "willing obedience."

That is why I think *Paradise Lost* was written under the shadow of Calvin. Officially, the great enemy in the poem is Satan, whose name means "The Adversary." There are also a scattering of subsidiary and episodic enemies, such as Charles II, the Restoration court, and the Pope. Unofficially, however, the greatest enemy proves most unexpectedly to be Calvin's God, the shadowy authority figure later excoriated by Blake, Shelley, and others down to William Empson, Stanley Fish, and beyond. This is not to say that Calvin's God is Milton's God; indeed, they are opposites. Far from giving freedom as a gift, Calvin's God allows his creatures no freedom. Therefore, he is *not* the God to whom we are introduced in the poem. Nevertheless, somehow he hovers over the poem as the ultimate, menacing threat: as Belial's God, who reads our secret thoughts; as Mammon's God, who demands humiliating hymns and prostrations; as Satan's God, who assaults us with thunder; for a time as Eve's God, who keeps us subservient. This is the God of power, the God of thunder and revenge, the God of arbitrary Will, who swallows up resistance and refuses to permit individuation or separation from his stifling rule. He is not, in fact, the God whom we see or hear speaking in the poem, not the God who encourages Adam to think for himself and ask for a wife, yet somehow he is the God whom many readers imagine there, not only because many of the characters see him thus but because, I would suggest, he is the God with whom Milton constantly argues, everywhere in the poem, even in the speeches spoken by God himself. Many readers have asked, with whom is God arguing? Why is he so defensive? Or, if his tone is not properly heard as defensive, why does he harp on these particular theological issues and no others while he dismisses his ostensible adversary, Satan, with a few scornful words? He does so, I think, because for Milton these and no others are the supremely important issues.

Miltonists have remarked that Milton seldom cites Calvin in his prose works, considering Calvin's great importance. When he does so, his references are respectful but brief, and are usually to be found where Milton addresses readers for whom Calvin's authority has weight. The most interesting of these passages appears in the late tract *Of True Religion.* There, while urging tolerance among the various Protestant factions, he discusses some of the charges they bring against one another. He does not attack Calvin himself, but he knows the usual charges. "The Calvinist is taxt with Predestination, and to make God the Author of Sin; not with any dishonourable thought of God, but it may be over zealously asserting his absolute power, not without plea of Scripture."[11] Milton's phrasing twists and vacillates uncharacteristically. He leaves us with the impression that, to preserve Protestant fellowship, we should not tax Calvinists with their beliefs. Still, they may indeed "over zealously" assert God's "absolute power." They may indeed make Him responsible for sin, with or without their plea of Scripture. Surely it is significant that the particular charge that God is responsible for sin is precisely the one that the whole of *Paradise Lost* was written to refute, if we believe that Milton is serious about wanting to "justify the ways of God to men" (1.26).

The charge that God is responsible for the fall and for sin in general, because nothing can happen unless He wills it, has no obvious relation to Catholicism or Anglican Prelacy. If anything, most Protestants accused Catholics of underestimating the importance of grace and predestination. But although Calvinists did not themselves accuse God of responsibility for sin, such a charge seemed to many to follow logically from their uncompromising views on election and predestination. Thus Calvin — or Calvinism misunderstood — opened the door to putting the blame on God for sin and the fall, as well as for feeling a suffocating fear of the total loss of freedom. It may be objected that Milton does not attack Calvin by name in *Paradise Lost* any more than he attacks a particular king, bishop, or pope. Indeed, I do not think he means to attack Calvin at all. Rather, he attacks the dark shadow of Calvin: the fearful God whom Calvin evokes among those who cannot accept his arguments yet cannot quite dismiss them.

At this point I should like to turn again briefly to Descartes, because it can be argued that Descartes's prodigious innovation stemmed from fears very similar to what motivated Milton. On the night of 10 November 1619, after an arduous week spent clearing his mind of every philosophical tradition and assumption, Descartes had three strange dreams, which he credited with giving him the central *aperçu* that he developed in the *Discourse on Method* a decade later. Although Descartes's preparation during the preceding week was intensely skeptical — namely, to doubt everything — he was terrified of the nihilistic void opened by skepticism. In the first dream, Descartes found himself walking down a street, frightened by phantoms. His right side was crippled, so he had to lean to the left in order to walk. A sudden gust of wind "spun him about three or four times on his left foot. Hardly able to stand, he noticed a school in front of him . . . and entered it 'to find a refuge, and a remedy for his disorder'; he hoped to reach the school church and to pray there." Then, just as he approached the church, he began to change his mind. But the wind at his back pushed him forward. He resisted, and successfully turned aside. The rest is history. As Michael Keefer notes, in a provocative interpretation of this dream, "What seems really to have frightened Descartes . . . was not so much his own disability, or the humiliation of being spun around like a top, as the discovery that the wind that attacked him was furthering his decision to seek refuge in a church."[12] Descartes resisted entering the church because in his dream the wind began to seem demonic, akin to the phantoms that had first frightened him into seeking shelter. Yet how odd that an ill wind should seek to drive him into shelter, or demons to drive him into a church. His solution to the nightmarish conundrum recalls an old proverb: "Damned if you do and damned if you don't."

Descartes declined the utter freedom offered by skepticism because he feared emptiness. Yet he resisted the wind that drove him into church — not against his will, but in accordance with it. Evidently, the wind must have made him suspect that his will was not really his own. It is a curious paradox. Descartes prided himself as an orthodox Catholic, yet his method of building a bulwark against doubt, "I think, therefore I am," proved immensely detrimental to traditional religion. Was the wind that tried to drive him into church but instead persuaded him to turn aside demonic or divine? Perhaps it was both. Keefer suggests that, for Descartes, the wind covertly represents Calvinism. In other words, it represents what I have called Calvin's shadow — the fearful, even demonic, God, who threatens to annihilate the self and disallow all exercise of free will.[13] One refuge from the skeptical despair that troubled the seventeenth century was Calvinist determinism; the other was the bedrock of the Cartesian self. I think they were twin-born opposites. Thus similar pressures operated on Milton and Descartes. Both were religious. They agreed, in differing fashion, that freedom is a gift of God. But, on a deeper level, the threat that God might swallow them up and deprive them of independent will drove them toward a new kind of individual autonomy. To borrow Satan's words and use them in a context Milton would have thoroughly disapproved, the new individualism to which Milton himself unwittingly contributed was "self-begot, self rais'd" (5.860). Because of the hidden fear that the living God might actually be Calvin's God or rather the dark shadow of Calvin's God, Descartes and Milton could no longer take for granted the notion — on behalf of which Milton and his God so repeatedly and fervently argue — that free will can survive under the sway of providence. It was as if, in spite of themselves, they could not abide the wind of God blowing at their backs. That is why Milton was the first to teach us how to misread his poem.

Premonitions of Autonomy

We should do Milton the justice of admitting that he really was an advocate of willing service, as modeled by Raphael and Abdiel. "Freely we serve / Because we freely love." That trusting message lies at the heart of *Paradise Lost*. But to love in that way can be hard. For Milton, at some deep level it involves more than confronting Satan, whose threats, after all, prove empty in the end. Instead, each individual must confront and wrestle, not with Satan, but with fear of the terrible omnipotence of God. We hear Milton's conflicting motives operating in a well-known passage in which God explains that he intends to leave room in the universe he is about to create for actions independent of his own providential causation. The logic of the passage is to assert once more that freedom is authorized by God himself. But the counterlogical force of the poetry undermines that logical statement, revealing something of Milton's troubled state of mind. For modern readers, enamored of self-sufficiency, God's assurances may seem to close down, rather than open up, the space, or wiggle-room, which freedom requires. At least many of my students react to the passage in this way, despite assurances to the contrary. God speaks:

> Boundless the Deep, because I am who fill
> Infinitude, nor vacuous the space.
> Though I uncircumscrib'd myself retire,
> And put not forth my goodness, which is free
> To act or not, Necessity and Chance
> Approach not mee, and what I will is Fate.
>
> (7.168–73)

Milton's God assures us that he will voluntarily "retire" or withdraw himself, in order to allow a space — physical, spiritual, and psychological — for natural contingency within which human and angelic free will can operate and, at choice, diverge from goodness. Ostensibly, this speech is reassuring. Logically and syntactically, the verb "to be" is a copula. To say "what I will is Fate" is the same as to say "Fate is what I will," or, by implication, "Don't worry about Fate, it's under my benevolent control." Such was the reassurance that Lady Philosophy gave Boethius in prison, and it remained a traditional consolation throughout the middle ages. According to the theologians, Christian Providence frees us from classical Fate. Therefore, in *The Nun's Priest's Tale*, even Chanticlere the rooster can reassure his wife Pertelote that God's foreknowledge does not diminish our freedom.

But Milton usually looks forward as well as backward, in this case to a time when divine Providence is thought of as constraining rather than ensuring human freedom. In poetry, word order is telling, and the last position in a line or passage is always emphatic. God's closing words clang ominously. What he says perfectly accords with the ancient, reassuring tradition, yet not Calvin himself could assert God's arbitrary will more forcefully: "what I will is Fate." Reassurance, or threat? As Descartes's nightmare implies, when skepticism reaches a certain point one can no longer be sure whether what he wills is ever truly free, and that God does not secretly do his willing for him and through him. If God is the author of freedom, as Milton devoutly hopes, then there is nothing to worry about. His omnipotence guarantees our freedom, just as Augustine and Boethius thought. If the contrary is true, however, omnipotence becomes an overwhelming threat. In that case, we must seize our autonomy *from* God. Like Satan, we must refuse service, defy or deny omnipotence, and, impossibly, try to raise and beget ourselves. No wonder Milton is anxious as he throws all his energies into resisting the path that Descartes took, a path leading down into the modern world.

Six

The Fall into Subjectivity

ଛ

Milton's "Paradise Within" and "Abyss of Fears and Horrors"

The Paradise Within

Related to Milton's concern for the nature of free will in *Paradise Lost* is its drive inward toward individuality, self-examination, and subjectivity. In his book *The Paradise Within*, Louis Martz argues that the whole epic may be conceived of as taking place within the mind of the poet — and by sympathetic extension (we may presume) in the minds of fit readers willing to follow him into those inward regions. "[T]his poem is an action of thoughts within a central, controlling intelligence that moves with inward eyes toward a recovery of Paradise." Martz rightly stresses the importance of the inward journey of the mind toward salvation, reminding us, as we draw toward the close of both the poem and his essay on it, that "the promised redemption consists primarily in the renewal of man's inner powers: those powers of the soul by which the bard has just pursued his triumphant journey of the mind toward Paradise."[1] Although salvation occurs objectively in history through the life and atonement of Jesus, it operates effectually upon each separate individual by taking an inward turn within his heart, mind, and soul by his response to grace. Michael instructs Adam, as he goes forth into exile in the fallen world, that above all he and Eve must cultivate the inward, spiritual virtues and perform deeds that flow from and are enabled by those virtues. Earlier in the poem Milton briefly summarizes the relation of the inward soul to outward deeds in his synecdochic phrase "Faith and faithful works" (*Paradise Lost*, 11.64). Deeds done without faith are empty. Milton subscribes broadly, but not strictly, to Luther's doctrine of salvation *sola fide*. To faith, Michael tells Adam to add patience, temperance, love, and the other virtues. These are the means by which faithful and virtuous deeds, enabled by grace, will issue from within the regenerate soul.

In his famous promise, Michael assures Adam that if he properly cultivates what many spiritual writers, drawing upon biblical imagery, have called the garden of the soul,

> Then wilt thou not be loath
> To leave this Paradise, but shalt possess
> A paradise within thee, happier far.
>
> (12.585–87)

So, instead of spending their days tending a physical garden filled with paradisal fruits and flowers, which, as Eve laments, they must abandon forever because such prelapsarian plants "never will in other Climate grow" (11.274), Adam and Eve shall henceforth learn to tend the gardens of their souls, to cultivate inward fruits and flowers of "Faith, / . . . vertue, Patience, Temperance [and] Love" (12.582–83). God will enable them to do so by his promised gift of grace, which he offers not mediated through churches, congregations, priests, or prelates but directly to individuals, specifically by means of his "Umpire *Conscience*," through which he will speak to and empower them from "within" the very centers of their minds and selves (3.194–95).

The importance of this inward turn in the journey toward salvation cannot be overestimated. *Paradise Lost* is, ultimately, a hopeful and consoling poem, a divine comedy that anticipates a happy ending as time nears its close, when mankind will cross to the far side of the abyss that separates time from eternity. Nevertheless, although a happy outcome is assured, *Paradise Lost* also tells and shows us that just as the world will "tend from bad to worse" (12.106), so will the Church, even the Reformed churches, human institutions that are inextricably parts of the world. Perhaps for that reason among others, Milton does not give his poem a happy ending like Dante's, but rather a distinctly mixed one. From the death of the last apostle until the Last Judgment, according to Milton's stern vision of Christian history in *Paradise Lost*, "carnal power shall force / On every conscience." The churches will typically impair rather than help their members. "[S]o shall the World go on, / To good malignant, to bad men benign . . . till the day / Appear of respiration to the just" (12.521–22, 537–40). The Reformation provided Milton with much of his theology, as it provided him earlier with hopes of earthly reform, but in *Paradise Lost* he no longer finds its ameliorating effect on the churches worth mentioning. There will be no truly reformed church until the Last Judgment.[2] As Michael explains, even in the time of the apostles the Holy Spirit does not inspire and work through the Church and its ministers, but through individual conversion: "His Spirit within them, and the Law of Faith / Working through love, upon thir hearts shall write, / To guide them in all truth" (12.488–90). Similarly, Jesus tells us in *Paradise Regained* that his chosen way is not conquest, prescription, or worldly rule, but "By winning words to conquer willing hearts, / And make persuasion do the work of fear" (1.222–23). Therefore, when history reaches its happy ending, as the Son of God rises into heaven "with the multitude of my redeem'd" (3.260), he will bring with him not organized churches, or even those within particular churches who are loyal and responsive to the graces they claim to channel through the sacraments and apostolic authority, but elect individuals. Those who follow the guidance of other men will at best end up in the Paradise of Fools. As we saw in the previous chapter, Milton does not speak of election in the strict Calvinist sense but refers to those who respond internally with faith, love, patience, and the other virtues Michael enumerates to the grace that God offers to all: "The rest shall hear me call, and oft be warn'd" (3.185).[3] Under the guidance of "Umpire *Conscience*" (3.195) they will cultivate the "paradise within [them] happier far" (12.587).

The Abyss of Fears and Horrors

Nonetheless, although the promised ending of the tale of history will be happy for those who respond to grace and cultivate the virtues of the mind, throughout the poem another, darker process of internalization works counter to grace and virtue. Milton first and often associates the journey into the mind, the growth of self-consciousness and subjectivity, not with the blissful journey to heaven but with the tragic double fall of Satan and of Adam and Eve. Internalization may lead to heaven, but it begins with the Fall and may lead down into hell. The Fall brings in its train, together with Sin and Death, born in the first Fall and actualized in the second, self-consciousness, the obsessive habit of anguished soliloquizing, and an inward, spiraling fall into ever-expanding depths of terror, loss, and loneliness. Satan learns this terrible lesson in his earliest moments alone with himself, when he first has leisure to pause and take stock:

> Me miserable! Which way shall I fly
> Infinite wrath, and infinite despair?
> Which way I fly is Hell; myself am Hell;
> And in the lowest deep a lower deep
> Still threat'ning to devour me opens wide,
> To which the Hell I suffer seems a Heav'n.
>
> (4.73–78)

The contrast is stark: the inward self can become "a paradise within thee" or "Myself am Hell." Such is the fallen Satan's realization as he turns his eyes inward for the first time and, with that mental act, arrives at a terrible precipice from which he falls ever deeper and deeper into subjectivity and solipsism. "The mind is its own place," he had boasted earlier to Beelzebub, in a mood of pride, determination, and stubborn defiance, "and in itself / Can make a Heav'n of Hell, a Hell of Heav'n" (1.254–55). At that time, however, he was making outward rhetoric, talking and persuading more than thinking, not allowing himself to pause in self-examination or to look within the mind he characterizes. His early confidence in the power of the self-reliant mind to exert control over objective reality proves sorely misplaced. The autonomous mind cannot, of its own power, even retreat safely within the fortress of its thoughts when fate is outwardly adverse, a Stoic practice that Milton rejects. As long as the would-be autonomous individual rejects divine love and grace, which the poem informs us are the necessary supports of free will and of the power to cultivate a paradise within, it turns out that the mind ceases to be its own place. It loses control not only over the outward world of matter and events but even over its own inward mental processes.

The failure of the will to achieve its intention is accompanied by a corresponding failure of the intellect to comprehend its situation. When he makes his defiant boast Satan is in effect denying not only the true nature and limitations of the mind but the objective reality of hell. Yet all the while he boasts, he stands within hell, sees it with his eyes, hears it with his ears, and feels it through the soles of his feet. As long as he denies the objective reality of any part of the created universe — consequent on his hatred and denial of the Creator of the universe — he rejects the only available foundations upon which his reason might rest. Thus, although he is supremely intelligent, Satan utterly lacks workable principles on which to base his logic. He lacks the Christian-Aristotelian moral virtue of Prudence, which Milton sometimes refers to in his prose works as "Christian prudence," and the Christian-Platonic faculty of Right Reason.[4] The Aristotelian-Thomistic tradition, which Milton inherited and upon which he drew, understood that logical reasoning relies on the cardinal virtue of prudence, that virtue which enables its possessor to comprehend truth, reality, that which exists. Milton, who speaks often and favorably of prudence, mentions "Christian prudence" and "sacred prudence," and several times associates prudence with liberty, as in *Tetrachordon*: "[P]rudence guides us in the liberty which God hath left to us."[5] The related Platonic tradition, on which Milton also draws, speaks of *recta ratio*, or right reason. God exchanges his golden scepter for an iron rod to punish Satan and his followers precisely because they "reason for their law refuse, / Right reason for thir Law" (6.41–42). Since the time of Machiavelli, the word "prudence" has in common usage become increasingly more instrumental and pragmatic, not to say cynical. It is seldom thought of as a virtue but rather as an aid to *virtù* or as an amoral means of achieving desired results. Since the rise of the New Science, reason has in common usage likewise been divorced from rightness, to become more instrumental, less ethical and moral. A comparable rejection of rational foundations on which to build their arguments explains why the devilish philosophers, despite their presumably superior logical powers, are like Satan condemned to circle perpetually in their thoughts and find "no end, in wand'ring mazes lost" (2.561).

Since Satan, like the other fallen angels, loses control of the foundations of reason and will, he falls inevitably into helpless spirals of inward despair, as Milton so vividly shows us in his soliloquy. For the damned, the mind is not a stoic refuge but an inescapable trap.

Like Satan, Adam also falls into isolation and the habit of soliloquy after his fall. He first resolves to eat the forbidden fruit and commit the original sin because, drawn by his intense love of Eve, he firmly determines that they "never shall be parted, bliss or woe" (9.916). "Certain my resolution is to Die," he exclaims, "How can I live without thee?" (9.908–09). He would rather part from God and from life than from Eve. Nevertheless the Fall soon evolves into precisely what he most feared and condemned himself to death to avoid: the loss of her company, separation, isolation. It turns out that there is no true community outside of the love of God. As yet the human community consists of only two people, who no longer speak to each other. In book 10 we find Adam — having quarreled bitterly with Eve at the end of book 9, each blaming the other for his loss — alone, driven into himself in the manner of Satan. Milton appropriately describes him as "hid in gloomiest shade, / To sorrow abandon'd, but worse felt within, / And in a troubl'd Sea of passion tost" (10.716–18). His lengthy soliloquy that follows, extending for 142 lines, although modeled on dramatic convention, is unprecedented for the subtlety, reach, and comprehensiveness with which it depicts inward thoughts and feelings. It is precisely what Milton had promised to do some twenty years earlier in *The Reason of Church-Government* (1642), as soon as he had leisure to write poetry again: "to paint out and describe . . . with a solid and treatable smoothness . . . the wily subtleties and refluxes of man's thoughts from within" (670). With the exception of Augustine's *Confessions*, and much briefer passages in Shakespeare, nothing approaching the extraordinary depth of Milton's portrayal of the inward workings of the mind can be found in literature until after the ripening of the novel at the hands of Samuel Richardson and Jane Austen, or until Wordsworth's *Prelude* — a work pervasively conscious of and in rivalry with *Paradise Lost*.

As soon as Adam turns his thoughts inward, they lead him inevitably to the same awful brink discovered by Satan, and Adam likewise falls into the terrible depths of uncontrollable subjectivity. When Eve fell earlier, she echoed Satan's patterns of speech because she had heard him talk and his mode of language suited her new thoughts and aspirations.[6] Adam cannot have overheard Satan's soliloquy, yet his own soliloquy echoes Satan's words because he endures the same experience:

> Thus what thou desir'st
> And what thou fear'st, alike destroys all hope
> Of refuge, and concludes thee miserable
> Beyond all past example and futúre,
> To *Satan* only like both crime and doom.
> O Conscience, into what Abyss of fears
> And horrors hast thou driv'n me; out of which
> I find no way, from deep to deeper plung'd!
>
> (10.837–44)

For Milton, there is no way for the individual to escape from the endless abyss of subjectivity into which all the efforts of his mind to escape only plunge and entangle him further: no way, that is, except by means of an external rescue. The theological situation, similar to the familiar poststructuralist dilemma of absence and *différance*, is that there is no way for mortal man to reach God past the barrier of transcendence or difference, into a region that Augustine in the *Confessions* argues is beyond time and the material universe. If man cannot reach God, then the only possible solution to his dilemma is for God to reach man.

So says Augustine: "You were with me, but I was not with you. . . . You called me; you cried aloud to me; you broke my barrier of deafness. You shone upon me; your radiance enveloped me; you put my blindness to flight."⁷ The philosophical or metaphysical situation is similar to the theological situation. There is no way to transcend the I-centered world of the self, of language, of the perceived phenomena, to encounter the underlying substrate of reality, unless reality pierces the barrier from the other side and intrudes itself upon the self. That is clearly impossible unless we assign to "reality" qualities of agency and intentionality which, without romantic mystification, belong properly only to a person — that is, unless we assume that reality is or resembles God. Descartes claimed that he could ascertain with confidence the existence of God within a philosophical system beginning with the thinking self, but few if any philosophers who have succeeded him have been able to elucidate this crucial yet highly dubious aspect of his thought or to build further on it. For example, from a related position Thomas Nagel has argued recently that to escape the utter relativism of the post-Cartesian subject one must posit the existence of objective rationality, without which philosophical argument is pointless. But, Nagel continues, universal rationality, in which human thinking accords significantly with the nature of things at a deep level, is hard to account for without bringing God into the picture, a philosophical move he raises but strongly prefers to avoid.⁸ One may argue, as Milton implicitly does, that without the Divine Logos rationality is meaningless, but to one who begins with the thinking subject such an argument will almost certainly be found unpalatable. Indeed, one might begin with the subject but be forced at the end of the argument to deny the subject's certainty or centrality. Or, to put it another way, if God exists at all, He — as the Alpha and Omega, "from whom / All things proceed, and up to him return" (5.469–70) — is far too important to remain at the level of a contingent, secondary proof. Descartes does not say that he wishes to put God at the periphery, but on this point his argument has been generally thought to be incoherent.

Pain and Vertigo

Related to the sheer inward fall into subjectivity in both Satan's soliloquy and Adam's are elements familiar from traditional analyses of the inward discourses of guilt. The experience of guilt can spiral downward into an abyss of damnation or it can point upward from the abyss toward the possibility of renewal, by means of examination of conscience, conviction of sin, contrition, repentance, and the painful mental processes that lead to conversion, regeneration, and the paradise within. Mortal man can repent and resume his journey; but Satan cannot. Unable to respond to love with love, he is incapable of repentance, compunction, or softening of the heart. A commonplace of Christian psychology is that one of the chief functions of conscience is, when it is disregarded, to inflict inward pain on the guilty, to "heap coals of fire" on their heads. Echoing Proverbs 25:22, Paul advises the Romans not to take vengeance on their enemies and persecutors but instead to rouse their consciences by returning good for evil, which will work on their enemies from within, moving them to reconsider their ways, either to continue suffering or to repent. "Therefore if thine enemy hunger, feed him; if he thirst, give him drink: for in so doing thou shalt heap coals of fire on his head" (Romans 12:20). Because of the difference in their situations, Satan can only continue to suffer, while Adam can repent. But both begin by suffering the same inward experience: guilt wakens conscience, conscience wakens pain, terror, and despair, and the soul falls into the inner abyss. Satan's plunge into the depths begins precisely when "conscience wakes despair / That slumber'd" (4.23–24). The same thing happens to Adam: "O Conscience, into what Abyss of fears / And horrors thou hast driv'n me" (10.842–43). To the painful "coals of fire" provided by the Bible, Milton adds his own characteristic trope: disorientation, nausea, and vertigo, a fall into the void.

In *Paradise Regained*, when Satan tempts Jesus to expel the monstrous Emperor Tiberius from his throne by force as punishment for his sins, Jesus replies: "Let his tormentor Conscience find him out" (4.130). In its way, conscience is a worse punishment than vengeance, more inward, intimate, and inescapable. Unlike vengeance, however, its torments may point the victim toward repentance. Milton often portrays the inward workings of guilt leading to conviction of sin and repentance as excruciatingly painful, sometimes as a throbbing disease of the soul, sometimes as a sharp, medicinal probing that wounds as it cures. As we have already seen in chapter 3 when Spenser's Penance and his associates work their cure on Redcross, the curative process that Spenser describes is intensely — even morbidly — painful. As the spiritual physicians or torturers starve and excise Redcross's ulcers and his gangrenous flesh, "his torment often was so great, / That like a Lyon he would cry and rore, / And rend his flesh, and his owne synewes eat" (*The Faerie Queene*, 1.10.28).

Milton often uses imagery similar to Spenser's to describe the painful lashings of conscience in a guilty soul. The *locus classicus* is *Samson Agonistes*:

> My griefs not only pain me
> As a ling'ring disease,
> But finding no redress, ferment and rage,
> Nor less than wounds immedicable
> Rankle, and fester, and gangrene,
> To black mortification.
> Thoughts my Tormentors arm'd with deadly stings
> Mangle my apprehensive tenderest parts,
> Exasperate, exulcerate, and raise
> Dire inflammation....
>
> (617–26)

At this stage in his life Samson feels that no "cooling herb" or "med'cinal liquor," "Nor breath of Vernal Air from snowy Alp" (626–28) can cure him or ease his pain. These are Paul's true coals of fire. Only repentance, forgiveness, grace, and regeneration can ease the pain. What Samson does not yet recognize is that his cure is already at work, that the medicinal probing has begun, which is why his pain is more intense at this stage than it was when the action of the play began.

When Satan falls, he brings into existence new things with new names. Among the dreadful things and names that spring from his head, proceeding from his first inward act of defiance and rejection, are "sin," "death," "guilt," "shame," and "pain." When the sword of Michael shears deep into his right side during the War in Heaven, "then Satan first knew pain, / And writh'd him to and fro convolv'd" (6.327-28). He is carried from the battle "Gnashing for anguish and despite and shame" (6.340). So, after their fall, Adam and Eve first know shame, guilt, pain, and mortality. Along with physical pain, mental and spiritual pain enter the world. They are both penalties and cures for sin. Just as God provides death both as the just punishment for transgression and as the bitter cure for sinful suffering ("so Death becomes / His final remedy," 11.61-62), he provides physical and mental pain as necessary gifts to warn sufferers, so they will seek a cure for their wounds, their diseases, their sinful states while there is yet time. Analogously, although contemporary man is more than usually reluctant to suffer pain, physicians recognize it to be an indispensable symptom revealing deeper problems, therefore a salutary warning.

After his fall Adam's condition so closely resembles Samson's that Milton calls our attention to it in his well-known simile of Adam rising from sleep like Samson from the "Harlot-lap" of Dalila (9.1059-62). Yet, unlike Samson, Adam says little about pain, disease, or torment in his soliloquy. He is filled with "dread," "fear," "misery," "shame," "woe," and "horror" — key words on which his thoughts ring changes. The closest he comes to suffering pain is in his anxious wish that he could die at once, so that "no fear of worse /

To mee and to my offspring would torment me / With cruel expectation" (10.780–82). That is, his chief suffering is not present pain but anticipation of future pain, when the torturer will begin to do his work in earnest. Those who are physically diseased can experience two different and distinct kinds of suffering. One is pain. The other, which can be even worse, is vertigo, dizziness, and nausea. As we have already seen, Milton adds to the biblical trope of pain his own characteristic trope of vertigo from the first moment of the Fall. Satan first experiences both pain and vertigo not in his duel with Michael or his soliloquy on Mount Niphates, but at the initiating subjective moment of his revolt, as described to him by his daughter Sin:

> All on a sudden miserable pain
> Surpris'd thee, dim thine eyes, and dizzy swum
> In darkness, while thy head flames thick and wide
> Threw forth.
>
> (2.752–55)

I would argue that just as Milton uses spiritual pain as the natural signifier for the guilty pangs of conscience, so he uses vertigo, dizziness, and the sense of falling as a signifier for spiritual loss and disorientation, for forfeiture of faith, certainty, and mental foundations, for precisely what I would call the fall into subjectivity. Sartre speaks from the heart of a similar kind of alienation in his aptly titled *La Nausée*. The fall into subjectivity has a particular richness of meaning in connection with *Paradise Lost*. Some of the pain of falling into sin is suggestively evoked in Milton's first description of Satan's fall, when the "Almighty Power" hurls him "headlong flaming from th' Ethereal Sky / With hideous ruin and combustion down / To bottomless perdition" (1.44–47). It is painful, certainly, to imagine being set on fire and thrown down like a burning brand. More than pain, however, what the passage evokes is vertigo. The first thing we are told is that Satan is hurled from Heaven upside down, head first; the next, that the abyss into which he is thrown is "bottomless."

Numerous readers have remarked how, in his second recollection of the angels' fall, Milton appeals to our sense of kinœsthesia. He imaginatively evokes our sense of balance and of bodily orientation, a sense additional to the five traditional senses, for which the more recent medical term is vestibular, since it has been identified with the inner ear. When things go awry, physically or spiritually, the sense of orientation is transformed into a sense of disorientation. As Mulciber falls, he tumbles and rotates in a leisurely, strangely beautiful fashion, until we see as if from below how swift his fall really is. As he falls we participate with him in what it feels like to be thrown bodily from an immense height, to plunge through vast reaches of space, to hurtle downward faster and faster as subjective time slows to a crawl.

> And how he fell
> From Heav'n, they fabl'd, thrown by angry *Jove*
> Sheer o'er the Crystal Battlements: from Morn
> To Noon he fell, from Noon to dewy Eve,
> A Summer's day; and with the setting Sun
> Dropt from the Zenith like a falling Star,
> On Lemnos th' Aegean Isle.
>
> (1.740–46)

The tales of Marsyas and Philomel have taught generations of artists how to transform painful suffering into beautiful artifacts. But Milton does not allow us to rest even in that consolation.

> Thus they relate,
> Erring; for he with this rebellious rout
> Fell long before; nor aught avail'd him now
> To have built in Heav'n high Tow'rs; nor did he scape
> By all his Engines, but was headlong sent
> With his industrious crew to build in hell.
>
> (1.746–51)

Milton gives us another taste of helpless, vertiginous motion when Satan, after standing for a moment poised "on the brink of Hell" (2.918) to survey Chaos, hurls himself outward into the primal abyss:

> At last his Sail-broad Vans
> He spreads for flight, and in the surging smoke
> Uplifted spurns the ground, thence many a League
> As in a cloudy Chair ascending rides
> Audacious, but that seat soon failing, meets
> A vast vacuity: all unawares
> Flutt'ring his pennons vain plumb down he drops
> Ten thousand fadom deep, and to this hour
> Down had been falling, had not by ill chance
> The strong rebuff of some tumultuous cloud
> Instinct with Fire and Nitre hurried him
> As many miles aloft.
>
> (2.927–38)

It is hard to believe that anyone could have captured these dizzying sense experiences who lived long before it was possible to fly in bad weather and feel the sudden lurch of a downdraft, who never even felt the sensation of an elevator lurching to a stop.[9]

Milton tells us that Satan's dizzying and disorienting flight is governed by "chance." Perhaps Chaos is one of those regions, physical or spiritual, from which God tells us that he has voluntarily withdrawn his presence, thus relinquishing to chance and fortune all who dare to enter and put themselves outside his providential protection. If so, Satan's experience argues, as Boethius and others had long argued, that chance is not a reliable supporter of free agency, for it renders Satan passively helpless. Luckily for him, but unluckily for us, he escapes the threatened fate of falling forever into "vast vacuity," a hapless journey that according to traditional chronologies would have begun in the first days of the world and lasted more than five-and-a-half thousand years "to this hour" in which Milton wrote. But although Satan escapes falling forever into Chaos, this daunting moment serves as an outward sign of a similar, inward fall that he cannot escape: the loss of faith and certainty, the loss of intellectual footing and control, the loss of free will, as he plunges deeper and deeper into irremediable subjectivity. The inner life, potentially a way up to salvation, is also potentially a way down into bottomless perdition. The dizzy, nauseous, disorienting falls of Satan and Adam alike plunge them into the solipsistic void of the self.

Know Thyself

The inward fall is triggered by sin and guilt but in *Paradise Lost* not actualized until that moment when the eyes of the mind turn inward. Then the "Abyss of fears / And horrors" opens and reveals itself. Yet as the blind poet tells us, inward vision is also necessary for the spiritual life:

> So much the rather thou Celestial Light
> Shine inward, and the mind through all her powers
> Irradiate, there plant eyes, all mist from thence
> Purge and disperse, that I may see and tell
> Of things invisible to mortal sight.
>
> (3.51–55)

Since the time of Plato philosophers have said that the unexamined life is not worth living. *Nosce teipsum*, "know thyself," which begins in Plato as meditations on the relationship between the immortal soul and the eternal realm of Ideas — on Truth, Justice, Goodness, and Beauty as they converge in eternal Unity — has undergone many philosophical and religious revisions. In the middle ages, the Platonic ideal of self-knowledge, mediated and revised by Augustine, was chiefly realized in examination of conscience as a step leading to confession and conversion. By Milton's time introspection and examination of conscience were well established as salutary spiritual activities, necessary preludes to repentance and forgiveness. If anything, Protestantism rendered them more inward and private, concerns for the individual rather than the community. Yet as the present age has grown more and more inward-turning, self-consciousness and self-study seem to many to have lost their curative and restorative powers, giving rise instead mainly to doubt and anxiety.

C. S. Lewis was something of an authority on this modern dilemma, as Stephen Logan points out in a recent essay. From Samuel Alexander's *Space, Time and Deity* (1920) Lewis picked up the distinction, which he subsequently called an "indispensable tool of thought," between participating fully in an experience from within and consciously examining an experience from without.[10] An analogy would be the difference between looking at a natural scene through a pair of eyeglasses or refocusing your eyes on the glasses themselves. Or we might consider the twin poles of reading and literary criticism as represented by Victorian enthusiasts and postmodern deconstructionists, one type of reader giving himself with uncritical enjoyment to the experience, the other suspiciously holding back, fearful of ideological contamination, determined to demystify and dissect. As Logan argues, "The essential point is that these two forms of attention are mutually exclusive. If you analyze the taste of strawberries you are no longer experiencing it. You are experiencing instead the act of analysis." If this is true of the habit of analysis directed outward, it is even more true when analysis is directed inward. "If you become over-interested in the emotions produced in you by attention to a loved one, you cease attending to the loved one and cease to experience the emotions."[11] To put the matter in broader terms, if you spend too much time analyzing your life, you cease to live. Living is primary, analysis secondary.

Yet Milton, like most of his contemporaries, would argue that, in a fallen world, some degree of analysis and introspection, some thoughtful distinguishing between good and evil so as to choose the good, is necessary. In practice, such analytical activity is sometimes necessarily detailed, wearisome, and tedious, as in the myth of Psyche upon whom, as Milton reminds us in *Areopagitica,* Venus imposed the burden of "incessant labor to cull out and sort asunder" "those confused seeds." Acute analytical attention is often necessary to achieve the good life because "Good and evil we know in the field of this world grow up together almost inseparably; and the knowledge of good is . . . involved and interwoven with the knowledge of evil." The origin of this knotty problem, and therefore of the need for constant close analysis and introspection, was of course the Fall. "It was from out the rind of one apple tasted, that the knowledge of good and evil, as two twins cleaving together, leapt forth into the world"[12] It suits Milton's purpose in *Areopagitica* to leave the matter there, so as to give no grounds for the advocates of prior censorship to make their case for suppressing certain kinds of knowledge. We must be free to study and sort out as wide a selection of texts as possible, so as to make informed decisions. We must analyze to live. But we may remember that in Apuleius' version of the myth Psyche would never have finished the tedious, soul-destroying work of sorting out the seeds if she had not been helped by friendly ants. Human powers blanch and fail at such an impossible analytical task. In *Areopagitica,* Milton is confident that careful reasoning can sort out the seeds, can know good by looking very closely at evil and carefully distinguishing between the two. "Let her and Falsehood grapple; who ever knew Truth put to the worse, in a free and open encounter?" (746). Yet the case is much different in *Paradise Lost*. After the failure to reform English government and religion, Milton is far less confident in the power of analytical reason to discriminate and choose correctly between truth and falsehood. As history unfolds in *Paradise Lost,* far from prevailing over falsehood, "Truth shall retire / Bestuck with sland'rous darts" (12.535–36). There is no likelihood that the seeds can be properly sorted.

In general, self-analysis and introspection work best when dealing with faults and failures. As Logan suggests, watching yourself love is unhealthy, but "If . . . you want to free yourself from a bad emotion, such as resentment, you can at least interrupt it by contemplating the emotion itself and know its cause."[13] Which is to say that ideally you should know yourself by focusing analytically on your faults, while refraining from too close or lingering an analysis of your strengths and virtues. But for Milton and the Christian-Classical tradition, that is impossible. It is difficult for people to weigh their faults impartially, or to distinguish their faults from their virtues in the first place. Such is the danger of the unexamined life. Discrimination, that is analysis, is the first task. Moreover, Michael does not instruct Adam only to peruse his inward faults and consult his conscience as he combs through his mind for sins to be purged and avoided, but above all to seek for the positive spiritual experience of "a paradise within thee happier far." No longer is it possible for a newly created Adam simply to "feel that I am happier than I know" (8.282). Once having fallen, he cannot escape the two-sided trap and gift of self-consciousness and self-examination.

Durum Genus

Although Milton was certainly an individualist by instinct and conviction, his poetry also reveals that he feared the isolation and loneliness entailed by fallen subjectivity. Before the fall, Adam and Eve evidently wandered apart from time to time, as Eve does during Adam's conversation with Raphael, but without ever thinking or feeling that they were alone. After the fall comes a new sense of separation, of exile, of "distance and distaste" (9.9), of banishment and alienation. We may think of "alienation" as a modern concept, perhaps as a Marxist term, but Milton's use of the word anticipates its modern sense of internal exile and estrangement from the community. Uriel, looking down from the sun, recognizes Satan's true nature not only from the passions that are revealed in his face, on which many Miltonists have remarked, but from his look or posture of alienation; he "soon discern'd his looks / Alien from Heav'n, with passions foul obscur'd" (4.570–71). Satan is out of place; he no longer belongs. Similarly Abdiel addresses Satan as "alienate from God" (5.877). Whole nations and churches can fall away from God and community in this manner, as is the case with "alienated *Judah*" and its "dark Idolatries" (1.456–57). At the opening of book 9, alienation is one aspect of the chasm that opens between heaven and Earth, God and Man: "foul distrust, and breach / Disloyal on the part of Man, revolt, and disobedience: On the part of Heav'n / Now alienated, distance and distaste" (9-6-8). As Satan tells Sin and Death, God has withdrawn his presence from the world, "Retiring, by his own doom alienated" (10.378), giving the hellish trio room to bridge the abyss from below and claim the abandoned world as their conquered empire.

With withdrawal and alienation come loss of community and a new sense of loneliness. Milton was well acquainted with loneliness. It is implicit in *Lycidas*, where the singer who once experienced youthful friendship, companionship, and community, has been forced by his encounter with death and loss to exchange companionable needs and pleasures for isolation:

> Meanwhile the Rural ditties were not mute,
> Temper'd to th'Oaten Flute;
> Rough *Satyrs* danc'd, and *Fauns* with clov'n heel
> From the glad sound would not be absent long,
> And old *Damaetas* lov'd to hear our song.
>   But O the heavy change, now thou art gone,
> Now thou art gone, and never must return!
>
>   (32–38)

Not even the religious consolation of Christ's Resurrection, the vision of Edward King's salvation and reception into the company of the saints, or the implied prospect of his own eternal life after death "In the blest Kingdoms meek of joy and love" (177) provides the singer of this "Monody" with relief from isolation or — at least at the moment — with a renewal of the communal companionship he once had and now has lost. His thoughts are eager, his music Doric, his mood hopeful as he confronts the future and pursues his chosen vocation. Still he remains alone in an empty landscape.

It was, of course, the death of his close friend, Charles Diodati, that most strongly brought home to Milton the essential loneliness of human beings in this world, painfully alienated from one another, discordant in their feelings, and — should they find companionship — faced with inevitable loss:

> Nos durum genus, et diris exercita fatis
> Gens, homines, aliena animis, et pectore discors,
> Vix sibi quisque parem de millibus invenit unum,
> Aut, si sors dederit tandem non aspera votis,
> Illum inopina dies, qua non speravis hora
> Surrupit, aeternum linquens in saecula damnum.
> (106–11)

"But we men are a painful race, a stock tormented by fate, with minds mutually alienated and hearts discordant. A man can hardly find a comrade for himself in a thousand; or, if one is granted to us by a fate at last not unkind to our prayers, a day and hour when we apprehend nothing snatches him away, leaving an eternal loss to all the years."[14]

The problem, for Milton as for modernity in general, arises from an absence of mediation and subsidiarity in the society he envisages. The Middle Ages, as described in chapters 2 and 4, were rich in mediating institutions and overlapping communities: feudal bonds of loyalty and obligation, the local parish community with its rites and sacraments, burial societies, and especially the various guilds and voluntary associations. The people of that time had a more communal sense of prayer and reconciliation, especially of intercessory prayer for others, including the dead. Since religion was then at the heart of the culture — and was at least the remote foundation of our present secular culture — this loss of intermediation is most readily seen in the realm of prayer and intercession. Dante's *Commedia* shows us a universe of intermediation and intercession, represented most obviously by Beatrice but also by Mary and the angels and saints whom we encounter in the *Paradiso*. Prayer by one person for another is constant and efficacious. Only the damned in the *Inferno* are lost to the Communion of Saints, cut off, individualized, isolated within themselves, unable to love and be loved. The angels and saints are given active parts to play in the economy of salvation. With the help of Virgil and through the mediation of Beatrice, Dante is led along his journey upward. With Beatrice's aid and the intercession of Bernard and Mary, Dante is able at the end of his journey to gaze at last on the heavenly radiance of the Trinity. All is accomplished through divine grace, without which nothing would be possible; but Dante's God freely and generously delegates his grace to his servants and is ready to hear intercessory prayers. By contrast, Milton's God uses angelic messengers to convey his word but gives them small scope to act in the economy of salvation. They do his will, carry out his orders unquestioningly, and communicate information but, as exemplified most clearly by the outcome of the first two days of the War in Heaven and by Satan's encounter with the angelic guard in Eden, they have little real power or opportunity to further God's providential plans. Nor are they asked or permitted to intercede with God for grace. In England, Anglicans and Puritans alike rejected the legitimacy of praying to the saints or of asking them to pray for them or their loved ones. Accordingly, in *Paradise Lost* only the Son has such delegated powers. He is the sole High Priest, King, Intercessor, and Advocate (11.14–44).

Milton's mentality is, of course, Protestant, but he carries matters further toward a fundamental individualism than most of his fellow Protestants as a result of his strong belief in the total individuation of grace. Just as Milton's angels and saints are essentially excluded from the active economy of salvation, so in his view are churches and nations. The first duty of the Church is to get out of the way and to let God work. There are perhaps two significant exceptions to this principle of total focus on the individual. One — rarely found in this life — is friendship, as exemplified by the figure of Charles Diodati. The other is marriage. Before the fall, Adam and Eve are helpmeets, mutual supports, and loving companions. After the fall they resume their close companionship. Even the line that feminists understandably find most troubling in the poem, "Hee for God only, shee for God in him" (4.299), seems determined to suggest, although with awkward asymmetry, what would otherwise be unthinkable to Milton, that grace can be mediated. Certainly it suggests that their communal relationship, in and under God, is close. Just so Eve's closing words to Adam: "thou to mee / Art all things under Heav'n, all places thou" (12.617–18). Milton further suggests that, after the Flood, there was a time when men lived "in joy unblam'd . . . Long time in peace by Families and Tribes / Under paternal rule" (12.22–24). So the intimate community provided by marriage might conceivably extend to families and even to whole tribes. But Nimrod brings this period of primitive peace to an end with his invention of tyranny, glory and empire, and seemingly it is never repeated. The possibilities for community and companionship are limited. Instead of focusing on communities, Milton gives us a vision of salvation history that famously puts all its emphasis on singular election and accomplishment, on a succession of figures representing the "one just Man"

(11.818, 890), anticipated and exemplified among the angels by Abdiel. This theme is, of course, biblical, but Milton noticeably elides any concomitant emphasis, which would have been equally biblical, on Israel as the chosen community or the first Christian fellowships depicted in Acts.

The Lonely Crowd

The sociologist David Riesman coined the telling phrase "the lonely crowd" to characterize what he describes as the typically modern condition of man: isolated individuals in a faceless, anonymous nation-state, with few mediating institutions.[15] Thomas Hobbes's frightfully inhuman image of Leviathan anticipates this typically modernist relationship between the individual and the state, with no vital communal institutions to intervene between them and moderate the psychological pressures. When he looks at humanity, Hobbes can see nothing but selfish individuals, who if given the chance would pit themselves against one another in a war of all against all. Therefore they must consent, from motives of self-protection, to be forcibly squeezed together willy nilly into the gigantic body pictured in the frontispiece to the first edition: a strange, monstrous mutation of the more human "body politic" posited by classical and medieval political thinkers.

When we look for the phenomenon of the lonely crowd in *Paradise Lost* we find it everywhere depicted after the fall: threatening, anonymous crowds, huge numbers of faceless angels or men, and among them lonely, isolated individuals. It is the characteristic situation of hell, where as Satan complains there is "neither joy nor love, but fierce desire" (4.509). Satan and Beelzebub consult with each other as fellow officers and politicians, as near equals in power, but not as friends. Typical is the mass rally convened when Satan addresses his defeated troops, which strangely anticipates the mass political rallies staged by modern totalitarian states under the leadership of Hitler, Stalin, or Mao:

> All in a moment through the gloom were seen
> Ten thousand Banners rise into the Air
> With Orient Colors waving: with them rose
> A Forest huge of Spears: and thronging Helms
> Appear'd, and serried Shields in thick array
> Of depth immeasurable; Anon they move
> In perfect *Phalanx* to the *Dorian* mood
> Of Flutes and soft Recorders.
>
> (1.544–51)

As Milton shows us, the devils can work together, can move in unison in perfect military order. Similarly they can agree after debate on a plan of action at the Great Consult. But Milton is surely ironic in his words of praise: "O shame to men! Devil with Devil damn'd / Firm concord holds" (496–97). What he shows us is not admirable: it is based on military and imperial convenience, not loving fellowship or community. The "concord" of the devils precisely resembles the situation of individuals in Hobbes's nation-state as leviathan.

Such a monolithic nation-state is the end product of Hobbes's argument for submission of the individual will to the general, since the contractual agreement or implied covenant to obey an absolute monarch is the surest means that a single person, thrust into a lawless and loveless world and concerned above all for his own survival, has to ensure self-protection and self-gratification. Hobbes does not advocate mediating or subsidiary institutions or voluntary associations of any kind. Suspicious of faction, he would consider them potentially divisive. They would undermine absolute power, which the state requires, in his view, to keep the peace against the disruptions of individual ambition, division of opinion, and the threat of civil war. For Hobbes, liberty consists paradoxically in absolute, arbitrary, unquestioning obedience to the sovereign power of the state: "The Liberty of a Subject,

Lyeth therefore only in those things, which in regulating their actions, the Soveraign hath prætermitted.... [N]othing the sovereign Representative can doe to a Subject, on what pretence soever, can properly be called Injustice, or Injury."[16] Milton, who certainly had no love of absolute rule, shows us in his hell an exaggerated picture of the Hobbesian state, exhibiting the perfectly disciplined unity of perfectly self-centered individuals. Completely absent from his hell are personal freedom, love, concern for others, and the possibility of personal relationships, such as any true community would allow and support.

That the angels had another kind of life, a more personal, intimate kind of companionship with one another before they fell, is suggested by several of Milton's scenes set in heaven among the loyal angels and by Raphael's hint to Adam concerning angelic love-making. "Let it suffice thee that thou know'st us happy," Raphael tells Adam, and then he extends the logic of that supposition: "without Love no happiness" (8.621–22). Evidently for Milton unhindered enjoyment of the beatific vision and basking in the love of God does not suffice for full happiness. There must also be close companionship among the inhabitants of heaven, a true society and a loving community. Whether we take Raphael's description of angelic lovemaking literally as a kind of sex or, with C. S. Lewis, more allegorically and spiritually,[17] it is evident that Milton wants the inhabitants of Heaven to escape the burden of loneliness, isolation, and frustration in love so often experienced in this world. There is a world of meaning in the earliest words chronologically that Satan speaks in *Paradise Lost*. He addresses them to Beelzebub the evening before the War in Heaven: "Sleep'st thou, Companion dear?" (5.673). His question must be read as the sugared beginning of a rhetorically skilled seduction to revolt and damnation, but if that is true then it must also be read as his expected and customary way of addressing his once dear and intimate friend, perhaps we should say his beloved friend, with whom he says he was used to share his inmost thoughts: "Thou to me thy thoughts / Wast wont, I mine to thee was wont to impart; / Both waking we were one; how then can now / Thy sleep dissent?" (5.676–79). Satan's rebellion, like Adam's, begins in, and is entangled with, a sense of estrangement from his closest companion and soul mate. It even begins with the avowal of hurt affection, like a lovers' quarrel.

We cannot imagine Satan or any of the devils speaking to each other in such a loving and intimate fashion after their fall. Satan's first words to Beelzebub in Hell are: "If thou beest hee; But O how fall'n! how chang'd / From him, who in the happy Realms of Light / Cloth'd with transcendent brightness didst outshine / Myriads though bright" (1.84–87). Among the many implications of the terrible (and mutual) transformation with which Satan's eyes are confronted is this: that Beelzebub, like his former "darling" Sin, is no longer good looking, no longer conceivable as an object of his love. In Satan's mind the past is instantly revised. He remembers or pretends to remember Beelzebub merely as a close military associate, a fellow rebel, a sharer in the desperate cause. After his fall, Satan can produce at best only a menacing, ironic parody of love, as he does in thoughts addressed silently to the unfallen Adam and Eve:

> League with you I seek
> And mutual amity so strait, so close,
> That I with you must dwell, or you with me
> Henceforth.
>
> (4.375–78)

Never again will Satan or his fellows be able to love each other truly, or even to speak to anyone about love and intimacy, as once they did in Heaven.

So also to a lesser extent with fallen men. Although human beings are still capable and needful of love, they will seldom find it. They will typically confuse love with lust and desire, "Marrying or prostituting, as befell, / Rape or adultery" (717–78). As incapable of true fellowship and community as of loving marriages, they will become the anonymous, slavish followers of tyrants or the willing dupes of churches. Even the most virtuous among them, as they walk hand-in-hand with a devoted and loving spouse must, like Adam and Eve, pursue the "paradise within" them "with wand'ring steps and slow," along a "solitary way" (12.648–49). Thus they will be spiritually isolated at best. After death, in eternity, they will know the full joy of unimpeded love in heaven, such as Milton anticipates with his "late espoused Saint" in Sonnet 23. But they cannot expect to find such unshadowed happiness in this life, caught up as they are in the drama of human history, which inevitably tends "from bad to worse."

The poet himself, who imagines and builds for us his marvelous vision of a paradise within, and who confidently declares that this new inward paradise can be happier far than the paradise that was lost, is nonetheless moved to compare himself to a bird that "Sings darkling, and in shadiest Covert hid" (3.39–40). He tells us that he is "cut off" "from the cheerful ways of men" (3.46–47). He is alone in the dark not only because he is blind but also because he writes from within the darkness and corruption of the fallen world, of which his blindness is emblematic: "On evil days though fall'n, and evil tongues; / In darkness, and with dangers compast round, / And solitude" (7.26–28). He finds some relief from the encroachments of solitude, isolation and loneliness — he is "yet not alone" altogether — only because of the nightly visitations of his Muse, a figure who (if not imaginary) represents both his divinely appointed vocation — the satisfaction of great things well made and well done — and the personal grace and enlightenment of the Holy Spirit. But to speak of his social nature, man is *durum genus*, a hard race, congenitally lonely.

Seldom may true friendship and companionship be found in this life. In the modern, individualist world toward which *Paradise Lost* points, religion will diminish from something found in churches, parishes, and voluntary societies as well as within the soul, something with social and communal as well as private aspects, into something found only within the minds of the fit few. Indeed those were the only places, according to Milton's radically Protestant, revisionist view of history, where true religion was ever to be found, written in the hearts of the elect by the Holy Spirit.

So it was even from the beginning, when God drove Adam and Eve from the Garden, when he sent Abraham into exile from his home and family, and when the Son resolved to be a messiah who would let inward persuasion, individual by individual, do the work of outward fear. In the future, toward which Milton sets his face along with Adam and Eve, true community and companionship of any real depth will be absent or rare. As Milton acknowledges concerning his epic vocation in *Epitaphium Damonis*, "Quid enim? omnia non licet uni, / Non sperasse uni licet omnia"; "What then? One man cannot do everything, nor [can one man] so much as hope to do everything."[18] He firmly resolves to try, but after the death of his one intimate friend his task will be lonely. If a man falls from grace into sin, he will tumble into dizzying inward depths of alienation and estrangement and may never again escape the bottomless pit of subjectivity. If aided by grace he rises again, he can expect only inward consolation of his hurts and continuing loneliness. As he journeys toward the future, a whole world will unfold before him "where to choose." The possibilities are endless. God may send an angel to instruct him, but not to guide him. The distant goal of his journey, Michael assures Adam — perhaps in due course even the present inward state of his mind — will be "happier far" than the paradise he has lost. Yet each exile is doomed either to fall into himself and be forever lost or to pick himself up after each lapse, enabled by the power of grace, and travel onward alone, with conscience as his inward guide, sometimes with a companion to give mutual aid and comfort but still essentially alone — until that happy day of "respiration to the just."

SEVEN

Theoretical Considerations and Conclusion

I have left until the end some theoretical matters which might have been introduced earlier, because as far as possible I have tried to let literary works and cultural practices speak for themselves, and to view them more in the context of earlier literary works and cultures than of our own. The purpose of "theory" is too often simply to force discussion into a framework or "discourse" of the theorist's own choosing. As it happens, many recent postmodernist theories and ideologies have their remote origins in just those cultural changes we have been considering. Using today's presuppositions to understand how we have arrived at today's presuppositions would be circular. Thus, for example, the interesting question raised by *Hamlet* is not why our remote ancestors prayed for the dead and felt themselves to be in solidarity with them, but how and why they ceased to do so. Admittedly, I have based my work on certain assumptions and philosophical principles, among them the conviction that, although cultural change and resultant changing subjective assumptions have played and continue to play an indispensable role in human history, nonetheless objective reality exists and should be dealt with as forthrightly as possible. I understand that to be critically objective is hard (some would say impossible) and that positions must be taken, but I hope that through the body of this work mine have been clear enough not to require an elaborate theoretical account of them before turning to the task at hand.

The aim of the book has been to show that, broadly speaking, subjectivity and individuality — the sense that an individual human being has his own "insides," feelings, and identity — go back a long way into the past, at least as far back as *The Wanderer* in England and to Virgil and Ovid in antiquity, but that the individual's internal sense of himself began to undergo a critical change of direction about the time of Luther, Shakespeare, Descartes, and Milton. The ancient experience of exile produced somewhat different results from the modern experience of alienation. Aeneas consented willingly to suppress his human, personal feelings, whereas if he had been a Romantic hero (into which he was often transformed in later redactions), he would have considered it his gravest, most integral duty to respect his own feelings: that is, to be true to himself. The experience of the inner depths of the self was originally more or less congruent with tradition and with the individual's sense of himself as a member of society and a participant in his family and community. Gradually this sense of self split away from externally obligating definitions, and it became almost necessary to repudiate them in order to realize a different kind of self-definition, more private, more revolutionary, more anxious to escape from customs and debts owed to one's ancestors, which were now regarded as oppressive and self-destructive.

The evidence suggests that exile, the destruction of one's tribe or city, and other unusual social and psychological pressures have always driven people into themselves, and that once within themselves they have found there vast imaginative depths, much like those that a Romantic or a modern writer might encounter. But they did not, apparently, find revolution there, or individual autonomy, or moral relativity, or the theory of possessive individualism, ways of thinking that underlie the modern liberal politics and psychology of both the left and the right. Thus a wide expanse of western literature suggests that people have remained in some ways the same over the millennia but in other important ways have changed decisively. Harold Bloom puts his finger on one critical aspect of this change when he considers the significance of Shakespeare's Hamlet. For Bloom, Hamlet marks the birth of a new perceptual age, because he, "more than anyone else in Shakespeare . . . is the free artist of himself. His exaltation and his torment alike stem from his continuous meditation upon his own image."[1] Bloom is not the first to suggest that Hamlet represents something new in western thought. But the critical aspect of his insight, in my view, is that Hamlet's constant activity of self-creation — by overlooking and correcting his own thought processes — although it makes him the vaulting and admirable figure he has always seemed to be in the eyes of Shakespeare's audiences, also contains a corrosive element of rejection and nihilism at its core.

Hamlet's combination of flamboyant individualism and introspective nihilism originates with Shakespeare's transformation of Marlowe's overreacher into a new kind of tragic hero. This self-constructed individualist amalgam passes from Shakespeare to Milton, then to the Romantics and the moderns. Bloom touches on the core issue: "The intellectual nihilism of *Paradise Lost*'s Satan properly begins within the abyss within Hamlet's capacious consciousness; but the nihilistic accents of Milton's ruined angel are first heard in Iago, the original sufferer of a sense of injured merit."[2] Bloom persuasively argues that it takes more than the New Historicist theory of the circulation of cultural energies to explain the emergence of Iago and Hamlet, Edmund, and Macbeth. It took Shakespeare's unique genius to create these historically portentous figures. But to that recognition, one may add another with which a New Historicist could agree, that this series of extraordinary invented characters (to the list of which we should append Shakespeare's remarkable exponent of autonomous individualism in politics, Coriolanus) appeared on the stage of the world in the ripeness of time, when conditions were ready and the balance of history was about to tip toward autonomous individualism — toward everyone's becoming a "free artist of the self." It was, after all, Marlowe (and before him, Machiavelli and others) who showed Shakespeare how to mix the heroic with the villainous, the noble with the nihilistic. In England and in Europe minds were increasingly ready to recognize and assimilate Shakespeare's extraordinary series of fictional characters into themselves. After all, theater requires a receptive audience, although that audience may be asked to receive into themselves things that they never consciously heard or thought of before. It is not contradictory to conclude that Shakespeare was a superb manipulator of what Greenblatt calls social energy *as well as* a supreme artist.[3] Indeed, common sense affirms that for a public dramatist neither of these achievements would have been possible without the other.

Human Nature and Human Culture

In the present intellectual climate of the academy, permanence rather than change in human nature and human history is what most needs to be accounted for. The question is not so much why moderns are different from their ancestors as how they might be, in any essential regards, still the same. It is unlikely that any brief argument can break down the widely prevailing antipathy against such concepts as "human nature" or to such descriptives — whether applied to authors or to texts — as "universal" and "transcendent." Nevertheless, we may remind ourselves that some of our contemporary assumptions — which are among the end results of the very process of modernist internalization and individualization we are investigating — are so strongly entrenched in our own culture that they make the effort of seeing things differently, as the past might have seen them, extremely difficult. Paradoxically, proponents of the doctrine of cultural relativism and advocates of tolerance in human affairs often adhere to certain ideological positions unbendingly. It has been increasingly fashionable among academics even before the rise of self-conscious postmodernism to take for granted as a fundamental axiom of critical and political discourse that human nature is infinitely malleable. It is no longer even possible to use the phrase "human nature" without risk of rebuke.

Older views, such as those embodied in the title of Theodore Spencer's now unfashionable book, *Shakespeare and the Nature of Man*, seem quaint. On its publication, the *New York Herald Tribune Book Review* hailed Spencer's book as "the most distinguished contribution to our understanding of Shakespeare's mind and purposes since the publication of A. C. Bradley's *Shakespearean Tragedy*."[4] Ironically, Bradley himself, once the touchstone of excellence, is now more often deplored than admired — because he writes about Shakespeare's plays, and especially about his characters, as if they were universal and transcendent. Josef Pieper, who was on the intellectual scene at the time, credits Jean-Paul Sartre with originating the now conventional wisdom that rejects "human nature" as a respectable term. In 1947 Sartre bluntly wrote: "Il n'y a pas de nature humaine."[5] If Sartre was the first to put this supposition in such direct and sweeping words, nevertheless he owed a debt to the cultural anthropologists, to the tradition of Franz Boas, Ruth Benedict, Margaret Mead, and their French confrères and descendants. He only made more explicit and dogmatic what they had already made widely fashionable.

Already a star in her field, widely read in introductory courses, Mead became a household name in the 1960s, because she told popularizers of the counterculture what they wanted to hear. Her chief message was that there is no universal human nature. Each culture is different from every other culture. Before the cultural revolution of 1968, she argued, ours was the most "repressed" of cultures. Mead's mission was to teach us that we can be what we want to be, do what we want to do, because we are what our cultures make us. Consequently we can seize the high ground and take into our hands the power to remake our culture.[6] As Sartre faded from his high postwar eminence, Michel Foucault rose to prominence among Americans newly fascinated by French theory. Although theoretically at odds with Sartre, nonetheless Foucault lent new strength to cultural-anthropological ways of thinking, in particular to the increasingly popular view that there is no nature, only culture. Many current branches of feminism and of gender theory, to instance just two of today's most influential academic movements, have taken as their ideological cornerstones the doctrine that men and women have the ability to construct and deconstruct themselves purely by the manipulation of language — and thereby to become the manipulators of culture. For example, in *St. Foucault*, David M. Halperin explains why Foucault's theory of gender construction is so important to postmodern "queer theory" and gender studies generally. The critical point is "Foucault's decision to treat sexuality not as a biological or psychological drive but as an effect of discourse, as the product of modern systems of knowledge and power."[7] In this regard, the early, linguistic Foucault was already more radical than the later Foucault who turned more overtly to the history of sexuality. Over the years of the twentieth century, terms have altered depending on the system in use, from anthropological "culture," to the "existential condition" or Malraux's *"condition humaine"* (quite different from "human nature"), to neo-

Saussurian "systems of discourse," to Richard Rorty's consensual construction of legal norms and values. Still, the gist has remained the same: "*Il n'y a pas de nature humaine.*" There is only culture. With Derrida it becomes: "*Il n'y a pas d'hors texte,*" since culture is linguistically determined. Culture-constructivist theories impinge on many aspects of human life, but at present the field of gender and especially of gay and lesbian studies marks the cutting edge, where one finds the greatest heat of conviction and controversy.[8]

Under the benevolent rule of "multiculturalism," relativism grows uncontrollable. "Essentialism" and "totalization" become deadly academic insults. Typifying the trend toward social constructivism is an advertising blurb for a collection entitled *Rhetorics of Self-Making*, edited by Debbora Battaglia: "Departing from an essentialist concept of the self, this highly original work advances the cross-cultural study of selfhood."[9] "Rhetorics of self-making" fittingly describes the current belief that the "self" is a cultural-linguistic construction, contested by competing ideological rhetorics. The excitement of the ideological chase may account for the blurb-writer's claim that such a view is "highly original," since at the time of its appearance it was largely conventional. Just what "essentialism" means is not always clear, since it slides from broad philosophical attacks against belief in objective reality, nature, universality, goodness, or truth, to innuendos that the "essentialist" in question thinks that nothing ever changes or, worse, is guilty of racism, sexism, and classism. Speaking broadly, all one need do to be considered an essentialist is to assert that something "real" or "natural" exists out there, something that cannot, without damaging consequences, be altered or controlled by the prevailing systems of discourse and desire. It might puzzle a detached observer how belief in something real or objective, brought into connection with criticism of literary texts, should be thought likely to erupt in prejudice against disadvantaged social groups. Rather, it seems logical that belief in the existence of truth lends essential support to social justice. Can justice be established and accorded to others without submission to truth? Can we judge a case without knowing the facts? Knowing the facts is insufficient to ensure that justice will be done, but it is a good preliminary.

The elimination of human nature may be the *reductio ad absurdum* of instrumental reason, as it descends to us from Bacon, Descartes, Hobbes, and Locke. If reason is reduced to a servant, whose function is to obtain for us what we want, then why not turn to looser instrumental methods that can gain what we want even more quickly, with fewer headaches? Bacon, of course, said that knowledge should be regarded not as a servant but as a spouse — yet the wife Bacon had in mind has no purpose for being other than usefulness. "But as both heaven and earth do conspire and contribute to the use and benefit of man, so the end ought to be, from both philosophies to separate and reject vain speculations and whatsoever is empty and void, and to preserve and augment whatsoever is solid and fruitful, that knowledge may not be as a courtesan, for pleasure and vanity only, or as a bond-woman, to acquire and gain to her master's use, but as a spouse, for generation, fruit, and comfort."[10] Bacon begins with the unexamined assumption that man's "end" is not heaven but that heaven and earth conspire instrumentally toward his well-being and "comfort" on earth; and although he denies that knowledge should be a bond-woman serving her master's "use," he has only just said that heaven and earth conspire for man's "use and benefit." His insistence that knowledge rightly used is not a servant but a wife, who brings not money but fruit and progeny, shifts the metaphor but obfuscates the logic.

Before leaving these questions of human nature and human culture, I should repeat that it is not my intention to argue that human nature is unchangeable. Rather, some things change and others stay the same. The possibilities of change are not limitless. Even such immense historical changes in attitude as those we touch on in this book do not erase all elements of commonality among disparate human cultures. Such a position is supported by biology as well as history, anthropology, and metaphysics. We are in part, so to speak, "hard-wired," mind and body, so there are limits to what any possible transformation of the internal software can do. But I am less concerned to lay down a new and precise "theory" than to open up conceptual space against current assumptions, to consider the past with fresh eyes.

Paradoxically, just as the end result of the modern descent into greater and greater preoccupation with the autonomous self has been to put the existence of the self into question, so the end result of the belief that all cultures are infinitely malleable has been to render cultures other than our own "opaque." Multiculturalism urges that we respect other cultures. It also holds, however, that we cannot truly understand or judge them, even though we should admire them. These conflicting views lead to difficulties. For example, New Historicists have argued that each micro-period of English history differs radically from every other micro-period. Nevertheless, for practical purposes, it seems that most periods of English literature are similar, because they share certain regrettable "structural" characteristics. One and all, they are dominated by ruthless, hegemonic, patriarchal cliques, whose sole preoccupation is to oppress others and to manipulate the culture to their advantage. By definition, we cannot understand these men of the past. They differ so radically from us that their minds are closed books. We can understand them no more than Columbus understood the first Indians he encountered on the beach in the New World. Men and women of the middle ages and the Renaissance may look human in portraits, they may seem to write about matters that concern us still, ultimately they may even have begotten us, but all such family resemblances are illusory. For there is no such thing as universal human nature on which to base a common understanding.

Who are those sinister men sitting around the council table, dressed in somber black suits and white ruffs, on the cover of Stephen Greenblatt's *Shakespearean Negotiations*? They are complete strangers to us, they are "others." Yet we suspect at a glance what they are up to. They are plotting repression. After having read Greenblatt's book (as one reads a Renaissance book to understand its frontispiece) we suspect that these confident, authoritarian figures might be discussing (between colonial and imperial projects) how far to let the King's Men at the Globe Theater — at the "margins" of their society on the other bank of the Thames — put authority into question, in order to give vent to popular discontentment and thus more effectively bottle it up.

Belief in cultural opacity can lead to strange consequences. Among at least some American academics, for example, it has reinforced the belief that, until the Renaissance — perhaps until as late as the seventeenth century — those human-looking creatures who walked upon the earth and talked to one another in languages we thought we could read had no inward depths. To a postmodern way of thinking, they simply had no insides, no "selves." If the statement sounds incredible when so baldly put, it is only because I translate into plain English assumptions usually couched in opaque theoretical terms. Even Anne Ferry, whom I single out because she writes far more carefully and sensibly about these matters than most, remarks on the great difficulty of knowing "whether sixteenth- and early seventeenth-century writers, without modern vocabularies for describing what we call the *real self* or the *inner life*, nevertheless conceived of inward experience in any sense to which our terminologies can intelligibly be applied." Ferry compares the human problem of knowing whether there was anything going on inside these ancestral figures to the scientific problem of knowing what goes on inside a Black

Hole.[11] She avoids jargon and observes admirable methodological caution throughout her book. Yet the difficulties she speaks of result, from the first, mostly from problems endemic to our culture, not to Renaissance culture and its supposed opacity. They result from our unquestioning assumption that there are — or can be — *absolute* cultural discontinuities between human beings. To extend Ferry's apt analogy of the black hole, we might call these imagined absolute cultural barriers "event horizons," beyond which, by definition, the observer simply cannot observe directly.[12]

Such an attitude toward historical cultural change is distinct from the attitude, readily found in Petrarch and Virgil, that our predecessors are *distant* from us, and thus require of us a considerable effort to understand and to sympathize with them.[13] It is as much as to say that the chasm between cultures past and present is too wide ever to cross or even to see across. To give Ferry due credit, after consenting to these contemporary assumptions she valiantly attempts, for the whole length of her book, to cross that discontinuity. The effort, however, handicapped as it is by self-imposed theoretical limitations, dooms her to political incorrectness. The more fashionable position is to resign the effort because by definition it is impossible. Then, in an instant, a critic can free him- or herself to view the past on his or her own terms, not *theirs*. The past cannot be understood or sympathized with. Utterly distanced and estranged, it can instead be used instrumentally to foster correct ideological positions in the present. One approach is to take a deplorable incident from history, mix it with a line or two from an old text, and then use this more or less arbitrary combination to make a political point bearing on our own situation. The intention may be admirable, but as has sometimes been said, there are more direct and effective ways to do politics and to right wrongs in the real world. New Historicism, which at its best offers great promise in throwing new light on past cultures and their literatures, has too often found it difficult to relinquish its ideological baggage. Caught between opposing impulses, as contemporary politics and the urge better to understand the past come into conflict, it has too often preferred to keep the politics and relinquish the past.

Where We Are Now: The Postmodernist Implosion of the Self

Thus, since we have broken with the past, it has become something of a commonplace that the origins of our particular sense of individuality and subjectivity go back to some time in the Renaissance or perhaps to the early seventeenth century, depending on the views of the scholar in question. Some medieval scholars have suggested that the limits should be pushed back further. Yet there is wide agreement that individuality, subjectivity, and self-consciousness are relatively recent phenomena. Paradoxically, this theoretical consensus is based largely on the current view that human nature is socially constructed and therefore radically changeable from culture to culture, a view now adapted into the heart of postmodernism. High modernists in the Whig tradition could argue that self-consciousness, individualism, and freedom evolved gradually, beginning about the time of the Greeks.[14] Postmodernists are more likely to say that they arose suddenly, at a relatively late moment in history. Yet as we have seen, among postmodernists belief in the rise of the autonomous individual, having reached its terminus, has abruptly collapsed, resulting in a complete reversal of high-modernist confidence in the ever-expanding freedom of the liberal subject and the autonomous self.

Although postmodernism even more than modernism argues the right of each individual to "do his own thing" — and especially supports the rights of individuals belonging to oppressed groups, such as women and persons of color — at the same time it denies in theory that such things as individuals actually exist. We are not individuals; we are merely nodes in the prevailing discourse. This collapse of the self, I would suggest, is not unrelated to the Satanic predicament discussed in chapter 6, which Milton poetically represents by the trope of a dizzying vertigo that results from plunging ever more deeply into the depths of the self without reference to the objective universe and without hope of escape. The predicament can be traced back to radical Protestant notions of individual grace and to such theoretical developments as Descartes' thinking and doubting self, as well as, more recently, to Boas's cultural construction and the neo-Saussurean "prison house of language."[15] But as the fashion has moved from structuralism to poststructuralism and as anthropology has joined hands with linguistics, instead of reversing structuralist theories, poststructuralism has taken them to even greater extremes. According to Foucault, whose views have so widely influenced critical practices such as new historicism, gender studies, and culture studies, the "subject" or "self" is merely an illusion, emanating from the ever-changing "discourse" that creates the illusions of culture — much as classical Marxists might speak of a cultural "superstructure" thrown up by the material developments of history. Thus Foucault takes the dissolution of human nature a step further than Sartre, to the dissolution of the self.

"How, under what conditions, and in what forms can something like a subject appear in the order of discourse?" Foucault asks. "What place can it occupy in each type of discourse, what functions can it assume, and by obeying what rules? In short, it is a matter of depriving the subject (or its substitute) of its role as originator, and of analyzing the subject as a variable and complex function of discourse."[16] Thus material objects are said to manipulate and actually to create the illusion of the subjective self. Thus we escape the self of Descartes, Milton, and Shakespeare and make a move to return to the objective world by denying that the self exists, simply reversing the polarities of the Cartesian mind-body problem. The postmodernist objective world, however, is purely material, so it offers no way to account for "subjects" as real, as more than secondary epiphenomena. In former times, according to this fairly common view, the "discourse" or cultural superstructure was constituted mainly by various hegemonic villains: patriarchs, priests, and princes, who seized and accumulated power and authority by use of what has variously been called introjection (Freud), positive reinforcement (B. J. Skinner), social control (Stanley Milgram), or manipulation of cultural energies (Stephen Greenblatt).[17] Or to put the matter in fashionable Althusserian terms, history is a "field of contestation," in which authors, subjects, and texts alike are merely "ideological constructions," illusions of mental activity or of human records produced by purely material developments.[18]

Certainly it would be foolish to argue that human nature is fixed, that it is everywhere always the same. Having previously written several books concerning cultural change and transformation as witnessed in literature, I have no possible interest in doing so. Nor would I have written a book such as this present one if such were my belief. But it seems equally questionable to argue that human nature is infinitely malleable. Experience tells us otherwise. Just as when we meet and speak with strangers whose backgrounds and beliefs are unknown to us, so when we read the *Iliad, The Song of Roland, The Thousand and One Nights,* and *The Tale of Genji,* we begin to recognize certain common elements of humanity in each of these great works and, however wide the gap, still find it possible to empathize with the stories and the characters, at the same time that we recognize important differences in assumptions, attitudes, feelings, and values. Like strangers, as we read their stories these characters may surprise us by their deeds and their attitudes, however well we think we have come to know them. Yet they are not entirely alien to our understanding. To believe that they were would not only be defeatist, it would end — good intentions to the contrary — in a kind of demonization of other cultures, a retreat toward the kind of thinking that recognizes only one's own tribe as human and all others as dark and not worth knowing. It would invite that very contempt for the other that it so rightly deplores.

As yet the cheerful nihilism of the postmodernists remains largely an academic phenomenon, but it is spreading into the politics of the larger culture. Perhaps as postmodernism spreads the imperial self of modernity will implode, as postmodernism continues to deconstruct the foundations of Enlightenment confidence. Yet it is still the case that most people remain steeped in or are moving toward the cultural assumptions of western modernity — a modernity that now influences large regions of the world beyond what we ordinarily think of as the west. Such people have an increasingly individualistic and subjective sense of themselves in relation to the world and to others. Our most authentic selves are now our most intimately inward, subjective selves. And we desire to push our individuality as close to absolute autonomy as we can practically manage or psychologically construct. At the same time we long for community, for solidarity with others. We fear that our individuality, fiercely as we prize it, may in the end be only selfish and ungenerous toward others. But if it comes to a choice, who would give up individuality, the freedom to be true to oneself?

Such questions cannot be quickly answered. Still they are worth asking. The thesis of this book has been that, in all likelihood, people have always had an inner sense of themselves, a consciousness of inward depths, and that they have always had at least some sense of individuality, but that the nature of the private self and its relation to the communal and social realms has nonetheless altered over the centuries. To understand the change requires methods partly anthropological, partly sociological, and partly historical, not to speak of the importance of philosophy and theology. But it also requires recourse to literature, since only literature (in the broad sense that includes good writing in any genre such as *The Anatomy of Melancholy* or the *Dialogues* of Plato) provides windows into regions of the human heart, mind, and soul and into human relations, which might otherwise be inaccessible. Literature illuminates culture and history; history and culture illuminate literature. I conclude with some mild, tentative observations concerning the last two writers we have looked at, Shakespeare and Milton, and what they have to tell us about subsequent developments in the history of subjectivity.

Ambivalent Freedom and Subjectivity

There are at least two versions of freedom and subjectivity in Shakespeare and Milton, on which later writers, political thinkers, and others who have been influential in the transformation of western culture have repeatedly drawn. One, about which I have said little, is the inextricably public ideal of rational political freedom upon which the Whig Enlightenment tradition later built. This tradition found useful reinforcement in *Areopagitica* and in Milton's other prose tracts, as well as in the progressive nationalism in some of Shakespeare's history plays, embodied in such figures as Prince Hal or Henry V and John of Gaunt. The optimistic ideal of modern nationhood as the champion of freedom for the people and the guarantor of free personal subjectivity emerged into full flower under the authorship of "John Milton, Englishman" and William Shakespeare, who (in at least one of his personae) might also have signed himself "Englishman." Emergent imperial and colonial policies were viewed as means not just to control the world and amass power, but also to spread the new birth of freedom.[19] It is well known that the great Whig politicians of England and the American founding fathers studied Milton's prose works carefully with political freedom in mind. It is also known that English and American patriots repeatedly turned to Milton and Shakespeare for comfort and reassurance in times of cultural crisis. Wordsworth invoked Milton in response to the French Revolution; English propagandists and filmmakers turned to both writers in the confrontation with Hitler. No doubt this nationalistic vision of political freedom has had some ill effects, since it has provided cover for many an imperial and colonial excess, but in itself it is bright and optimistic. The individual self is authorized to be free after it has helped to free the political nation. Once having done so, the free self draws further energy and confidence from the national myths, such as are evoked by the names of Runymede, Agincourt, Bosworth Field, Dunbar Field, and the Battle of Britain. In this vein, Milton characteristically writes in *The Reason of Church Government* that he cannot feel free within himself, cannot attend to private business or even write poetry, until he has helped to free his country from oppression, in this instance from the "impertinent yoke of prelaty, under whose inquisitorious and tyrannical duncery no free and splendid wit can flourish."[20] For the individual to be free, the nation must first be free. And when one nation has been freed, its solemn and noble duty is to free others.

But neither Shakespeare nor Milton remains perpetually optimistic about political freedom. Shakespeare conceals his views behind the masks and ironies of drama, and even *in persona* Prince Hal is not all sweetness and light. Although *Paradise Lost* has much in common with *Areopagitica*, its reading of history and of the reformative power of politics is far more pessimistic. Rather than free the nation, it is better to turn and seek the paradise within. That, too, is potentially a bright paradise. Yet in both Shakespeare and Milton one also finds a second, darker version of the free self, an isolated, private, sometimes nihilistic version of subjectivity, in which the individual is exiled from or withdraws from the nation and society into his inner self. *Hamlet* and *Paradise Lost* have deeply influenced the way in which subsequent generations have developed this darker, more rebellious and corrosive sense of individuality and subjectivity. Hamlet and Adam, Edmund, Iago, and Satan are among the most influential exemplars of this kind of complex subjectivity. Although their stories are very different, all are tragically alienated from their surroundings — as the result of varying degrees of guilt and personal responsibility — and thus are forced to discover that they no longer fit properly into their societies and worlds. They feel themselves to be out of joint with their times, yet condemned to live on in worlds from which the natural sense of citizenship and community has vanished. What is significant about their influence upon later generations, however, is that instead of being exemplars of error and of guilt, of suffering and of tragic fall into exile, they become simply normative of what human beings ought to be. They become models for admiration and emulation. By contrast, we can imagine that Anglo-Saxon audiences would have admired the brave stoicism of the Wanderer and would have hoped to show similar fortitude in adversity; but none would have wished, even for a moment, to join him in the bitter taste of exile.

The role of Satan in this transformative cultural and psychological process is familiar enough, but perhaps insufficient attention has been paid to the influence of Milton's inward-turning, disobedient Adam on future generations.[21] Voltaire wants to love like Adam; Coleridge and Wordsworth want to plunge with him into the vast depths of subjectivity. Enlightenment readers, Romantic readers and modern readers all identify in various ways, if not with Satan, then with Hamlet and Adam. What Hamlet and Adam — and their creators — originally experienced as an anguished fall into subjectivity and a woeful loss of community begins to seem normal, inevitable, even desirable. Laurence Olivier is only one of a long succession of Hamlets who revel in the role and (as Petrarchan sonneteers say about love) find the suffering sweet.

Most Miltonists writing in the middle of the twentieth century, during the period of high modernism or still under the influence of modernist values, were scholars enough to recognize that Milton's considered theological position is that the fall is sinful, woeful, and tragic. Still, many preferred to think that, *pacé* Milton, the fall was a good thing, because it allowed human beings to get on with the business of living richer, fuller, and more human lives. If Adam and Eve had remained in paradise unfallen, life would have been very different: unnatural and boring. There would have been no cities, no art and architecture, no excitement, no warfare, no glory and empire; also no self-examination, no inner depths of subjectivity, no self-consciousness, no modernity, no scholarship, and no ideology or theory. Probably we would still be living "by Families and Tribes" (12.23) and, like the prelapsarian Adam, each of us would innocently "feel that I am happier than I know" (8.282) — a state of mind intolerable to any good modernist in need of literary irony and complexity, still less to a postmodernist, for whom living the unexamined life entails supine acquiescence to mystification and hegemony.

Hamlet and Adam are both the flawed heroes of their tales, whereas Edmund, Iago, and Satan are magnificent villains. To insist on the distinction in a more than technical or conventional sense makes the modern or postmodern reader somewhat uncomfortable. When dealing with matters of traditional good and evil, heroism and villainy, we prefer irony or resort to enclosing quotation marks. That attitude, of course, begins famously with Blake's transvaluation of Satan from villain to subterranean hero. Nevertheless, Satan has always belonged properly to the Enlightenment anti-religionists (who consider him somewhat *bêtise* yet a useful tool to *écraser l'infame*) and to the great rebels: Blake, Shelley, Byron, Lermontov, Joyce, Harold Bloom.[22] But for those uncomfortable with assuming a Satanic role, the same dark, private, resentful, solipsistic, and ultimately nihilistic subjectivity can be found in two certified heroes, Hamlet and Adam. Adam, it is true, finds subjectivity dizzying and disorienting, while at times Hamlet revels in his private madness. Yet in the private lives of both characters there are close juxtapositions between the admirable and the terrible, juxtapositions that blur traditional boundaries. Moreover in Adam there is the further, significant juxtaposition between his soliloquizing and the motivation for his fall: his love-life, which was vastly influential on the formation of Enlightenment and Romantic views about love within marriage.[23] Milton's immediate successors admire Adam's sacrifice of the world for love even as they deplore his disobedience. However that may be, the new Miltonic model of mutual and exclusive married love, which contains within it strong elements of private feeling and rejection of the world, will subsequently be defined, like the private self, by its antipathy to the political, the social, and the public. The private self and privacy within marriage will come to resemble each other, because both achieve their authenticity from within. But, we may wonder, after God and the world have been rejected, on what foundation does that inner authenticity ultimately rest?

Appendix

Further Considerations on Penance

The Biblical Basis of Confession

Over the centuries, the Church always had some means of restoring sinners internally to a state of grace and externally to full communion with itself as the Body of Christ by means of various penitential rites, which incorporated confession, contrition, penance, forgiveness, and reconciliation. Scholars generally agree that the history of these penitential rites, while unchanging in some respects, has been marked by significant long-term evolutionary development toward increasing internalization, privacy, and leniency. So, as is true of most human affairs, the history of penance is characterized both by continuity and change.

An important recent historian of penance, Thomas Tentler, observes that rites of forgiveness and reconciliation have always incorporated at least four basic, continuing elements:

> From the earliest centuries of the church there has been some kind of ecclesiastical ritual to restore baptized Christians who have committed serious sins, fallen from grace, and forfeited their right to full participation in the body of the faithful. There

is, moreover, a rough continuity between the institutions of forgiveness in the early church and those that were known on the eve of the Reformation. Throughout the history of this ritual of forgiveness four substantial elements persist, even though they receive varying emphasis from century to century. First, to be forgiven, sinners have always been required to feel sorrow at having lapsed. Second, they have consistently made some kind of explicit confession of their sins or sinfulness. Third, they have assumed, or had imposed, on them, some kind of penitential exercises. And fourth, they have participated in an ecclesiastical ritual performed with the aid of priests who pronounce penitents absolved from sin or reconciled with the communion of believers.[1]

Authority to forgive sins is broadly based on the theology of the Atonement and on the Son's power, as God and Man, to absolve men from their guilt.[2] The specifically priestly authority to forgive sins, which Tentler mentions as one of the four continuing elements of the rite, was traditionally believed to have been delegated by Jesus to Peter and the Apostles. Delegation is perhaps too simple a term; it was generally agreed that only Christ could forgive sins but that He had promised to extend His power sacramentally through priests acting in His name.[3] So qualified, the authority delegated to bishops and through them to priests was based on Christ's words to the apostles at their first meeting after the Resurrection, as described in St. John's Gospel: "Then said Jesus to them again, Peace be unto you: as my Father hath sent me, even so I send you. And when he had said this, he breathed on them, and saith unto them, Receive ye the Holy Ghost: Whose soever sins ye remit, they are remitted unto them; and whose soever sins ye retain, they are retained" (John 20:21–23).[4]

Centralization of the delegated authority to forgive or to retain sins in the office of the papacy and in Church Councils summoned or authorized by the pope was based on another text: "And I say unto thee, That thou art Peter, and upon this rock I will build my church; and the gates of hell shall not prevail against it. And I will give unto thee the keys of the kingdom of heaven: and whatsoever thou shalt bind on earth shall be bound in heaven: and whatsoever thou shalt loose on earth shall be loosed in heaven" (Matthew 17:18–19). Here too the centralizing authority represented by the keys is closely associated with the power to absolve or to retain sins.[5] Another significant text in this connection is 2 Corinthians 5, especially verse 18: "And all things are of God, who hath reconciled us to himself by Jesus Christ, and hath given to us the ministry of reconciliation."[6] Throughout the middle ages the ordinary practice was for the pope and councils to regulate penance through pronouncements, encyclicals, and codes of canon law, and for the diocesan bishops in turn to reserve to themselves forgiveness of certain kinds of serious sins and to delegate to their parochial priests and to members of religious orders within their dioceses (later especially Franciscans and Dominicans) the authority, variously delimited, to forgive less serious sins.[7] Some transgressions — of which the murder of St. Thomas à Becket and the personal and political complications resulting from the "Great Matter" of Henry VIII are two well-known examples — were too grave or public to be resolved except by the papal legate or the pope himself.

Chaucer: The Pardoner and The Pastor

Many readers and some critics have drawn a one-sided or misleading picture of penance as it was practiced in the middle ages from Chaucer's *Pardoner's Tale*. Chaucer's Pardoner offers ready ammunition for those who view the medieval Church as a combination of superstitious credulity and corrupt chicanery. He is obviously the very model of everything a pardoner should not be. He is venal, corrupt, and hungry only for that *radix malorum*, money. He knows just how to break the seal of the confessional: not openly, which would get him into trouble with the ecclesiastical courts and the bishop, but covertly; naming no names but making it widely clear whom he means. He sells fake relics and pardons, he has no interest in the "correccioun of synne" (404), and he demands not heartfelt contrition of his penitents but — contrary to the policy of the Church — good coins or payment in kind.[8] Worst of all, he takes no interest in the ultimate fate of those he shrives:

> I rekke nevere, whan that they been beryed,
> Though that hir soules goon a-blakeberyed!
> (405–06)

Those folk are dead and gone, after all; there is no more profit to be made from them. The Pardoner takes an even more pragmatic view of confession than might a modern sociologist. His despicable character and behavior reveal him to be a negative exemplar, whom Chaucer holds up for his audience's blame and execration.

When his tale is done, the Pardoner displays a last gift antithetical to his office: he is a bringer of discord rather than of peace, a breaker not a restorer of the community. He is no better at mending society than souls. He and the Host quarrel violently, threatening the fellowship among the pilgrims. The Knight must step in and restore order by persuading the two of them to stop quarreling and exchange the kiss of peace. The Knight plays what should have been the Pardoner's role. Nevertheless, in spite of his manifold failings, the Pardoner is clearly an expert at his game. If his sermons are as effective as his tale, he has probably saved more souls than he ever meant to. His brilliant technique would drive sinners to confession in droves. According to the orthodox Catholic view, a priest's inward sinfulness does not detract from the efficacy of the sacrament he administers so long as he observes the basic forms. God employs weak and sinful instruments. Despite the Pardoner's underlying corruption, it remains true that his sermons and his tale are powerful instruments, apt in spite of his indifference to their welfare to lead many of his listeners to conviction of sin, repentance, and forgiveness.

Chaucer reserves his more direct exposition of the importance of penance until the end of *The Canterbury Tales* (as we now have them). The Parson — Chaucer's most admirable figure — represents penance out of all other possible values. Chaucer might, for example, have had the Parson give his sermon on the Eucharist, which was under attack at the time by Wyclif and others. As Miri Rubin suggests, the rapid spread of the Feast of Corpus Christi and of Corpus Christi Fraternities shows how important the issue of Christ's real presence in the sacrament was at that time in popular Catholic piety.[9] But instead Chaucer chose to end *The Canterbury Tales* with penance, giving it the most rhetorically significant position in the tales. Presumably he saw in the sacrament of penance — if only people could be persuaded to make proper use of it — the best solution to all the sins, quarrels, and moral failings of his pilgrims, who are a microcosm of society.

The Parson's sermon on penance is a compendium of the manuals, the thought, and the practice of Chaucer's time.[10] Like *Handlyng Synne*, it takes an orderly approach, including among its major points for exposition the three parts of penance, the six reasons to confess, and the seven deadly sins. The Parson is aware that penance can be either public or private, although he speaks not of an evolution from public to private but of three degrees of publicness, depending on the nature of the offense and the status of the offender. His explanation, based on authority, canon law, and practice,[11] is so lucid that it deserves quotation:

> The speces of Penitence been three. That oon of hem is solmpne, another is commune, and the thridde is privee./ Thilke penance that is solempne is in two maneres; as to be put out of hooly chirche in Lente for slaughtre of children, and swich manner thyng./ Another is, whan a man hath synned openly, of which synne the fame is openly spoken in the contree, and

> thanne hooly chirche by juggement destreyneth hym for to do open penaunce./ Commune penaunce is that preestes enjoynen men communly in certeyn caas, as for to goon peraventure naked in pilgrimages, or barefoot./ Pryvee penaunce is thilke that men doon alday for privee synnes, of whiche we shryve use prively and receyve privee penaunce. (101–06)

Public, flagrant, or joint sins receive public penances, but in most instances penances are private. On the whole, a reading of the Parson's sermon confirms that his view of sin is mainly personal, private, and interior.

Undoubtedly Chaucer was aware of the social and communal effects of sin, for they are visible throughout *The Canterbury Tales*. But he seems to have concluded that the social good would best be served by means of individual renovation and spiritual renewal. So the tenor of the Parson's sermon carries out his promise, which he makes in his prologue:

> And Jhesu, for his grace, wit me sende
> To shewe yow the wey, in this viage,
> Of thilke parfit glorious pilgrymage
> That highte Jerusalem celestial.
> (48–51)

In this respect, that he puts the individual's ultimate goal of salvation above and prior to the social good, Chaucer anticipates Milton, who thought that the social benefits of a virtuous republic could only be brought into being and preserved by the personal moral choices of a critical mass of virtuous individuals. Milton's view is often thought symptomatic of the rise in his time of a market economy together with the ideals of liberal individualism, and it is sometimes opposed to older values of feudal corporatism.[12] For Milton, individual merit is more important than noble blood, and the nation is built upon the individual virtues of its citizens. But historical Christianity itself has an element of free individuality, together with notions of communal responsibility, and the Christian individual freedom on which Milton builds has ancient roots.

The message of Chaucer's Parson calls to mind Chaucer's own message to Sir Philip de la Vache in "Truth":

> That thee is sent, receyve in buxumnesse;
> The wrastling for this world axeth a fal.
> Her is non hoom, her nis but wildernesse:
> Forth, pilgrim, forth! Forth, beste, out of thy stal!
> Know thy contree, look up, thank God of al;
> Hold the heye wey, and lat thy gost thee lede,
> And trouthe thee shal delivere, it is no drede.
>
> (15–21)

If society is to be bettered, it will be bettered by those who "Flee fro the prees" and seek their "hevenlich mede." Chaucer was not by nature ascetic, eremitic, or unworldly. What he means by this advice to flee from the world is that one must put first things first, then everything else will fall into place. Individual choice, freedom, and subjectivity are not modern inventions, although in the unfolding of modernity they have sometimes been extended to grotesque and unsustainable extremes. True community has traditionally been achieved not by the denial or suppression of individuality, but by a proper balance between the needs of the individual and the family, the household, and society.

Notes

Notes to Preface

1. Homer, the *Odyssey*, trans. Robert Fitzgerald (New York: Vintage Classics, 1990), 5.156–66.
2. Erich Auerbach, *Mimesis: The Representation of Reality in Western Literature*, trans. Willard Trask (Princeton: Princeton University Press, 1953; Garden City: Doubleday Anchor, 1957), p. 4.
3. Virgil, *The Aeneid*, trans. Allen Mandelbaum (New York: Bantam Books, 1981), 4.373–83.
4. W. R. Johnson, *Darkness Visible* (Berkeley: University of California Press, 1976), pp. 84–87.
5. St. Augustine, *Confessions*, trans. Henry Chadwick, The World's Classics (Oxford: Oxford University Press, 1991), pp. 146–47 (8.8.19–20).

Notes to Chapter One

1. Ronald A. Knox, *Enthusiasm: A Chapter in the History of Religion with Special Relevance to the Seventeenth and Eighteenth Centuries* (London: Oxford University Press, 1950).
2. Significantly, Virgilian "subjectivity" begins with the first eclogue's treatment of exile from a farm and finds its fullest statement in the exile of Aeneas and his followers from Troy. Exile is the common theme, with a known basis in Virgil's experience. One might propose similar origins for Petrarchan subjectivity. The *Confessions* is only one of many places in which Augustine takes an inward turn. See, e.g., *De vera Religione* (39.72): "Noli foras ire, in teipsum redi; in interiore homine habitat veritas" [Do not go outward, return into yourself; truth dwells in the inward man] (my translation).

3. Anne Ferry, *The "Inward" Language: Sonnets of Wyatt, Sidney, Shakespeare, Donne* (Chicago: University of Chicago Press, 1983), p. 7. Among numerous other studies arguing that "subjectivity" was a Renaissance innovation, are Joel Fineman's influential book, *Shakespeare's Perjured Eye: The Invention of Poetic Subjectivity in the Sonnets* (Berkeley: University of California Press, 1986) and Stephen A. Greenblatt, "Psychoanalysis and Renaissance Culture," *Learning to Curse: Essays in Early Modern Culture* (New York: Routledge, 1990), pp. 131–45. Sara van den Berg's essay, "The Passing of the Elizabethan Court," *Ben Jonson Journal* 1 (1994): 31–61, exemplifies how much we now take for granted that seventeenth century political and economic events produced a new "subjectivity" never seen before.

4. *Sir Thomas Browne's Pseudoxia Epidemica*, ed. Robin Robbins (Oxford: Clarendon Press, 1981), 1:31 (1.3.4).

5. Bacon, *The Advancement of Learning*, 1.3.4. In a letter to me commenting on this chapter in draft, Edward W. Tayler points out that establishing just what Browne and Bacon meant by individual is "tricky." He argues that Henry More was first (c. 1642) to think of individuals in the modern sense, in "The First Individual," *Soundings of Things Done: Essays in Early Modern Literature in Honor of S. K. Heninger Jr.*, ed. Peter E. Medine and Joseph Wittreich (Newark: University of Delaware Press, 1997), pp. 251–59. Tayler's comment persuades me that Bacon's meaning lies somewhere between "inseparable" and "unique," as does Milton's (see below).

6. *Complete Prose Works of John Milton*, ed. Don M. Wolfe et al. (New Haven: Yale University Press, 1953–82), 1:712. Milton is arguing whether the word "angel" in Revelation 2 is singular or collective. He did not originate the paired terms "individual" and "collective" in this passage but cites them from Bishop Joseph Hall's attack on his *Apology for Smectymnuus*. Milton assigns them to the Remonstrant, who accuses Milton of interpretive error: "[Y]our shift is that the Angell is heere taken collectively, not individually." In an interpretive maneuver which the Yale editor finds hard to "fathom" or approve, Milton had earlier assumed in *The Apology* that "angel" was collective, but without using Hall's paired terms. Thus Hall, not Milton, has the linguistic priority, although Milton finds the innovation much to his purpose.

7. See "individual" and its variants in *A Concordance to the English Prose of John Milton*, compiled by Laurence Sterne and Harold H. Kollmeier (Binghamton, NY: Medieval & Renaissance Texts & Studies, 1985).

8. *Complete Prose Works*, 2:316. Milton often uses "individual" to the same purpose in *Tetrachordon* (1645), to argue that traditional interpreters err when they separate proof texts from their contexts.

9. On the development of Milton's thinking under the difficult pres-

sures of reconciling personal experience in marriage with conventional readings of the Bible, see Edward W. Tayler, "Milton's Grim Laughter and Second Choices," in *Poetry and Epistemology: Turning Points in the History of Poetic Knowledge*, ed. Roland Hagenbüchle and Laura Skandera (Regensburg: Postet, 1986), pp. 72–93 and Anthony Low, *The Reinvention of Love: Poetry, Politics and Culture from Sidney to Milton* (Cambridge: Cambridge University Press, 1993). On remarkable innovations in Milton's writings about divorce, see John G. Halkett, *Milton and the Idea of Matrimony: A Study of the Divorce Tracts and Paradise Lost* (New Haven: Yale University Press, 1970). On divorce before and after the Reformation, see Georges Duby, *Medieval Marriage: Two Models from Twelfth-Century France*, trans. Elborg Forster (Baltimore: Johns Hopkins University Press, 1978); Christopher N. L. Brooke, *The Medieval Idea of Marriage* (Oxford: Oxford University Press, 1989); Leo Miller, *John Milton Among the Polygamophiles* (New York: Loewenthal Press, 1974); and Lawrence Stone, *Broken Lives: Separation and Divorce in England 1640–1857* (New York: Oxford University Press, 1993).

10. The modern quarrel originates with Bernard F. Huppé, "*The Wanderer*: Theme and Structure," *JEGP* 42 (1943): 516–38. Huppé postulates that the poem has two separate speakers, the wanderer and the wise man. Classic unified readings of the poem and central character are offered by R. M. Lumiansky, "The Dramatic Structure of the Old English *Wanderer*," *Neophilologus* 34 (1949): 104–12, and Stanley B. Greenfield, "*The Wanderer*: A Reconsideration of Theme and Structure," *JEGP* 50 (1951): 451–65. E. G. Stanley puts the wanderer in context in "Old English Poetic Diction and the Interpretation of *The Wanderer, The Seafarer,* and *The Penitent's Prayer*," *Anglia* 73 (1955): 413–66. James L. Rosier, "The Literal-Figurative Identity of *The Wanderer*," *PMLA* 79 (1964): 366–69 argues that the poem's indebtedness to its predecessors does not lessen the unified impression made by its central character. John C. Pope, "Dramatic Voices in *The Wanderer* and *The Seafarer*," in *Essential Articles for the Study of Old English Poetry*, ed. Jess B. Bessinger, Jr. and Stanley J. Kahrl (Hamden, CT: Archon Books, 1968), pp. 532–70, revives Huppé's dialogue theory. More recently, Carol Braun Pasternack, "Anonymous Polyphony and *The Wanderer*'s Textuality," *Anglo-Saxon England* 20 (1991): 99–122, goes much further, combining theories of orality with poststructuralism to argue for the anonymity, impersonality, indeed the nonexistence as a person, of the wanderer. Pasternack's essay is in tune with the times, but the consensus may still be represented by Bruce Mitchell and Fred C. Robinson, *A Guide to Old English*, 5th ed. (Oxford: Blackwell, 1992): "*The Wanderer* is . . . a dramatic monologue briefly introduced by the Christian poet and briefly concluded by him with a terse exhortation to seek comfort in God the Father. The monologue itself is spoken by a heroic-age nobleman whose

assessment of life's meaning shows no awareness of Christian enlightenment" (208).

11. An excellent introduction to social psychology and its implications for criticism is Lawrence Danson, "Jonsonian Comedy and the Discovery of the Social Self," *PMLA* 99 (1984): 179–93.

12. I put "earlier" in quotation marks because the historical process is not always linear. One may, for example, speak of "early" and "late" classical cultures, although both precede England's "early" period. Alasdair MacIntyre's discussion of the Homeric hero and his society in *Whose Justice, Which Rationality?* (Notre Dame: University of Notre Dame Press, 1988), pp. 12–29, illumines identity in a tenth century English poem.

13. Prominent among them, Stephen Greenblatt issues ten New Historicist commandments, the first of which is: "There can be no appeals to genius as the sole origin of the energies of great art" (*Shakespearean Negotiations: The Circulation of Social Energy in Renaissance England* [Berkeley: University of California Press, 1988], p. 12). Greenblatt distinguishes himself from Moses by dividing his commandments into seven "abjurations" and three "generative principles." His qualification — "sole" — gives this rule credibility but is slippery and soon lost from sight.

14. I should mention Roland Barthes as a significant source of these influential ideas and more recently Michel Foucault, who asserts more sweepingly that the very idea of "man . . . is probably no more than a kind of rift in the order of things" (*The Order of Things: An Archaeology of the Human Sciences* [New York: Random House, 1970], p. xxiii).

15. In writing this, I am reminded of a graduate class I took with Francis P. Magoun, Jr., many years ago. Middle English, he remarked, typically expresses smaller and more delicate feelings than Old English. As proof, he compared the M.E. lament, "well-a-day," with its O.E. cognate: "WAH . . . LA . . . WAH!" At 40 years' remove, I still remember the elegant briskness with which he spoke the former phrase, and the prolonged, heartfelt wail of the latter.

16. See Anthony Low, *The Reinvention of Love*, chaps. 2 and 6.

17. The literature on the subject has grown immense; two classic treatments are Anthony Esler, *The Aspiring Mind of the Elizabethan Younger Generation* (Durham: Duke University Press, 1966), and Lawrence Stone, *The Crisis of the Aristocracy: 1558–1641* (Oxford: Clarendon Press, 1965). Typifying extreme discontent with problems in the patronage system is Bossola in Webster's *The Duchess of Malfi*.

18. Stanley B. Greenfield, "The Formulaic Expression of the Theme of 'Exile' in Anglo-Saxon Poetry," *Speculum* 30 (1955): 200–06. Robert E. Bjork, "Sundor æt Rune: The Voluntary Exile of the Wanderer," *Neophilologus* 73 (1989): 119–29. "Though perhaps the most intense

and painful experience one can have within Anglo-Saxon society, exile is nevertheless an accepted (even expected) part of Anglo-Saxon life, a part that both the culture and the language accommodate" (p. 119).

19. Early Old English scholars argued that Christian elements in Old English verse were superficial intrusions into purely pagan originals. Dorothy Whitelock (see note below) was influential in challenging that view. J. E. Cross, "On the Genre of *The Wanderer*," *Neophilologus* 45 (1961): 63–75, offers a balanced view of how far "Christian" readings of the poem may be taken. He argues that the wanderer's exile is actual before it is Christian-allegorical and notes that in the consolation the poet mixes classical and Christian authorities inextricably. Mitchell and Robinson argue that the wanderer is a pagan of the heroic age, while the framing poet who interprets his story is Christian. I find no problem with that view provided that we recognize the immense sympathy the poet shows for the wanderer's experience and reactions to that experience — and expects his audience to feel. The wanderer is not just an exemplum of pagan error: his pain, stoicism, and contempt for the world are adopted, not repudiated, by the Christian poet.

20. The text of *The Wanderer* is from George Philip Krapp and Elliot van Kirk Dobbie, eds., *The Exeter Book, The Anglo-Saxon Poetic Records* (New York: Columbia University Press, 1936), 3:134–37, lines 114–15; translations are mine. I have also consulted T. P. Dunning and A. J. Bliss, eds, *The Wanderer* (London: Methuen, 1969).

21. Dorothy Whitelock, "The Interpretation of *The Seafarer*," in *Essential Articles for the Study of Old English Poetry*, ed. Jess B. Bessinger, Jr. and Stanley J. Kahrl (Hamden, CT: Archon Books, 1968), p. 450. Clair McPherson, "The Sea a Desert: Early English Spirituality and *The Seafarer*," *American Benedictine Review* 38 (1987): 115–26.

22. *Gebideð* is ambiguous; it may mean that the wanderer lives long enough to find favor or that he lives on still awaiting it.

23. If *The Wanderer* was composed in the tenth century, a Senecan influence through the monasteries is more likely than if it was composed earlier. The case is unproven.

24. Robert Bellah, et al., *Habits of the Heart* (Berkeley: University of California Press, 1985), pp. 56–62. Charles Taylor, *Sources of the Self: The Making of the Modern Identity* (Cambridge: Harvard University Press, 1989), p. 39.

25. Taylor, *Sources of the Self*, p. 36; see also Jerome Bruner, "The Transactional Self," in his *Actual Minds, Possible Worlds* (Cambridge: Harvard University Press, 1986), p. 60.

26. Speaking about a much later period, Taylor distinguishes Martin Luther's spiritual crisis, which he characterizes as "turning around the acute sense of condemnation and irremediable exile" resulting

from his break with the institutional Church, from our "modern sense of meaninglessness, or lack of purpose, or emptiness" (p. 28). Luther, by substituting an alternative system for the one against which he rebelled — a system he justified in part by insisting that it was more traditional than Catholicism — in this respect may be said to represent a half-way point from the wanderer's response to exile to those characteristic of Nietzsche and his postmodern heirs.

27. MacIntyre, *Whose Justice?*, p. 15. But when, for example, Achilles chooses to return Hector's body to Priam, he reveals that areté may rise to a higher level than the audience might anticipate. And it can be argued that in the *Odyssey* Odysseus learns a different kind of areté from what he exemplified in the *Iliad*. Although classicists dispute their exact meanings, *aretē* and *dikē* may be roughly translated as excellence and justice.

28. It is easy to overemphasize a Christian Anglo-Saxon's resignation to "fate." As Dunning and Bliss argue, *wyrd* more likely means "what comes to pass" (p. 72) or what is brought about by providence (as explained by Boethius), rather than something decreed in spite of the gods by immortal beings like the Greek Fates or Scandinavian Norns.

29. The italics and translation are mine.

30. Dunning and Bliss's awkward-sounding gloss for *cwidegiedd*, "spoken utterance" (p. 44) clearly conveys the wanderer's longing for any least speech with lost companions. Demetrius undergoes a similar hallucinatory experience in the *Aeneid* (11.271-74).

31. See, for example, Frank Kermode, *Romantic Image* (London: Routledge & Kegan Paul, 1957).

32. See Peter Clemoes, "*Mens cogitans* in *The Seafarer* and *The Wanderer*," in *Medieval Literature and Civilization*, ed. D. A. Piersall and R. A. Waldron (London: University of London, Athlone Press, 1969), pp. 62-77.

Notes to Chapter Two

1. Stanley Fish, *There's No Such Thing as Free Speech and It's a Good Thing, Too* (Oxford: Oxford University Press, 1994), p. 57; cited by R. V. Young, *At War with the Word: Literary Theory and Liberal Education* (Wilmington: ISI Books, 1999), p. 31, who provides evidence to flesh out Fish's remark.

2. John F. Crosby, "Conscience and Superego: A Phenomenological Analysis of Their Difference and Relation," *Logos* 1 (1998): 190. I draw upon Crosby's illuminating discussion throughout this paragraph.

3. See, e.g., Victor Turner, *The Ritual Process: Structure and Anti-Structure* (Chicago: University of Chicago Press, 1969). The distinction is ancient, deriving (as Turner's terminology suggests) from the classical Latin *privitas, societas* and *communitas*.

4. See Joseph Cardinal Ratzinger, *Principles of Catholic Theology*, trans. Sister Mary Frances McCarthy (San Francisco: Ignatius Press, 1987), pp. 15–55.

5. Owen Barfield, *Poetic Diction: A Study in Meaning* (London: Faber and Faber, 1928); *Saving the Appearances: A Study in Idolatry* (London: Faber and Faber, 1957).

6. Thomas N. Tentler, *Sin and Confession on the Eve of the Reformation* (Princeton: Princeton University Press, 1977), pp. 12–13.

7. Nicetas, *Explicatio Symbolorum* 10, *Patrologia Latina* 52:871B; cited in commentary on "The Communion of Saints," *Catechism of the Catholic Church*, p. 247, sec. 946. The *Catechism* adds: "The communion of saints is the Church." On the biblical basis of confession and some further basic background, see Appendix A.

8. Larry D. Benson, ed., *The Riverside Chaucer*, 3rd ed. (Boston: Houghton Mifflin, 1987), p. 298.

9. St. Ambrose, *De poenitentia* (2.10.95) in *Patrologiae cursus completus . . . Series latina*, ed. J.-P. Migne (Paris, 1844–1890), 16:520. Cited by Tentler, *Sin and Confession*, p. 4.

10. See Pierre J. Payer, *Sex and the Penitentials* (Toronto: University of Toronto Press, 1984) and R. C. Mortimer, *The Origins of Private Penance in the Western Church* (Oxford: Oxford University Press, 1939).

11. The habit of taking practical advice from respected elders in Britain while obeying the Pope's central authority in Rome is exemplified in early Lives of Saints Willibord, Boniface, and Sturm, who converted the Germans in the seventh and eighth centuries. See C. H. Talbot, ed. and trans., *The Anglo-Saxon Missionaries in Germany* (London: Sheed and Ward, 1954).

12. Payer, *Sex and the Penitentials*, p. 60.

13. Ibid., p. 58.

14. Ibid., p. 86.

15. John Bossy, "The Social History of Confession in the Age of the Reformation," *Transactions of the Royal Historical Society*, 5th ser. 25 (1975): 21. See also Bossy's companion piece, "The Mass as a Social Institution 1200–1700," *Past and Present* 100 (1983): 29–61.

16. Playing on his readers' antipathy, Milton does it the honor of calling it, in *Areopagitica*, "the most Antichristian Councel." See the *Complete Prose Works of John Milton*, ed. Don M. Wolfe et al. (New Haven: Yale University Press, 1959), 2:505.

17. Bossy, "Social History of Confession," 23. Contrary to Bossy, see, for example, chap. 14 of the Decree Concerning Justification (sixth session of the Council of Trent; January 13, 1547).

18. Reversing the long movement toward a culture of privatization, Vatican Council II and *The Catechism of the Catholic Church* call penance the "sacrament of reconciliation" (to God and the community of the faithful).

19. Bossy, "The Social History of Confession," p. 24.

20. On the spread of the confessional, see Bossy, "The Social History of Confession," pp. 28–33.

21. Eamon Duffy, *The Stripping of the Altars* (New Haven: Yale University Press, 1992), pl. 19. For the carved font mentioned below see pl. 20.

22. In the *Summa*, Aquinas states that laying-on of hands is not part of the "form" of the sacrament, which consists only in the words "Ego te absolvo, in nomine Patris, et Filii, et Spiritus Sancti." But the practice was customary. Bossy mentions that well after the Council of Trent Cardinal Borromeo advocated laying-on of hands as good traditional practice, even though the confessional booth made it physically impossible (p. 29).

23. On the complex cross currents of authority among the various levels and branches of Church and state, see, for example, R. N. Swanson, *Church and Society in Late Medieval England* (Oxford: Basil Blackwell, 1989); and A. Hamilton Thompson, *The English Clergy and their Organization in the Later Middle Ages* (Oxford: Clarendon Press, 1947). As Thompson's opening pages suggest, the whole history of the medieval church can, if one wishes, be told as a neverending series of shifting rivalries. "Among English medieval dioceses York was preeminent for the importance of the spiritual republics within its borders which claimed exemption from the ordinary jurisdiction of the diocesan; while in addition it included certain outlying districts in which the archbishop's authority was open to question from other prelates. The rights of the archbishop within his province were strictly limited. The bishops of the small diocese of Carlisle owned his authority; but from the middle of the twelfth century his claim to metropolitan jurisdiction over the Scottish sees was acknowledged only by the bishops of Galloway, and the last consecration of a bishop of Galloway by an archbishop of York took place in 1294, though the formal profession of obedience was maintained until a later date. The efforts of Archbishop Romeyn and his successors to bring the proud spirit of Antony Bek into subjection had been signally defeated; for Bek and the chapter of Durham, though at war among themselves, were of one mind when their metropolitan proposed to assert himself in their midst" (1). And so on.

24. Duffy, pl. 20.

25. Jacobus, "cautum est etiam facies habere tectas ut sola vox possit audiri," in Tentler, *Sin and Confession*, p. 84, n. 2.

26. Ann Eljenholm Nichols, "The Etiquette of Pre-Reformation Confession in East Anglia," *The Sixteenth Century Journal* 17 (1986): 158.

27. Bossy, "The Social History of Confession," p. 24. Robert Raymo, who has carefully read the manuals used in England, tells me he does not find this to be a customary complaint.

28. Lea, *The History of Auricular Confession*, 1:354, cited by Bossy, "The Social History of Confession," p. 24, n. 10.

29. Bossy, "The Social History of Confession," p. 25.

30. St. Thomas, *Summa*, 3.86.3. Also: "It is impossible for Penance to take one sin away without another. First because . . . without grace no sin can be forgiven. Now every mortal sin is opposed to grace and excludes it." He cites a treatise attributed to Augustine, *De vera et falsa pænitentia*: "There are many who repent having sinned, but not completely; for they except certain things which give them pleasure, forgetting that our Lord delivered from the devil the man who was both dumb and deaf, whereby he shows us that we are never healed unless it be from all sins."

31. Robert Mannyng of Brunne, *Handlying Synne*, ed. Idelle Sullens (Binghamton: Medieval & Renaissance Texts & Studies, 1983), p. xiii.

32. "The Parson's Tale," l. 1005, in *The Riverside Chaucer*, ed. Larry D. Benson, 3d ed. (Boston: Houghton Mifflin, 1987).

33. Lawrence G. Duggan, "Fear and Confession on the Eve of the Reformation," *Archiv für Reformationsgesichte* 75 (1984): 168–69, 165.

34. Ibid., "Fear and Confession," pp. 168, 172.

35. Duggan, "Fear and Confession," p. 165. Steven E. Ozment, *The Reformation in the Cities: The Appeal of Protestantism to Sixteenth-Century Germany and Switzerland* (New Haven: Yale University Press, 1975), pp. 12, 28, 118–19, 176–77 and *The Age of Reform 1250–1550: An Intellectual and Religious History of Late Medieval and Reformation Europe* (New Haven: Yale University Press, 1980), pp. 209, 216–19. Tentler, *Sin and Confession*, pp. 21–26, 52–53 and especially Thomas N. Tentler, "The Summa for Confessors as an Instrument of Social Control," in Charles Trinkhaus and H. Oberman, eds., *The Pursuit of Holiness in Late Medieval and Renaissance Religion* (Leiden, 1974), pp. 103–37.

36. "A Discussion on How Confession Should be Made" [1520] in *Luther's Works*, ed. Helmut T. Lehman, et al. (Philadelphia: Fortress Press, 1970), 39:35.

37. J. J. Scarisbrick, *The Reformation and the English People* (Oxford: Basil Blackwell, 1984); Duffy, *The Stripping of the Altars*; see also Christopher Haigh, *English Reformations: Religion, Politics, and Society under the Tudors* (Oxford: Clarendon Press, 1993); David Cressy, *Bonfires & Bells: National Memory and the Protestant Calendar in Elizabethan and Stuart England* (Berkeley: University of California Press, 1989); and Colin Richmond, "The English Gentry and Religion, c. 1500," in *Religious Belief and Ecclesiastical Careers in Late Medieval England*, ed. Christopher Harper-Bill (Woodbridge: Boydell Press, 1991).

38. Jonathan Hughes, *Pastors and Visionaries: Religion and Secular Life in Late Medieval Yorkshire* (Woodbridge: Boydell Press, 1988), p. 131.

39. In addition to Hughes, *Pastors and Visionaries*, see the excellent survey of popular catechetical methods in chapter 2 of Duffy's *Stripping of the Altars*, pp. 53–87.

40. Hughes, *Pastors and Visionaries*, p. 144.

41. Although Rolle initiated a new movement toward inward spirituality, he was not without predecessors. See Thomas H. Bestul, "Devotional Writing in England between Anselm and Richard Rolle," in *Mysticism: Medieval & Modern*, ed. Valerie M. Lagorio (Salzburg: Institut für Anglistik und Amerikanistik Universität Salzburg, 1986), pp. 12–28.

42. Hughes, *Pastors and Visionaries*, p. 121.

43. These reasons are given *passim* in 1–2.73, "Of the Comparison of One Sin with Another," and elsewhere in the general discussion of sin.

44. Payer, *Sex and the Penitentials*, pp. 46–47.

45. Bossy, "The Social History of Confession," pp. 36–37, n. 39.

46. That the story is a joke is further suggested by the name of the collection from which Bossy takes it, *Motti e facezie del piovano Arlotto*, ed. G. B. Folena (Milan and Naples, 1953), pp. 34–35. As with confessing the sins of others, it might have happened but is hardly normative.

47. Pope John Paul II, *Apostolic Exhortation on Reconciliation and Penance*, Sixth Assembly of the General Synod of Bishops (1984), sec. 16; quoted from "Reconcil.zip," Catholic Forum, CompuServe. The citation in square brackets is in the original text.

48. Tentler, *Sin and Confession*, p. 52.

49. Jean Delumeau, *Sin and Fear: The Emergence of a Western Guilt Culture 13th–18th Centuries*, trans. Eric Nicholson (New York: St. Martin's Press, 1990). Ozment's thesis in *The Reformation in the Cities* and *The Age of Reform* (see n. 35 above), that the Reformation represented a casting-off of unbearable anxieties caused by medieval confession, is also unlikely. To the contrary, confession was widely popular. The typical Protestant complaint was not that it was burdensome, but that it made forgiveness too easy, mechanical, and automatic.

50. Quotations are taken from the openings of the graces of shrift (ll. 11,907–12,296).

51. The methodology is fundamental to Bacon's thought and to that of the Royal Society and its heirs; see especially *The Proficience and Advancement of Learning* and the *Novum Organum*. Others who deserve mention in this context are Machiavelli, Guicciardini, Hobbes, and Descartes. On Descartes see Stephen M. Fallon, *Milton Among the Philosophers: Poetry and Materialism in Seventeenth-Century England* (Ithaca: Cornell University Press, 1991), p. 25.

52. J. R. R. Tolkien and E. V. Gordon, eds., *Sir Gawain and the Green Knight* (Oxford: Clarendon Press, 1930), p. xvi.

53. Theodore Silverstein, ed., *Sir Gawain and the Green Knight: A New Critical Edition* (Chicago: University of Chicago Press, 1974). Quotations are from this edition; translations — as literal as I can reasonably manage — are mine. Scholars have often suggested that the unknown author of *Gawain* was a priest. As Tolkien and Gordon note, he is equally expert in moral and spiritual matters and in aristocratic concerns such as clothing, armor, courtly love, and the hunt.

54. On the communal significance of the Mass, see Bossy, "The Mass as a Social Institution." For profound analysis of the changing meaning of the community in Jewish, Classical, Christian, and Enlightenment societies, see Joseph Ratzinger, *The Meaning of Christian Brotherhood* (New York: Sheed and Ward, 1966; reprinted San Francisco: Ignatius Press, 1993). Sung mass and matins were commonly celebrated in medieval England, even on weekdays in small parishes; see Peter Heath, *The English Parish Clergy*, pp. 4–6, 19–20.

55. He says he will never tell it to a "lance." Marie Boroff translates: "nor say to a soul" in her translation first printed in 1967 and reprinted in M. H. Abrams, ed., *The Norton Anthology of English Literature* 7th ed. (New York: W. W. Norton, 2000), vol. 1. "Lance" — literally the weapon — is synecdochic for "man" or "person." The alliterative scheme requires an L-sound, but the poet may have chosen this word to denote not just any man but a man of honor who bears the chivalric weapon.

Notes to Chapter Three

1. Leo Miller, *John Milton Among the Polygamophiles* (New York: Loewenthal Press, 1974). Miller's particular concern is polygamy, which seems an easy case; yet early dissertations in theology and shifting opinions of authoritative figures such as Luther suggest otherwise.

2. Christopher Haigh, "The Recent Historiography of the English Reformation," in *The English Reformation Revised*, ed. Christopher Haigh (Cambridge: Cambridge University Press, 1987), pp. 19–33; also Haigh, *English Reformations: Religion, Politics, and Society under the Tudors* (Cambridge: Cambridge University Press, 1993).

3. As a typical example, see Julian Cornwall, *Revolt of the Peasantry 1549* (London: Routledge & Kegan Paul, 1977). Cornwall sympathizes with the peasants but has little interest in their religion, even though they declared it the cause of their revolt. Masses of new primary data have become available; in addition to books already mentioned, see Margaret Bowker, *The Secular Clergy in the Diocese of Lincoln* (Cambridge: Cambridge University Press, 1968) and other studies cited by Haigh in "Recent Historiography."

4. Bossy, "The Social History of Confession," p. 27, n. 15.

5. In "The Sacrament of Penance" (1519), in *Luther's Works*, ed.

Helmut T. Lehman, et al. (Philadelphia: Fortress Press, 1970), 35:5–22, Luther still treats penance as a sacrament; a position he drops in "A Discussion on How Confession Should be Made" (1520), *Luther's Works*, 39:25–47. But the sacramental nature of penance is already made tenuous in the earlier work by Luther's insistence that only belief makes absolution efficacious because only belief lifts the burden of guilt, as well as by his argument that "the keys have not been given to St. Peter but to you and me" (p. 16), as an aspect of the priesthood of all believers. In the later work, although he no longer calls it a sacrament, Luther still recognizes the need for formal confession. Likewise in "The Babylonian Captivity" (1520), he writes: "Without doubt, confession of sins is necessary" (Martin Luther, *Selections from His Writings*, ed. John Dillenberger [Chicago: Quadrangal Books, 1961], p. 319). The *Augsburg Confession* (1530), Melancthon, and other early Lutheran confessional documents take the same position.

6. Bossy, "The Social History of Confession," p. 26.
7. Ibid., p. 27.
8. Ibid., p. 26. As Bossy suggests, all the secret sins Luther specifically mentions involve sexual imaginings and transgressions, although his reference to the ninth and tenth commandments might implicitly include coveting a neighbor's house or his ox as well as his wife (see below).
9. *Luther's Works*, 39:42, 44.
10. Ibid., 39:36–37.
11. See the discussion in John T. McNeill, *A History of the Cure of Souls* (New York: Harper and Brothers, 1951), pp. 174–76.
12. Bossy, "The Social History of Confession," pp. 26–27, quoting from *Babylonian Captivity*.
13. *Luther's Works*, 39:33.
14. See McNeill, *Cure of Souls*, pp. 218–36; and on General Confession, G. J. Cuming, *A History of Anglican Liturgy* (London: Macmillan, 1969), pp. 61–64.
15. See Martin Ingram, *Church Courts, Sex and Marriage in England, 1570–1640* (Cambridge: Cambridge University Press, 1987). Since Ingram's only concern is to examine the post-Reformation ecclesiastical courts, which he does extremely well, a reader might underestimate their continuity with late-medieval ecclesiastical courts.
16. See M. M. Goldsmith, "Hobbes on Law," *The Cambridge Companion to Hobbes*, ed. Tom Sorell (Cambridge: Cambridge University Press, 1996), pp. 274–304.
17. On continental treatments of this theme in Rousseau, Goethe, and Flaubert, see Tony Tanner, *Adultery in the Novel: Contract and Transgression* (Baltimore: Johns Hopkins University Press, 1979). Tanner argues that the novel is generically synonymous with transgression.

A contributing factor to the novel's success might be modern culture's inability to deal constructively with some kinds of transgression, resulting in a variety of comic, tragic, or irresolvable situations, hard on protagonists but rich in artistic possibilities, and relevant to what the traditional novel does best: portray individuals in conflict with their societies.

18. *Luther's Works*, 39:32.

19. *The Works of Edmund Spenser: A Variorum Edition*, vol. 1, ed. Edwin Greenlaw et al. (Baltimore: Johns Hopkins Press, 1932). All quotations from Spenser are taken from this edition, hereafter cited as *Spenser Variorum*.

20. Quoted from John Wilson, "The Fairy Queen," *Blackwoods Magazine* 36 (1834): 429 in *Spenser Variorum*, 1:496.

21. David Cressy, *Bonfires and Bells: National Memory and the Protestant Calendar in Elizabethan and Stuart England* (Berkeley: University of California Press, 1989), pp. 20–21.

22. Although she says nothing about the House of Pride, Rosemond Tuve demonstrates numerous continuities between medieval and Renaissance allegories in *Allegorical Imagery: Some Medieval Books and Their Posterity* (Princeton: Princeton University Press, 1966).

23. Milton retains Augustine's concept of evil as lack, but Satan's heroic individualism obscures this fact. See Peter A. Fiore, *Milton and Augustine: Patterns of Augustinian Thought in "Paradise Lost"* (University Park: Pennsylvania State University Press, 1981), pp. 12–22; also Stephen M. Fallon, *Milton Among the Philosophers: Poetry and Materialism in Seventeenth-Century England* (Ithaca: Cornell University Press, 1991), pp. 168–93.

24. See especially the notes and apparatus in Edmund Spenser, *Books I and II of "The Faerie Queene,"* ed. Robert Kellogg and Oliver Steele (New York: Odyssey Press, 1965).

25. Gerald Morgan, "Holiness as the First of Spenser's Aristotelian Moral Virtues," *Modern Language Review* 81 (1986): 817–37. On St. Thomas's influence, see C. B. Schmitt, *Aristotle and the Renaissance* (Cambridge: Harvard University Press, 1983); Schmitt, "Philosophy and Science in Sixteenth-Century Universities: Some Preliminary Comments," in *The Cultural Context of Medieval Learning*, ed. J. E. Murdoch and E. D. Sylla (Dordrecht, 1975), pp. 113–21; and W. T. Costello, *The Scholastic Curriculum at Early Seventeenth-Century Cambridge* (Cambridge: Harvard University Press, 1958). Tuve acutely but briefly remarks on Spenser's and Aquinas's placement of holiness among the moral virtues (*Allegorical Imagery*, p. 68).

26. Originally, New Critics justified this dismissal by T. S. Eliot's observation that poets are no more reliable critics of their own poems than anyone else. Poems are self-sufficient artifacts. Although

this position is now thoroughly discredited, the argument has lingered.

27. *The Summa of St. Thomas Aquinas*, trans. Fathers of the English Dominican Province (New York: Benziger Brothers, 1947), 2:1533–34 (2–2.81.8). All quotations from the *Summa* are from this edition. See Morgan, "Holiness," p. 821.

28. *The Works of John Selden* (London, 1726), 3:1760, as cited by Morgan, "Holiness," p. 821; Donne, "Satire III," l. 43.

29. Cicero, *Rhetoric* (2.53) as cited in *Summa* (2–2.81.1).

30. Augustine, *De vera Religione* (55); cited in *Summa* (2–2.81.2).

31. *Summa* (2–2.81.6).

32. Morgan, "Holiness," p. 821.

33. *Summa* (2–2.82, 83, 89, 90).

34. For Milton, baptism was the *sine qua non*; his two favorite Bible verses were John 3:16 ("God so loved the world, that he gave his only begotten Son") and Matthew 28:19 ("Go ye therefore, and teach all nations, baptizing them in the name of the Father, and of the Son, and of the Holy Ghost"). See Michael Bauman, *A Scripture Index to John Milton's De doctrina christiana* (Binghamton: Medieval & Renaissance Texts & Studies, 1989), p. 175.

35. *Complete Prose Works of John Milton*, ed. Don M. Wolfe et al. (New Haven: Yale University Press, 1973), 6:294. Doubt has been cast on Milton's authorship of this work; he seems to invoke the Holy Spirit under the name of Urania in *Paradise Lost*.

36. Emile Legouis, *Spenser* (Paris, 1924), pp. 233–37; cited in *Spenser Variorum*, 1:441; F. M. Padelford, "The Spiritual Allegory of the *Faerie Queene*, Book One," *JEGP* 22 (1923): 1–17, cited in *Spenser Variorum*, 1:439. For more recent discussion, see Darryl J. Gless, *Interpretation and Theology in Spenser* (Cambridge: Cambridge University Press, 1994), pp. 142–71.

37. Although there were significant differences between Reformers and Catholics on the issue of faith and works, it was something of a Protestant canard to argue that Catholics held that good deeds could be efficacious without grace. As indicated by many discussions among medieval theologians and confirmed by the Council of Trent (see chapter 2 above) it was never an orthodox Catholic position that good works unaided by grace could absolve from sin.

38. *Everyman*, in *Medieval Drama*, ed. David Bevington (Boston: Houghton Mifflin, 1975), pp. 939–63; all quotations from the poem use this edition. Square brackets are supplied by Bevington.

39. Una is defined largely in opposition to Duessa, a figure whose religious and political significance has been far more carefully studied than hers. See, e.g., D. Douglas Waters, *Duessa as Theological Satire* (Columbia: University of Missouri Press, 1970), and Richard A. McCabe, "The Masks of Duessa: Spenser, Mary Queen of Scots, and James VI,"

English Literary Renaissance 17 (1987): 224–42. The only recent study that devotes much attention to Una as a romance object is Richard A. Levin, "The Legend of the Redcrosse Knight and Una: or Of the Love of a Good Woman," *Studies in English Literature* 31 (1991): 1–24. But Levin does not try to deal with the implications that their love (which he finds critics have neglected) has for the political and religious allegory.

40. F. M. Padelford, "The Spiritual Allegory of the *Faerie Queene*, Book One," in the Spenser *Variorum*, 1:433–34. I refer to early comments from the variorum for much the same reason that Jonathan Goldberg does in *Endlesse Worke: Spenser and the Structures of Discourse* (Baltimore: Johns Hopkins University Press, 1981); they raise many issues neglected by more sophisticated intermediate criticism.

41. As its title suggests, the whole argument of Jonathan Goldberg's *Endlesse Worke* is to say that nothing in *The Faerie Queene*, including marriages, is ever closed or resolved. Kenneth Gross elegantly restates the developing consensus in *Spenserian Poetics: Idolatry, Iconoclasm, and Magic* (Ithaca: Cornell University Press, 1985), p. 130: "Book I's Eden of the end becomes, if not the original Eden of loss, then, strangely, an Eden of deferral, even while the interrupted marriage foreshadows all later deferrals in the poem."

42. See Barbara Kiefer Lewalski, *Protestant Poetics and the Seventeenth-Century Religious Lyric* (Princeton: Princeton University Press, 1979), p. 304. The most influential source in England for this reading of Revelation was John Bale, *The Image of Both Churches* (London, 1548), p. 404. The underlying importance to Protestantism (and modernity) of the displacement of the "true" Church by a false one through most of Christian history is well argued by Anthony Kemp, *The Estrangement of the Past* (Oxford: Oxford University Press, 1991).

43. See *Faerie Queene* 1.3.30 and David Lee Miller, *The Poem's Two Bodies: The Poetics of the 1590 "Faerie Queene"* (Princeton: Princeton University Press, 1988), p. 83.

44. Padelford, "Spiritual Allegory," 1:434. I discuss this topic in *The Reinvention of Love*, esp. pp. 65–86, where further citations are given.

45. See William M. Lamont, *Godly Rule: Politics and Religion 1603–60* (London: Macmillan, 1969), pp. 28–55; the preamble is cited from p. 34.

46. McCabe, "Masks of Duessa," p. 227.

47. On the betrothal as unbreakable, see 1.12.36–37.

48. *The Poems of John Donne*, ed. Herbert J. C. Grierson (London: Oxford University Press, 1912), 1:330.

49. *Poems of John Donne*, 1:158, ll. 95–97; *Complete Prose Works of John Milton*, 2:543.

50. John Calvin, *Institutes of the Christian Religion*, trans. Ford Lewis Battles, ed. John T. McNeill (Philadelphia: Westminster Press, 1960),

2:976 (3.24.8). The unbearable problem of the fate of children led some later Calvinists to retreat from individual election to the presumption that God accords election to families and especially to children of the elect. The two views, seen in Books I and II of *Pilgrim's Progress*, found historical expression in the Massachusetts Bay Colony.

51. For evidence of Donne's knowledge of the traditional trope, which he understands to represent an indissoluble marriage between Christ and the soul, in his Sermon preached before the King at Whitehall, 24 February 1625/26, see Low, *The Reinvention of Love*, p. 65.

Notes to Chapter Four

1. Gertrude Stein, *The Making of Americans* (New York: Albert & Charles Boni, 1926; Normal Illinois: Dalkey Archive Press, 1995), p. 3.

2. After this chapter was written (mostly in 1995) and a shorter version appeared in *English Literary Renaissance* 29 (1999): 443–67, Stephen Greenblatt's *Hamlet in Purgatory* (Princeton: Princeton University Press, 2001) was published. Since our studies developed independently, it seems best simply to cite Greenblatt here without attempting to add further cross references.

3. Stein, *Everybody's Autobiography* (New York: Cooper Square Publishers, 1971), pp. 133, 142; see also pp. 132, 138–39. *The Diary of Virginia Woolf*, ed. Anne Olivier Bell assisted by Andrew McNellie (New York: Harcourt Brace Jovanovich, 1980), 3:208; see also Vara S. Neverow, *The Diacritics of Desire: Virginia Woolf and the Rhetoric of Modernism and Feminism* (Ann Arbor: University Microfilms International, 1989), which brought this passage to my attention. J. Hillis Miller, "The Critic As Host," *Deconstruction and Criticism* (New York: Continuum, 1979), p. 251.

4. The secular-minded object because it makes modernism seem inversely parasitic on religion; Christians object because it seems to deny the continuing vitality of their religion. Christianity thrives today in America, but has been declared marginal by political and cultural arbiters. If one defines secularization as the weakening of bonds between religion and the dominant culture, not the weakening of religion itself, its prevalence in modern times is evident.

5. All Shakespeare's works except *Hamlet* are cited from *The Complete Poems and Plays of William Shakespeare*, ed. William Allan Neilson and Charles Jarvis Hill (Cambridge: Houghton Mifflin, Riverside Press, 1942). In *How Milton Works* (Cambridge: Harvard University Press, 2001), pp. 511–18, which came to my attention as this book was going to press, Stanley Fish discusses how Satan in *Paradise Lost* internally re-creates himself at the moment of his fall.

6. To Tillyard one may add Arthur O. Lovejoy, *The Great Chain of*

Being: A Study of the History of an Idea (Cambridge: Harvard University Press, 1936).

7. Although my focus is on *Hamlet*, not on the facts of Shakespeare's life, I should mention the recent revival of interest in the theory that Shakespeare was Catholic. See especially Richard Wilson's "Shakespeare and the Jesuits," on the internet at http://www.lancs.ac.uk/users/english/research/shakespeare/jesuits.html, expanded from his "Shakespeare and the Jesuits: New Connections Supporting the Theory of the Lost Catholic Years in Lancashire," *Times Literary Supplement* (Dec. 19, 1997): 11–13. Among recent studies on Catholic elements or tendencies in the plays, see especially the essays by David N. Beauregard, OMV, in *Renascence, Ben Jonson Journal, Religion and the Arts*, and elsewhere.

8. For a detailed study with no axe to grind (except occasional overeagerness to debunk pious accounts), see Jacques Le Goff, *The Birth of Purgatory*, trans. Arthur Goldhammer (Chicago: University of Chicago Press, 1984).

9. See, e.g., R. N. Swanson, *Church and Society in Late Medieval England* (Oxford: Basil Blackwell, 1989). The Crown's chief interest in fraternities, as with other religious activities, was to license them for stiff fees, leading historians to suspect that many went unrecorded.

10. Caroline M. Barron, "The Parish Fraternities of Medieval London," *The Church in Pre-Reformation Society*, ed. Barron and Christopher Harper-Bill (Woodbridge: Boydell Press, 1985), p. 33.

11. Miri Rubin, "Corpus Christi Fraternities and Late Medieval Piety," *Voluntary Religion*, ed. W. J. Sheils and Diana Wood (Oxford: Basil Blackwell, 1986), pp. 103–04. J. J. Scarisbrick, *The Reformation and the English People* (Oxford: Basil Blackwell, 1984), pp. 19–20.

12. See John Bossy, "The Mass as a Social Institution 1200–1700," *Past and Present* 100 (1983): 39.

13. Colin Richmond, "The English Gentry and Religion, *c.* 1500," *Religious Beliefs and Ecclesiastical Careers in Late Medieval England*, ed. Christopher Harper-Bill (Woodbridge: Boydell Press, 1991), pp. 121–25.

14. W. K. Jordan, *Edward VI: The Threshold of Power* (Cambridge: Harvard University Press, 1970), p. 181.

15. Theo Brown, *The Fate of the Dead: A Study in Folk Eschatology in the West Country after the Reformation* (London: D. S. Brewer and Rowman and Littlefield for The Folklore Society, 1979), p. 15.

16. For a good general history, see Alan Kreider, *English Chantries: The Road to Dissolution* (Cambridge: Harvard University Press, 1979).

17. Virginia R. Bainbridge, *Gilds in the Medieval Countryside: Social and Religious Change in Cambridgeshire c. 1350–1558* (Woodbridge: Boydell Press, 1997), pp. 96–97. David Cressy, *Birth Marriage and Death: Ritual, Religion and the Life-Cycle in Tudor and Stuart*

England (Oxford: Oxford University Press, 1997), pp. 396–420, suggests that old customs of burial rite, prayer, and remembrance lingered among recusant nonconformists for several generations, usually in secret.

18. Edward T. Bonahue, Jr., "Citizen History: Stow's *Survey of London*," *Studies in English Literature* 38 (1998): 74. Bonahue cites John Stow, *Survey of London*, ed. C. L. Kingsford (Oxford: Clarendon Press, 1908), 1:253.

19. See Latimer's "Sermon of the Plow," first published as *A notable Sermon of the reverende father Maister Hughe Latemer, whiche he preached at the Shrouds at paules churche in London, on the xviii. daye of January* (London, 1548).

20. Scarisbrick, *Reformation and the English People*, pp. 92–93.

21. *The Works of John Milton*, vol. 2, ed. Frank Allen Patterson, et al. (New York: Columbia University Press, 1931).

22. All quotations from *Hamlet* are from The Arden Shakespeare, second series, ed. Harold Jenkins, gen. eds. Una Ellis-Fermor et al. (London: Methuen, 1982; Routledge, 1989).

23. Purgatory is usually mentioned but briefly, with the notable exception of John Dover Wilson, *What Happens in Hamlet* (Cambridge: Cambridge University Press, 1964), pp. 60–86. Eleanor Prosser discusses the issue at length in *Hamlet and Revenge*, 2d ed. (Stanford: Stanford University Press, 1971), pp. 97–143, but concludes that the Ghost's identity is ambiguous. In the Arden Shakespeare Jenkins alludes to purgatory when he cites More's *Supplication of Souls* to gloss "fast," but his remark that "hell, after all, was physical, and its torments often included hunger" (1.5.11n) implies that we are dealing with hell, not purgatory.

24. *Hamlet* 1.5.12n.

25. The Q1 stage direction includes "Priest" among those who enter with Ophelia's corpse at 5.1.211; Q2 omits this. F has *"Priest"* as speech-head at 5.1.219 and 228; Q2 has *"Doct."* The early editions do not list *Dramatis Personae*.

26. Letter to the Editor, *Culture Wars* 20 (2001): 9, 47.

27. Thomas Becon, *Comparison of the Lord's Supper and Mass* (1564), cited in the *Oxford English Dictionary*, which says that "housel" went out of use in the sixteenth century.

28. *Hamlet*, 1.5.77n.

29. See Guy Bedouelle, "The Consultations of the Universities and Scholars Concerning the 'Great Matter' of King Henry VIII," in *The Bible in the Sixteenth Century*, ed. David C. Steinmetz. Durham: Duke University Press, 1990, pp. 21–36, 200–02.

30. Le Goff, *The Birth of Purgatory*, p. 82.

31. Dover Wilson, *What Happens in Hamlet*, pp. 60–86.

32. Brown, *The Fate of the Dead*; Norman Cohn, *The Pursuit of the Millennium*, 2d ed. (New York: Harper & Brothers, 1961).

33. *Hamlet*, 1.5.138n. Jenkins quotes a prominent Protestant authority, Lewes Lavater, *Of Ghosts and Spirits Walking by Night*, trans. R. H. (London, 1572), 3.6.

34. Saint Augustine, *Confessions* (9.13.36–37), as cited in Le Goff, *The Birth of Purgatory*, p. 65. Goldhammer credits R. S. Pine-Coffin as translator; probably from the Penguin edition or the Chicago Great Books. On the efficacy of Masses for the dead, see Bossy, "Mass as a Social Institution."

35. See Le Goff, pp. 63ff.

36. Ibid., p. 45, quoting from Salomon Reinach, "De l'origine des prières pour les morts," *Revue des Etudes juives* 41 (1900): 164.

37. Virgil, *Aeneid* 6.373, 376. In *Virgil*, trans. H. Rushton Fairclough, Loeb Classical Library (Cambridge: Harvard University Press, 1953), 1:532; my translation.

38. Dover Wilson, *What Happens in Hamlet*, p. 72.

39. Le Goff, *The Birth of Purgatory*, pp. 193–201.

40. In e-mail exchanges with me, R. B. Mullin and David N. Beauregard, OMV, have helped clarify Church of England practice on the burial of suicides. Richmond S. H. Noble, in *Shakespeare's Biblical Knowledge and Use of the Book of Common Prayer* (London: SPCK, 1935), quoting Canon 68 of Church of England, *Canons and Constitutions* (1604), says: "no minister was to refuse to bury any corpse brought to the churchyard unless 'the party deceased were denounced excommunicated *majori excommunicatione*, for some grievous and notorious crime, and no man able to testify of his repentance'" (p. 84). As Fr. Beauregard notes, "Here suicide is not specified as being a grievous crime, but custom would most probably have presumed it so." By 1662, Mullin adds, the Book of Common Prayer specifies in "The Order of Burial of the Dead" that "the Office ensuing is not to be used for any that die unbaptized, or excommunicate, or have laid violent hands upon themselves." Suicide is now clearly specified; it was not thought necessary to do so in earlier editions. Church cemeteries were further opened to those buried without Church of England rites in the Burial Amendment Act of 1880. According to Cressy, in *Birth Marriage and Death*, baptized Catholics, nonconformists, and offenders who died before resolving excommunication were usually allowed burial in consecrated ground. Unbaptized babies were "often given the benefit of the doubt." Only "suicide or irreversible excommunication" forfeited the traditional right that "had continued for more than a thousand years and was unbroken by the protestant reformation" (p. 465).

41. Martin Holmes, *The Guns of Elsinore: A New Approach to 'Hamlet'* (London: Chatto & Windus, 1964), p. 156.

42. Edmund Spenser, "The Ruines of Time" (line 196), in *The Works of Edmund Spenser* (Baltimore: Johns Hopkins University Press, 1947), 8:42.

43. The stage direction at 5.1.211 reads *"corse"* in Q2 and *"Coffin"* in Q1 and F. All read "The corse they follow" in the text (5.1.211).

44. See G. W. Pigman, III, *Grief and English Renaissance Elegy* (Cambridge: Cambridge University Press, 1985), pp. 16–39. For a recent study of psychological attitudes toward the dead, see Heather Dubrow, "The Message from Marcade: Parental Death in Tudor and Stuart England," in *Attending to Women in Early Modern England*, ed. Betty S. Travitsky and Adele F. Seeff (Newark: University of Delaware Press, 1994), pp. 147–67.

45. Matthew Parker, *A Funeral Sermon . . . Preached at S. Maries in Cambridge, Anno 1551, at the buriall of . . . Martin Bucer*, trans. Thomas Newton (London, 1587), sig. A4^v, cited by Pigman, *Grief and English Renaissance Elegy*, p. 29. I have regularized u and v.

46. Augustine, *City of God* (21.24), as cited by Le Goff, *The Birth of Purgatory*, p. 67.

47. Cited by Bossy, "Mass as a Social Institution," p. 43.

48. Alastair Fowler, "The Case Against Hamlet," *Times Literary Supplement* (December 22, 1995), p. 7.

49. Bossy, "Mass as a Social Institution," p. 43.

50. For vivid details, see Eamon Duffy, *The Stripping of the Altars*, pp. 454–58.

51. George William Rutler, *A Crisis of Saints: Essays on People and Principles* (San Francisco: Ignatius Press, 1995), pp. 118–19.

52. Bainbridge, *Gilds in the Medieval Countryside*, p. 97.

Notes to Chapter Five

1. *Of Education*, in John Milton, *Complete Poems and Major Prose*, ed. Merritt Y. Hughes (New York: Odyssey Press, 1957), pp. 631, 635; p. 635, n. 54. All quotations are from this edition; prose is cited by page, poetry by line number.

2. Alasdair MacIntyre gives an excellent description of the process in two books: *After Virtue: A Study in Moral Theory*, 2d edition (Notre Dame: University of Notre Dame Press, 1984) and *Whose Justice? Which Rationality?* (Notre Dame: University of Notre Dame Press, 1988).

3. For a fuller discussion of Milton's essentially Arminian position with regard to grace, see Dennis Richard Danielson, *Milton's Good God: A Study in Literary Theodicy* (Cambridge: Cambridge University Press, 1982). Georgia B. Christopher, *Milton and the Science of the Saints* (Princeton: Princeton University Press, 1982), acutely discusses the theological issues without, however, sufficiently distinguishing Milton's position from Calvin's.

4. C. S. Lewis, *A Preface to "Paradise Lost"* (Oxford: Oxford University Press, 1942), p. 70.

5. *St. Augustine's Enchiridion: Or Manual to Laurentius Concerning Faith, Hope, and Charity*, trans. Ernest Evans (London: S.P.C.K., 1953) p. 28 (IX.30).

6. To an extent,"Anglican" is an anachronistic term, since it sees the sixteenth and seventeenth centuries as the Oxford Movement saw them. Still, it is a convenient shorthand for the Elizabethan establishment and the Church which grew from it.

7. See Stephen M. Fallon, "'Elect Above the Rest': Theology as Self-Representation in Milton," in *Milton and Heresy*, ed. Stephen B. Dobranski and John P. Rumrich (Cambridge: Cambridge University Press, 1998), pp. 93–116. Fallon accounts for this passage as an "incompletely assimilated gesture" in Milton's "self-construction as a heroic and select servant of God" (p. 110). He cites earlier commentary, including Maurice Kelley, *This Great Argument: A Study of Milton's De Doctrina Christiana as a Gloss upon Paradise Lost* (Princeton: Princeton University Press, 1941), pp. 14–20. One might also mention Christopher Hill, *Milton and the English Revolution* (New York: Viking Press, 1977), who puts Milton in the company of "left" or "radical" Arminians (pp. 268–78). I find Milton's view that some individuals are specially elect even though all are called less unusual or contradictory than Fallon does, since there is considerable biblical support for it in the calling of the patriarchs and prophets and in the Pauline text cited just below.

8. Much of this paragraph, and the use of Bunyan as an example, stems from a response by Ralph C. Wood and David Lyle Jeffries to a talk I gave at Baylor (based on chapter 6 below).

9. The fullest recent discussion of Milton and Descartes is Stephen M. Fallon, *Milton Among the Philosophers: Poetry and Materialism in Seventeenth-Century England* (Ithaca: Cornell University Press, 1991). Fallon's focus is chiefly on the significance of Descartes for modern materialism, mine on modern subjectivity.

10. Robert Thomas Fallon, *Divided Empire: Milton's Political Imagery* (University Park: Pennsylvania State University Press, 1995).

11. *The Works of John Milton*, ed. Frank A. Patterson, et al. (New York: Columbia University Press, 1932), 6:169.

12. Michael H. Keefer, "The Dreamer's Path: Descartes and the Sixteenth Century," *Renaissance Quarterly* 49 (1996): 36–37. In describing the dream I paraphrase as well as quote from Keefer.

13. Ibid., p. 68.

Notes to Chapter Six

1. Louis L. Martz, *The Paradise Within: Studies in Vaughan, Traherne, and Milton* (New Haven: Yale University Press, 1964), pp. 106, 166. Further along these lines, see also Martz's *The Poem of the Mind:*

Essays on Poetry English and American (London: Oxford University Press, 1966).

2. For more on Milton's rejection of any and all Churches in historical time see my *The Reinvention of Love: Poetry, Politics and Culture from Sidney to Milton* (Cambridge: Cambridge University Press, 1993), pp. 158–77, 180–84.

3. See chapter 5.

4. On prudence, see Josef Pieper's excellent historical and philosophical analysis in *The Four Cardinal Virtues* (Notre Dame: University of Notre Dame Press, 1966), pp. 3–40; on *recta ratio* see Robert Hoopes, *Right Reason in the English Renaissance* (Cambridge: Harvard University Press, 1962).

5. *Complete Prose Works of John Milton*, ed. Ernest Sirluck (New Haven: Yale University Press, 1959), 2:688, hereafter cited as Yale Prose Works. See s.v. "prudence" and "prudent" in Laurence Sterne and Harold H. Kollmeier, eds., *A Concordance to the English Prose of John Milton* (Binghamton: Medieval & Renaissance Texts & Studies, 1985). Milton is familiar with the Thomistic rearrangement of the Aristotelian virtues, "Piety, Justice, Prudence, Temperance" (*Eikonoklastes*, Yale Prose Works 3:542), where piety corresponds with Spenser's Holiness in Book I of *The Faerie Queene*, as well as the classical version, "valor, justice, constancy, prudence" (*Eikonoklastes*, Yale Prose Works 3:348). Rarely does Milton use the word in its cynical, modern, Machiavellian sense, as when Satan abruptly adjourns the Great Consult, "Prudent" lest another take credit for his bold venture (*PL* 2.468). Since Satan parodies the virtues, this usage is not surprising.

6. See Peter Berek, "'Plain' and 'Ornate' Styles and the Structure of *Paradise Lost*," PMLA 85 (1970): 237–46.

7. Augustine, *Confessions*, trans. R. S. Pine-Coffin (London: Penguin Books, 1961), pp. 231–32 (10.27).

8. Thomas Nagel, *The Last Word* (Oxford: Oxford University Press, 1999). For more on the implications of Nagel's argument, see the passage quoted from his book with responses by several contributors in Sandra Menssen, ed., "From a Logical Point of View," *Logos* 5 (2002): 157–83, which appeared as this book was going to press. For broad discussion of the theological implications of the postmodernist rejection of meaning, see R. V. Young, *At War with the Word: Literary Theory and Liberal Education* (Wilmington: ISI Books, 1999), pp. 31–58.

9. Similarly, it has often been said that Milton's technique of "stationing" anticipates the movies. John Collier contributes to the efforts of many writers to naturalize the epic for their times in *Milton's Paradise Lost: Screenplay for Cinema of the Mind* (New York: Alfred A. Knopf, 1973).

10. C. S. Lewis, *Surprised by Joy* (London: Geoffrey Bles, 1955),

p. 206; cited by Stephen Logan, "Old Western Man for Our Times," *Renascence* 51 (1998): 72.

11. Logan, "Old Western Man," p. 72.

12. Hughes, *Areopagitica*, p. 728.

13. Logan, "Old Western Man," p. 72. Stanley Fish, in *How Milton Works* (Cambridge: Harvard University Press, 2001), pp. 168–72, suggests with reference to the Lady in *Comus* that for Milton there are two ways of regarding the inner self, or as Fish puts it, two kinds "narcissism," one healthy, the other destructive. Fish kindly sent me a copy of his book as mine was going to press.

14. Translated by Hughes, p. 135.

15. David Riesman, in collaboration with Reuel Denney and Nathan Glazer, *The Lonely Crowd: A Study of the Changing American Character* (New Haven: Yale University Press, 1950).

16. Thomas Hobbes, *Leviathan*, ed. C. B. MacPherson (London: Penguin Books, 1968), pp. 264–65 (2.21). On Milton and Hobbesian materialism, see Stephen M. Fallon, *Milton Among the Philosophers: Poetry and Materialism in Seventeenth-Century England* (Ithaca: Cornell University Press, 1991).

17. C. S. Lewis, *A Preface to Paradise Lost* (London: Oxford University Press, 1942), pp. 112–15. Because Milton tells us that one reason God creates Adam and Eve is to fill up the gap left by the fallen angels, we can deduce that the angelic population is probably fixed and therefore that whatever the angels enjoy with one another cannot be procreative sex, but rather some form of divinely sanctioned love, affection, intimacy, and companionship. Since the materiality of Milton's angels is itself unorthodox, the matter cannot be certainly resolved.

18. *Epitaphium Damonis*, 171–72; trans. Hughes p. 137.

Notes to Chapter Seven

1. Harold Bloom, *The Western Canon* (New York: Harcourt Brace, 1994), p. 73.

2. Bloom, p. 170. On Milton's debt to Shakespeare, see also Helen Gardner, "Milton's Satan and the Theme of Damnation in Elizabethan Tragedy," reprinted as appendix A in *A Reading of Paradise Lost* (Oxford: Clarendon Press, 1965), pp. 99–120.

3. Stephen Greenblatt, *Shakespearean Negotiations: The Circulation of Social Energy in Renaissance England* (Berkeley: University of California Press, 1988).

4. Theodore Spencer, *Shakespeare and the Nature of Man* (New York: Macmillan, 1942). The review is quoted on the cover of the Macmillan Paperback edition, 1961.

5. Jean-Paul Sartre, *Existentialism* (New York: Philosophical Library,

1947), p. 18; cited by Josef Pieper, *The Four Cardinal Virtues* (New York: Pantheon, 1954), who says that Sartre "originated this existentialist thesis" (pp. 49–50). For trenchant comments on the rejection of human nature from one of the least-loved of critics today, see also C. S. Lewis, *The Abolition of Man* (New York: Macmillan, 1947).

6. Mead's *Coming of Age in Samoa* (New York: Blue Ribbon Books, 1928) has been the single most widely influential anthropological study. The scientific value of the book was put into question by Derek Freeman, *Margaret Mead and Samoa* (Cambridge: Harvard University Press, 1983); in the succeeding controversy few of the disputants have discussed Mead's work on its merits — i.e., whether what she argues is demonstrably true or false on the evidence. It certainly appears that she projected her own psychological needs and desires upon the Samoans, making them seem more tolerant of casual sex and more guilt-free than they actually were.

7. David M. Halperin, *Saint Foucault* (Oxford University Press, 1995); quotation from the Oxford University Press catalog, "Literary Studies, 1994–95," p. 18.

8. See Eve K. Sedgwick, *Between Men* (New York: Columbia University Press, 1985), Jonathan Goldberg, *Sodometries: Renaissance Texts, Modern Sexualities* (Stanford: Stanford University Press, 1992), and Goldberg, ed., *Queering the Renaissance*, (Durham: Duke University Press, 1994). The problems such approaches pose for homosexuals and other advocates — in particular, that what has been socially "constructed" by one group may as easily be "deconstructed" by another — are tellingly posed by Joseph Cady in his review of Goldberg's *Sodometries* in *Renaissance Quarterly* 47 (1994): 675–78, and in his "'Masculine Love,' Renaissance Writing, and the 'New Invention' of Homosexuality," *Homosexuality in Renaissance and Enlightenment England*, ed. Claude J. Summers (Haworth Press, 1992), pp. 9–40, which suggest that these views are ahistorical. Cady's is, however, a minority voice against the established constructionist views.

9. Berkeley: University of California Press, 1995; the advertisement is in *PMLA* 110 (1995): 311.

10. Francis Bacon, *The Proficience and Advancement of Learning* (1605), in *Francis Bacon: A Selection of His Works*, ed. Sidney Warhaft (Toronto and London: Macmillan, 1965), pp. 235–36.

11. Anne Ferry, *The "Inward" Language: Sonnets of Wyatt, Sidney, Shakespeare, Donne* (Chicago: University of Chicago Press, 1983), p. xi. I repeat that I have chosen Ferry to represent the best and most sensible advocacy of such views. It would be easy to cite many more extreme or unthinking exponents. And there are some cracks in the façade of agreement. In *The Birth of the Modern Mind: Self, Consciousness, and the Invention of the Sonnet* (New York: Columbia University Press, 1989),

Paul Oppenheimer argues that subjectivity arose circa 1220, not 1620. More significantly, A. Kent Hieatt, in "The Alleged Early Modern Origin of the Self and History: Terminate or Regroup," *Spenser Studies* 10 (1992): 1–35, questions on commonsensical grounds the whole idea of a new birth of subjectivity.

12. Science fiction writers, responsive to popular cultural assumptions, have pioneered in expressing such views. Drawing on anthropology and advertising, Damon Knight's *Hell's Pavement* (New York: Lion Books, 1955) was among the first to examine the assumption, common in later science fiction, that people are what discontinuous cultures make them; Frederic Pohl's *Beyond the Blue Event Horizon* (New York: Ballantine Books, 1980) looks at the psychological implications of discontinuity.

13. In *The Light in Troy* (New Haven: Yale University Press, 1982), Thomas M. Greene argues that Petrarch felt distanced from the classical past. Virgil gives indications of a similar estrangement from his Greek predecessors.

14. On evolution of consciousness see Owen Barfield, *Saving the Appearances: A Study in Idolatry*, 2nd ed. (Middlebury: Wesleyan University Press, 1988).

15. Brian Vickers and others have argued that Saussure himself did not actually draw these conclusions. We possess only his reconstructed lecture notes, interpreted (perhaps incorrectly) by others. For convenience I call such views "neo-Saussurean."

16. "What is an Author?" in *The Foucault Reader*, ed. Paul Rabinow (New York: Random House, 1984), p. 110; cited in R. V. Young, *At War with the Word* (Wilmington: ISI Books, 1999), p. 89.

17. Briefly, introjection is the term preferred by Freud and psychoanalysis, positive reinforcement by the behaviorist school of B. J. Skinner, social control by sociologist Stanley Milgram, manipulation of cultural energies by Stephen Greenblatt and the new historicists. All these terms and views agree in positing that man is the product of purely material processes, a black box lacking free will or a created soul.

18. My paraphrase of Young, pp. 102–04, discussing and quoting introductory comments by Jean E. Howard and Marion F. O'Connor, eds., *Shakespeare Reproduced: The Text in History and Ideology* (London: Methuen, 1987), pp. 1–17.

19. More recently this policy was retooled and revived by Tony Blair, Gerhardt Schroeder, and Bill Clinton, whose massive bombing and occupation of parts of Yugoslavia had the avowed intent of teaching the tribal inhabitants to be free, tolerant, and modern.

20. Hughes, p. 671.

21. On the familiar story of Satan's influence on the Romantics and,

through them, modernity, see especially Lucy Newlin, *Paradise Lost and the Romantic Reader* (Oxford: Clarendon Press, 1993). Also of considerable interest is Valentin Boss, *Milton and the Rise of Russian Satanism* (Toronto: University of Toronto Press, 1991).

22. As Boss notes (pp. 85, 126), for Voltaire Satan's usefulness in attacking the Church was undermined by his disgusting relationship with Sin and Death. How influential Milton's Satan, as opposed to the Satan of his Catholic education, was on Joyce is debatable, yet it is hard to imagine Stephen Daedalus adopting the motto — and with it the Romantic stance — of *non serviam* without the tradition running from Milton through Blake and Byron (who is Stephen's hero).

23. See Low, *The Reinvention of Love: Poetry, Politics and Culture from Sidney to Milton* (Cambridge: Cambridge University Press, 1993), pp. 178–201. The discussion of privacy in Donne (pp. 31–64) is also relevant.

Notes to Appendix

1. Thomas N. Tentler, *Sin and Confession on the Eve of the Reformation* (Princeton: Princeton University Press, 1977), p. 3.

2. Even before the Reformation, the theology of the Atonement had a long history of development; see especially St. Anselm's influential treatise *Cur Deus homo?*

3. According to the *Catechism of the Catholic Church* (United States Catholic Conference, 1994), "Only God forgives sins" (p. 362; 1441); "The confessor is not the master of God's forgiveness, but its servant" (p. 368; 1466).

4. All biblical quotations are from the Holy Bible, Authorized or King James Version.

5. "Since ancient times the bishop, visible head of a particular Church, has thus rightfully been considered to be the one who principally has the power and ministry of reconciliation: he is the moderator of the penitential discipline. Priests, his collaborators, exercise it to the extent that they have received the commission either from their bishop (or religious superior) or the Pope, according to the law of the Church" (*Catechism of the Catholic Church*, p. 367; 1462).

6. The *Catechism of the Catholic Church* cites this verse in connection with the power of the keys (981; p. 256).

7. See, e.g., Edward V. Dargin, *Reserved Cases according to the Code of Canon Law*, unpublished dissertation (Washington: Catholic University of America, 1924); or Henry C. Lea's whiggishly biased but bountifully documented study, *The History of Auricular Confession* (Philadelphia and London, 1896), 1:314–46. Conflicts of authority between diocesan bishops and abbots of religious orders were a source

of frequent dispute, giving the laity some latitude in choosing their confessors.

8. As Lawrence G. Duggan remarks in "Fear and Confession," *Archiv für Reformationsgesichte* 75 (1984): 164, every council and synod for three hundred years following the Fourth Lateran Council forbade charging fees for confession. *The Riverside Chaucer*, ed. Larry D. Benson, 3rd edition (Boston: Houghton Mifflin, 1987). All quotations from Chaucer are from this edition, citations are to line number.

9. Miri Rubin, "Corpus Christi Fraternities and Late Medieval Piety," *Voluntary Religion*, ed. W. J. Sheils and Diana Wood, Papers Read at the . . . Ecclesiastical History Society (Oxford: Basil Blackwell, 1986), pp. 103–04.

10. Chaucer translated much of "The Parson's Tale" directly from the standard penitential manuals, especially the thirteenth century *Summa de poenitentia* of St. Raymund of Pennaforte and *Summa vitiorum* of William Peraldus. Siegfried Wenzel, in *Chaucer Review* 16 (1982): 248–51, suggests that the tale is generically a penitential manual, not a sermon — although many sermons were modeled closely on the manuals, making the distinction difficult.

11. These lines are based closely on the *Summa de poenitentia*. The synod of Breslau (1446) likewise speaks of three kinds of penance: public, solemn, and private, although Duggan suggests that by then the two public forms were uncommon ("Fear and Confession," p. 162).

12. See, for example, Andrew Milner, *John Milton and the English Revolution: A Study in the Sociology of Literature* (London: Macmillan, 1981).

INDEX

absolution, 63–64, 76
Acts of Restraint of Appeals (1533), 91–92
adultery, 41, 68
The Advancement of Learning (Bacon), 5, 212n5, 220n51
Aeneid, The (Virgil), xiv, xvii
Alexander, Samuel, 169
alienation. *See* exile
Amores (Ovid), xviii
The Anatomy of Melancholy, 198
Angelica, 62
Anglican Church, 66–67, 84, 91, 107, 148. *See also* Church of England
Anglicans, 135, 231n6
Annales school, xi, 25
anthropology, 187, 191
antiquity, xviii, 184
Apostles' Creed, 27
Aquinas, Saint Thomas, 28, 41, 72–74
Archbishop of Canterbury, 32
Archbishop of York, 32
Archdiocese of York, 38
Areopagitica (Milton), 130, 133–34, 198–99
Argonautica (Apollonius), vii, xvii
Aristotle, 72–74, 131
Auerbach, Erich, xv
Augburg Confession (Luther), 65
Augustine, Saint: on confession, 27–28; and *Confessions*, xiv, xix, 3, 116, 159–60, 211n2; on death, 117; on evil, 72; on popes, 32; on soul, x; on subjectivity, xix, 152
Austen, Jane, 160

Bacon, Sir Francis: and *The Advancement of Learning*, 5, 212n5, 220n51; and human nature, 190–91; and modern school, 46; and scientific method, xiii
Bainbridge, Virginia, 128
Barfield, Owen, 25
Barthelme, Donald, 116
Battaglia, Debbora, 189
Battle of Maldon, 17
Baylor University, xiv
Beatitudes, 64
Beauregard, David N., Fr., xiv

Becket, Saint Thomas á, 205
Bellah, Robert, 14–15
Benedict, Ruth, 187
Ben Johnson Journal, xiii
Beowulf, 13
Bernard de Clairvaux, Saint, 2
Bible, 5–6, 88, 162, 203–9
The Birth of Purgatory (Le Goff), 114
bishops, 39, 104, 107
Bjork Robert E., 11–12
Blake, William, 137, 146, 201
Bloom, Harold, 143, 185, 202
Boas, Franz, 187
Boethius, xix, 152
Boleyn, Anne, 113
Bonahue, Edward, 109
The Book of Common Prayer, 66–69, 91, 107, 135
Borromeo, Charles (Cardinal), 2, 31, 218n22
Bossy, John, 30–31, 33–34, 42–43, 62–63
Bradley, A. C., 187
Brown, Theo, 107
Browne, Sir Thomas, 5

Calvin, John, xix, 77, 95, 131–32, 139, 143–52
Calvinism, 138–39, 147–50
Canterbury Tales (Chaucer), 151, 205–9
Carew, Thomas, 11
Carleton, Sir Dudley, 11
Cartesian eras, 1, 143–52
Catholicism: allegiance to, 60, 77–78; and confession, 30, 63; and Decartes, 149; and laity, 110; and nationalism, 103; and Protestantism, 81, 89, 105, 145–46; and ritual, 78; and sacrament, xii; and sin, 148; and superstition, 118; theological disputes in, 1–2; universality of, 1, 37–38
Chanceries Act of 1547, 127
chastity, 64
Chaucer, Geoffrey, 28, 32, 35, 75, 151, 205–9, 237n10
chivalric rite, 55, 58–59, 76
Christianity: and chivalry, 55; divisions in, 1–2, 226n4; emphasis of, 13–14; in

England, 32; in Europe, 25; and guilt, 59
Christmas, 50–54
Church of England, 70, 74, 86, 89, 100, 107, 229n40. *See also* Anglican Church
Cicero, 73
clergy, 104–5
Cloud of Unknowing (anonymous), 39
Clusa, Jacobus de, 33
Cohn, Norman, 114
Coleridge, Samuel Taylor, 20
Columbus, Christopher, 191
communion of saints, xii
community: and confession, 30; and death, 27; definition of, 25; and prayer, 84; and Reformation, 26; and self, x; and subjectivity, xi, 128
confession: and Anglican Church, 66–67; Augustine on, 27–28; and Bible, 203–9; Bossy on, 30–31, 33–34; and Catholicism, 30, 63; and community, 30; and confessional booth, 31, 33–34, 81; Crammer on, 65; Duggan on, 35–36; in *The Faerie Queene*, 47, 79–82; in fourteenth century, 31–37; and guilt, 26; Luther on, 37, 62, 69; Nichols on, 33; parochial, 31–32; and penance, 25–26, 63, 84–85; and privacy, 33; and Protestantism, 62–70, 81; purposes of, 45–46, 65–66; and Reformation, x; and sacrament, xii, 65; and sin, xii; in *Sir Gawain and the Green Knight*, 47–49; and social control, 25–28; and transubstantiation, 107
Confessions (Augustine), xiv, xix, 3, 116, 159–60, 211n2
confirmation, 74
conscience, 24–25, 139–43, 162–65
Conscience Umpire, 129–53
Coriolanus (Shakespeare), 100–101
Corpus Christi fraternities, 105
Council of Ancyra, 42
Council of Paris (829), 29
Council of Trent, xi, 30, 62, 81, 131, 218n22
Counter-Reformation, x, xi, 2, 37, 105
Crammer, Thomas, 65
Cressy, David, 71
Crosby, John F., 24
Cross, J. E., 14
cultural relativism, 187
cultural transformation, 6
culture: European, 1–4, 31; human, 186–94; Mead on, 187–88; non-Christian, 117; and Reformation, 95–96; and religion, 95; structure of, 15, 183–84, 195

Dante, Alighieri, xii
The Dead Father (Barthelme), 116
Decretum (Gratian), 29
Defoe, Daniel, 68
Delumeau, Jean, 45
Derrida, Jacques, 189
Descartes, René, 129, 143–44, 148–50, 152, 184, 195

Dialogues of Plato, 198
Dickens, Charles, 68
Diodati, Charles, 142, 173–75
Discourse on Method (Descartes), 148
The Doctrine and Discipline of Divorce (Milton), 5–6
Donne, John, 10–11, 73, 93, 96
Dougherty, James, xiii
Downes, Geoffrey, 106
Duffy, Eamon, 32, 38
Duggan, Lawrence, 35–36
Duke of Buckingham, 11

Edwardian Prayerbook of 1549, 100
Edward VI, king of England, 108
Egerton, Sir Thomas, 10
elegiac lyric, 7
Eliot, George, 68
Eliot, T. S., 223–24n26
Empson, William, 146
England: Church of, 67, 70, 74, 86, 89, 100, 107, 229n40; monarchy of, 90–91; Parliament of, 91; and Reformation, 29, 32, 61–62, 104, 108, 110–14; and Renaissance, 4, 11
English Literary Renaissance, xiii
English Reformation, 108
Enlightenment, 21, 26, 97, 99 197, 201
Epitaphium Damonis (Milton), 181
Erasmus, Desiderius, 38
The Estrangement of the Past (Kemp), xii
Eucharist, 28, 74, 105
Europe: Christendom of, 1, 25; culture of, 1–4, 31; and Reformation, 1, 7, 61; and Renaissance, 45
Everyman, 62, 82–86, 90, 95
evil, 72, 223n23
exile: Bjork on, 11–12; definition of, 3, 14, 21; Donne on, 11; forms of, 7–11, 17–18, 21, 184–86; as literary theme, 200–201; and subjectivity, 11–19; suffering of, 15

The Faerie Queene (Spenser), xvii–xix, 62, 75–86, 79–82, 90, 93, 96–97
Fallon, Robert, 145, 231n7
Ferry, Anne, 4, 192–93, 212n3, 234n11
Fifth Lateran Council of 1516, 36–37
Fish, Stanley, 146
Fitzgerald, Sally, xiv
forgiveness, 59, 61, 81, 85, 203
fornication, 41–43
Foucault, Michel, 188–89, 195
Fourth Lateran Council of 1215, 29–30
Fowler, Alastair, 126
Francis of Sales, 2
fraternity, 104–6, 110
freedom, 130–43, 198–202, 208–9
free will, xix, xxi, 136–39
Freud, Sigmund, 23, 66, 99, 196

Gardner, Helen, 23
God, 46, 137, 140, 152
Greenblatt, Stephen, 186, 192, 196, 214n13

Greenfield, Stanley, 11
Gregory the Great (Saint), 32
Gropper, Johannes, 30
guilds, 104–5, 108
guilt: and Christianity, 45, 59; and confession, 26; Luther on, 66–67; and shame, 45, 68; and sin, 44–45; in *Sir Gawain and the Green Knight*, 55; in Western culture, 45

Halperin, David M, 188–89
Hamlet (Shakespeare): actor portrayal of, 201; Bloom on, 185; ghost in, 98–128, 111–14; themes in, ix–x, 100–103, 109–10, 119–27, 129, 183–85, 201
Handlyng Sinne (Mannyng), 34–35, 38, 40–46, 207
Hawthorne, Nathaniel, 68
Henry VIII, King, 89, 91–92, 113, 127, 205
Hilton, Walter, 39
Hobbes, Thomas, 67–68, 176–77, 190
Holmes, Martin, 120
Holy Day of Obligation, 54
holy orders, 74
Homer, xiv–xv, 142
Horace, 142
Hughes, Jonathan, 38
Hughes, Merritt, 130
human culture, 186–94
humanism, 37–38
human nature, 186–94
Hunt, Maurice, xiv
Huppe, Bernard, 8, 213n10

Ignatius of Loyola, 2
Iliad (Homer), 13, 196
individualism: and alienation, 2–3; extremity of, 16; and isolation, 3; liberal, 3, 208; Locke on, 4; and "the lonely crowd," 176–82; Milton on, xii, 6–7; roots of, 1, 4; and subjectivity, xi, 1–2, 194–95; as wanderer, 20–21; in *The Wanderer*, 8. See also self
Ingoldsthorpe, Joan, 106
inner self, ix
Institutes of the Christian Religion (Calvin), 77
Ireland, 28–29, 120
isolation, 3, 17–18, 52, 54. See also exile

James, Henry, 68
James I, 71, 91
Jews, 6, 140
John of Pouilly, 36
John of the Cross, 2
Johnson, W. K., xvii–xviii
Jordan, W. K., 107
Judaism, 24
Judt, Tony, ix
Julian of Norwich, 39
Kant, Immanuel, 24
Katherine of Aragon, 113
Keefer, Michael, 149

Kemp, Anthony, 15, 89, xii
Kempre, Margery, 39
Kierkegaard, Søren, 45
King Lear (Shakespeare), 101–2
Kinney, Arthur, xiv
Knox, Ronald, 2

Lamont, William, 91
last rites, 74
Lawrence, D. H., 116
Le Goff, Jacques, 114, 117
Lewalski, Barbara, 23
Lewis, C. S., 132, 169, 178, 233n17
liberalism, 3, 20–21
Locke, John, 4, 20
"lonely crowd" condition, 176–82
love, 135–43
Love, Nicholas, 39
Luther, Martin: and *Augsburg Confession*, 65; on commandments, 75; compared to Calvin, 146–48; on confession, 37, 62, 69; on guilt, 66–67; on sin, 37, 62–70

Machiavelli, Nicolo, 158, 186
Macintyre, Alasdair, 16
Making of Americans (Stein), 99
Malraux, Andre, 188–89
Mannyng, Robert, 34–35, 40–46
marriage, 6, 74, 92–93, 96, 127, 175
Martz, Louis L., ix, 23, 153–54
Marvell, Andrew, 75
Marxism, 2, 109
Mcpherson, Clair, 13
Mead, Margaret, 187–88, 234n6
Metamorphses (Ovid), xviii
metaphysics, 99, 191
Middle Ages, 1, 70–75, 108, 173
Milgram, Stanley, 23
Miller, J. Hillis, 99
Miller, Leo, 60
Milton, John: on Anglican Book of Common Prayer, 135; on Bible, 5; Bloom on, 143; on Calvin, 146–48; on conscience, 162–65, 181–82; and Diodato, 142, 173–75; on evil, 223n23; Fallon on, 145, 231n7; on freedom, 130–35, 208–9; on free will, 136–39; Hughes on, 130; on individualism, xii, 6–7, 169; Martz on, 153; and Protestantism, 105, 135; on self, 166–67, 184; on subjectivity, x, 5, 75, 195; on temptation, xix; works by: *Areopagitica*, 130, 133–34, 198–99; *Defensio Secunda (Second Defense)*, 130; *The Doctrine and Discipline of Divorce*, 5–6; *Of Education*, 130–34, 146; *Epitaphium Damonis*, 181; *Paradise Lost*, x–xi, 5, 110, 129, 130–33, 135–36, 142–44, 148, 153–57, 160–69, 176–77, 180–85, 201; *Paradise Regained*, 163; *The Ready and Easy Way*, 145; *The Reason of Church Government*, 159, 199; *Tetrachordon*, 158

Mine Own John Poyns (Wyatt), 52–53
modernism, 3–4, 18–19, 21, 46, 58, 66, 99–100, 194–98, 201, 226n4
Momma, Haruko, xiv
monarchy, 90–91
monasteries, 107–8
Montaigne, Michel, xii
More, Thomas, 38
Morgan, Gerald, 72–73
Mullin, Robert Bruce, xiv
Mulryan, John, xiii–xiv
multiculturalism, 191

Nagel, Thomas, 161
nationalism, 75, 103
Neoplatonism, 72
New Historicism, 191, 193–94
New York Herald Tribune Book Review, 187
Nichols, Ann, 33
Nietzsche, Friedrich Wilhelm, 20–21

obedience, 135–36; and freedom, 130–43
Odyssey (Homer), xiv–xv
OED. *See* Oxford English Dictionary
Of Education (Milton), 130–34, 146
Old English, 7–9, 11–12
Order for Visitation of the Sick, 67
Original Sin, xix–xx
Ovid, xi, xviii
Oxford English Dictionary (OED), 4–5
Ozmen, Steven, 37

Paradise Lost (Milton): on free will, 134; imagery in, 19, 144; Martz on, 153–54; publication of, xi; on sin, 148; themes in, 110, 129, 130–33, 136, 142, 153–57, 160–69, 176–78, 180–185, 201
Paradise Regained (Milton), 163
Pauline virtues, 63
Payer, Pierre, 29
penance: and confession, 25–26, 63, 84–85; definition of, 30–31, 46; Mannyng on, 46; rite of, 29, 45, 61, 80–81, 203–9; as sacrament, 47, 74; Spencer on, 78–79
Petrach, Francesco, xii, 193
Pieper, Josef, 187
Plato, x, 168, 198,
poetry, xviii–xix, 7–9, 11–12, 23, 223–24n26
Pope Boniface VIII, 36
Pope Clement VI, 38
Pope Innocent III, 29
Pope John Paul II, 43
Pope John XXII, 36
Pope Martin IV, 36
Pope Nicholas V, 36
popes: Augustine on, 32; Boniface VIII, 36; Clement V, 36; Clement VI, 38; image of, 145; Innocent III, 29; John Paul II, 43; Martin IV, 36; Nicholas V, 36; and papal league, 205; in Renaissance, 89–90. *See also* individual popes

postmodernism, 8, 21, 26, 99, 194–98
prayer, 84
Pricke of Conscience, 38
Prince Henry (1612), 10
Protestantism: allegiance to, 60, 93; birth of, 62–70, 81; and Catholicism, 81, 89, 105, 145–46; and confession, 62–70, 81; and English literature, xi; Kemp on, 89; and Milton, 135, 195; and nationalism, 91–93, 103; and scripture, 141; and self, x; and sin, 148
Pseudodoxia Epidemica (Browne), 5
psychology, 45–46, 65–66, 95
Purgatory: abolition of, 107–19, 128; Christian sense of, 106, xii; doctrine of, 105–6, 228n23; existence of, 76, 103–4; ghost from, 111–14; Jordan on, 107; Le Goff on, 117; Reformation view of, 103–6
Puritan Revolution, x

Quest de Sain Graal, 54

Raymo Robert R., xiii, xiv
The Ready and Easy Way (Milton), 145
The Reason of Church Government (Milton), 159, 199
reconciliation, 81, 203
Reformation: and Christianity, 1–2, 106–7; and commandments, 140; and community, 26; and confession, x, xii; and culture, 95–96; in England, 61–62, 104, 108, 110–14; in Europe, 1, 7, 60–61, 220n49; Miller on, 60; and Protestantism, 89; purgatory beliefs of, 103–6, 114
Reinach, Solomon, 117
religion: Cohn on, 114; and cultural criticism, 22–25, 95; definition of, 74; Shakespeare on, 103; in *Sir Gawain and the Green Knight*, 22–44, 51; and social control, 23–25; Spencer on, 72–73, 76–77, 87–88
Religion and Literature, xiii
Renaissance: and change, 1–2, 192; in England, xii, 11; in Europe, 45, 109; individualism in, 1; literature in, 11; patron system of, 9–10; politics in, 100, 113; popes in, 89–90; scholars, 4, 129, 194; subjectivity in, xvi, 212n3
repentance, x, 86–87
Rhetorics of Self-Making, 189
Richardson, Samuel, 68, 160
Richmond, Colin, 106
Riesman, David, 8, 176
Rolle, Richard, 76
Roman Congregation of Bishops and Regulars, 31
Romanticism, 3, 18–19, 21, 99, 185
Rorty, Richard, 189
Rubin, Miri, 105
Ryken, Leland, ix

242 Index

St. Francis de Sales, 38
St. Vincent de Paul, 38
Samson Agonistes (Milton), 163–64
Sartre, Jean-Paul, 187–88, 195
Satura, xiii
Scarisbrick, J. J., 38, 105–6
The Scarlet Letter (Hawthorne), 68
Seafarer, The (anonymous), 12–13
Second Defense (Milton), 130
Selden, John, 73
self, x, xii, xvi, 105, 194–95
Seneca, Lucius, 14
Servility and love, 135–43
Sessions, William A., xiv
seven deadly sins, 38, 44, 49, 71–72. *See also individual sins*
seven sacraments, 38, 74. *See also specific sacraments*
seven virtues, 38
Shakespeare, William: Bloom on, 185; Bradley on, 187; and culture, 9, 195; Greenblatt on, 186; on religion, 103; on self, 184; Theodore Spencer on, 187; Tillyard on, 102; works by: *Coriolanus*, 100–101; *Hamlet*, ix–x, 100–103, 109–10 118–28, 129, 183–85, 201; *King Lear*, 101–2; *Troilus and Cressida*, 102
Shakespeare and the Nature of Man (Theodore Spencer), 187
Shakespearean Negotiations? (Greenblatt), 192
Shakespearean Tragedy (Bradley), 187
Shelley, Percy Bysshe, 137
Shuger, Deborah, xiv
Sidney, Sir Philip, 10, 67
sin: and absolution, 58; Bossy on, 63; and Catholicism, 148; and confession, xii; definition of, 26; and forgiveness, 85; and guilt, 44–45; Luther on, 37, 62–70; Mannyng on, 41, 44; notions of, 81; Original, xix–xx; and penance, 29; private, 64–65; and Protestantism, 148; public, 64–65; and repentance, 61; and shame, 58
Sin and Confession on the Eve of the Reformation (Tentler), 26–27
Sir Gawain and the Green Knight (anonymous), 47–59, 61, 75, 97
social control, 25–28
The Song of Roland (anonymous), 13–14, 196
Sons and Lovers (Lawrence), 116
soul, x, 104
Space, Time and Deity (Alexander), 169
Spencer, Theodore, 187
Spenser, Edmund: on Anglican Church, 84; and church, 86–97; on conscience, 61, 69, 163; Cressy on, 71; Donne on, 93; and medieval heritage, 70–75; on religion, 72–73, 76–77, 87–88; works by: *The Faerie Queene*, xvii–xix, 62, 75–86, 90, 93, 96–97; *A View of the Present State of Ireland*, 70

Spenser Variorum, 70
Stein, Gertrude, 99
Stewart, Stanley, xiv
Stow, John, 109
Stripping of the Altars (Duffy), 32
subjectivity: Augustine on, xix; birth of, 20; and community, xi; definition of, ix, 3–4, 21; and exile, xi, 3, 11–19; and freedom, 198–202; and individuality, xi, 1–2, 194–95; Milton on, x; modern, 3; premodern, 19–21; in Renaissance, xvi, 212n3; and society, xi; in *The Wanderer*, 1–21
Summa (Aquinas), 28, 41, 218n22
Survey of London (Stow), 109

Tale of Genji, 196
Tale of Heike, 13
Taylor, Charles, 15–16
temptation, xix, 44, 55
Ten Commandments, 38, 49, 64–65, 140
Tentler, Thomas, 26–27, 30, 37, 203–4
Teresa of Avila (Saint), 2
Tetrachordon (Milton), 158
Theodulf of Orleans, 42
theology, 1, 30, 74, 136; in *Paradise Lost*, 136
Thirty-nine Articles (Church of England), 74
Thirty Years' War, 61, 93
Thoresby, John (archbishop of York), 38–39
Thousand and One Nights, 196
Tillyard, E. M. W., 102
Troilus and Cressida (Shakespeare), 102
Tudor kings, 90, 93
Turner, James, xiii
Turner, Victor, 25

Ulysses (Joyce), 116

View of the Present State of Ireland, A (Spencer), 70
Virgil, xi, xv–xviii, 3, 19, 142, 184, 193, 211n2

The Wanderer (anonymous): Christian virtues in, 13; compared to *Sir Gawain and the Green Knight*, 50–52; elements of, 7, 14, 18–19, 184, 215n19; Huppe on, 8; individuality in, 8; subjectivity in, xiv, 1–21
Weber, Max, 8
Werge, Thomas, xiii
Wharton, Edith, 68
Whitelock, Dorothy, 13
Wickenheiser, Robert, xiv
William of Ockham, xii
William of Pagula, 38
Wood, Ralph, xiv
Woolf, Virginia, 99
Wordsworth, William, 199
Wyatt, Sir Thomas, 10, 52–53, 151

Young, R. V., xiv